1981

A DISTINCTION OF STORIES

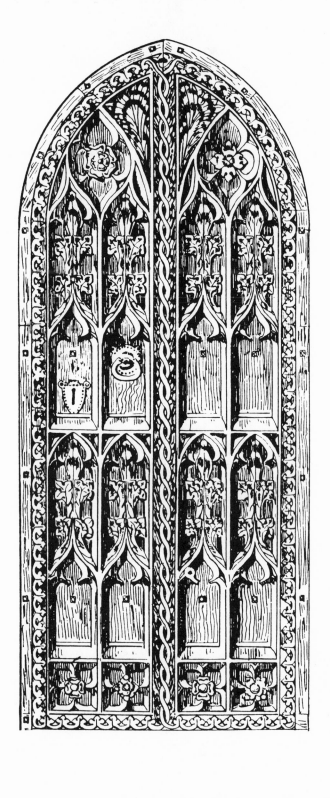

Judson Boyce Allen
and Theresa Anne Moritz

A DISTINCTION
OF STORIES

The Medieval Unity of Chaucer's
Fair Chain of Narratives
for Canterbury

OHIO STATE UNIVERSITY PRESS : COLUMBUS

Library of Congress Cataloging in Publication Data

Allen, Judson Boyce, 1932–
  A distinction of stories.

  Bibliography: p.
  Includes index.
  1. Chaucer, Geoffrey, d. 1400. Canterbury tales.
  2. Chaucer, Geoffrey, d. 1400—Technique.   3. Exempla.
  4. Rhetoric, Medieval.   I. Moritz, Theresa Anne, 1948–
  joint author.   II. Title.
  PR1874.A45   821'.1   80-26629
  ISBN 0-8142-0310-8

for Jacqueline Hewitt Allen
and Albert Frank Moritz

This love halt togidres peples
joyned with an holy boond, and
knytteth sacrement of mariages
of chaste loves; and love enditeth
lawes to trewe felawes.

CONTENTS

Preface

Collaboration is rare in literary criticism; whether because of the vanity of critics or the confidentiality of poetry, we cannot say. When it does happen, there is usually some easy division of credits. In our case, this division is quite impossible. Our collaboration is the result of a discovery, made at the beginning of a number of years of talk about Chaucer, that we were finishing each other's sentences, and finding both pleasure and profit in so doing.

In its present form, our reading of Chaucer's *Canterbury Tales* is new in three ways. In the first place, we go beyond the truism of criticism that Chaucer was fond of Ovid to find in medieval analyses of the form of the *Metamorphoses* as a collection basic guidance for our understanding of the form of Chaucer's own collection of tales. In the second place, and under this guidance, we propose a new order for the tales, based neither on the witness of some single "good" manuscript or group of manuscripts, nor on the geography between London and Canterbury. This order, indeed, is not the result or conclusion of any study of merely internal evidence; rather, it is a heuristic proposal guided by the external evidence of *Metamorphoses* commentary, and of other commentaries and manuals which define medieval procedures of literary organization. That this order, in the use of it, greatly facilitated our reading is gratifying. Nevertheless, what we wish ultimately to claim is not that our ordering is the only correct one, but rather that our method of reading, which takes the tales as an ordered series and reads them in terms of each other, is both medieval and permanently profitable. *Dispositio,* for the medieval sensibility, was a rhetorical strategy with discursive ends. Its purpose was to evoke in the reader or hearer that understanding of analogies existing between part and part which a heightened sense of the order of the parts produces. Hence the medieval emphasis on artificial orders; only for the most elementary of writers and speakers was the basis of *dispositio* required to be anything, such as geography, merely natural to the material being treated.

In the third place, we are quite conscious that Chaucer's stories, as we read them, have turned out to be not quite the same things as had been conventionally thought. In medieval terms, their *quidditas* is different. For us Chaucer's stories are not, except trivially, speeches or dramatic monologues. Neither are they, essentially, narrative plots, though most of them do, as stories, contain descriptions of completed actions. Rather, under the guidance of medieval critics and their theories, we have been led to see Chaucer's stories as examples—exempla. Seeing thus, we are obviously led to the thematic question, Examples of what? In answer to this question, we make a reading which is in part overtly thematic and find that Chaucer is, among other things, a superb political scientist. But we are also led to another and more subtle question: Examples in what way? An example is always properly particular; that which it exemplifies is universal or general. We thus confront the problem of the relation between universal and particular, under the mode of exemplification, in a way which permits value to be given to fictions, and which, in an age which some Chaucer critics accuse of being skeptically nominalist, permits us to discuss with some confidence both Chaucer's belief in definition and his method of making one. In this discussion we are interested both in method and in theme—or, in medieval terms, both in *modus* and in *sententia*. But we put *modus* first, and with a confidence authorized by the medieval critics, who made *forma tractatus* dependent on *forma tractandi*. Thus we have relatively more to say about relationships among stories, or among parts of stories, and relatively less to say about the thematic topics traditional among Chaucer critics as occasion for set-piece display. Respectful of Kittredge and Donaldson, for instance, we essay no *effictio* of the Wife of Bath. But we believe that we have made both clear and important a number of features of Chaucer's art whose existence has been previously obscured by too modern critical expectations.

What Chaucer is doing, we think, is making a normative definition of human society. Central to this definition is the structure of marriage. By the power of his strategy of exemplification, he uses this structure of marriage paradigmatically rather than merely as an exercise of sociological or psychological realism. In architectonically repeated stories of various marriages, Chaucer defines the norms of all types of properly conducted human relationships. In working to explain this definition, and Chaucer's concerns with it, we are perforce expressing concerns which are broadly ethical and political rather than narrowly aesthetic or literary. In this we have no discomfort, because here again we act under the authority of the medieval critics. Further, and in universal human terms, we hope also to affirm that great literature can be rhetorical in the classical moral sense without having any of its essential greatness compromised.

As is customary, we are happy to acknowledge our debt to previous critics, whose specifics are recorded in our notes. Especially where we differ or diverge from precedent, we are conscious of the great extent to which precedent permits us to take another step. Among these critics, however, we should take special note of some whose work cannot here be fully or even adequately acknowledged—the medieval authors of commentaries, glosses, manuals, and outlines, still largely unpublished, on whose work we ground our a priori assumptions. Full treatment of this material is another book, and cannot be included in this one. We cite sufficient preliminary studies of this material to make our presumptions clear, if not yet unarguable. At the same time we know that the true value of an apriority is its usefulness, not merely its historicity. Of that value we here make Chaucer's *Canterbury Tales* the judge.

In addition, we are happy to thank a number of friends and colleagues, who have read our work at some stage or other in its making, for their suggestions and criticism: John Alford, John McCabe, Charles Owen, Rossell Hope Robbins, R. A. Shoaf, and Paul Theiner. They have moderated our excesses, labeled our digressions, saved us from errors of fact and style, even while they encouraged us to believe that we were right about important matters. For the making of the bibliography, we thank Carol Briggs; for verification, proofreading, and the index, Judith Jablonski. Carol S. Sykes, of the Ohio State University Press, has transformed manuscript into book with an ideally helpful rigor. Finally, in our dedication we not only obey the preoccupation of the *Canterbury Tales,* but also honor and appreciate two particular people with whom, in the living form of our marriages, we discover our truth.

PART ONE

Definitions and Structures

Axioms of Unity
and Their Consequences

In the beginning of his *Les mots et les choses,* Michel Foucault quotes a cautionary joke which might well be recommended as the proper place of beginning for any critic who seeks to understand the literature of the past. The quotation is of Borges's encyclopedic Chinese classification of animals: belonging to the emperor, embalmed, tame, sucking pigs, sirens, fabulous, stray dogs, included in the present classifications, frenzied, innumerable, drawn with a very fine camel-hair brush, et cetera, having just broken the water pitcher, and that from a long way off look like flies.[1] It is a classification which, to Western minds, and perhaps to real Eastern ones as well, makes very little sense. Still, its matter-of-fact presentation makes a claim to truth which, even as it amuses us by its incongruity, also causes us to reexamine our cherished modes of formulating and classifying reality. Every system is equally arbitrary, until one considers what each is for; Borges's Chinese encyclopedia makes us realize how largely it is habit which accustoms us to find one such system a natural deposit from the way the world actually is, and another the fantasy of deluded persons made foreign to us by time, space, genius, or all three.

The problem to which Borges's irony addresses itself is peculiarly vivid for the literary critic because the critic's business is to account for something at once alien and contemporary. We deal with poems and stories which must be classified, analyzed, and assimilated as if they were a part of our own world, as indeed they are. At the same time we know that they survive from a possibly inscrutable past, and curiosity if not academic responsibility ensures that we try to deal with them in their own terms, even if those terms turn out to be as strange as Borges's classification of animals.

We have a number of methods for classifying the materials contained in Chaucer's *Canterbury Tales*. References to times and places in the links suggest that Chaucer would have arranged tales and interludes of conversation according to the geography of the pilgrimage route. The Parson's objections to storytelling, and the matter of his sermon, have led us to find in him a dramatic reversal of the worldly wandering represented by the story contest and its participants. Other methods for drawing together the diverse contents of the text have also been proposed. For example, the stories provide a representative collection of literary genres, from epic (at least in the opinion of some readers) to romance to fabliau to sermon. On the other hand, one may find in the poem descriptions of a number of fascinating people—some of them the pilgrims themselves, others characters in the tales which the pilgrims tell. Again, it is obvious that tales have tellers, and therefore the dramatic principle has concentrated on the psychological revelations of the pilgrims, whether in telling a tale or in talking together, as the unifying interest in all that Chaucer included in the poem. Finally, from manuscript evidence we have the witness of Chaucer's near contemporaries that the stories were arranged in groups, and these groups presented in a variety of orders.

All of these methods, with the exception of the last, are modern attempts to reconstruct Chaucer's irretrievably lost plan for the poem. The witness of manuscripts, which we preserve in editing the text, is still suspected of obscuring, rather than illuminating, authorial intentions. Using modern methods for classifying the contents of the poem, we have found much of interest in Chaucer, but the unity of his great collection eludes us. Nevertheless, there is a good deal of critical talk about the unity of the *Canterbury Tales,* which, although it is more often frustrated than not, does claim that we find the subject important, and that at an as yet inarticulate level we find a satisfaction in the poem, answering to our sense of the wholeness of things.

What we need is the right Chinese encyclopedia, that is, a naming of the poem's parts which not only identifies them properly as individual objects of interest but also reveals their character as units of an ordered, coherent presentation of a subject. We have determined to raise again the troublesome problem of the unity of the *Canterbury Tales* because our researches into medieval poetics and the medieval literary form, the story collection, have convinced us that organizational principles recognized and used in the Middle Ages have not been taken into account in modern efforts to understand the plan of Chaucer's story array. It seems surprising that, after thirty years and more of historical criticism, an aspect of medieval thought, especially one which we wish to argue is fundamental for understanding much of that age's poetry, should have eluded scholarly notice. We can only suggest that the range of historical method has been limited both by its own nature, as a fact-gathering procedure, and by an unwillingness to ask questions which cast doubt upon the preconceptions with which twentieth century readers approach the material.

The problem with historical criticism is that it has not yet gone far enough. Thus far, in our attempt to understand Chaucer's world and work, we have done extremely well in assembling the great body of facts which is the context of that world and its attitudes. We know a great deal about astrology and theology and mythology and medicine and many other things. We know the salient facts about most of the wars and diplomatic marriages, many of the crimes, and a fair number of the people, important and not so important. We know what books were available and where, and in many cases who read which ones. We have ourselves read a great many of these books and have puzzled over the fact that many of the ones which were most popular then are most boring now, even while we correlated the doctrinal or taxonomic facts which those books contained with the more allusive versions of the facts as found in our medieval poems. All of these things, which we have researched thoroughly and well, have to do with those aspects of the medieval culture which, from the modern point of view, we could call facts. We must be grateful for knowing them; our understanding of medieval art would be far poorer if we lacked them.

In the long run, however, facts are worse than useless if we do not know their proper relationships. It is a presumption of historical criticism that, since it is especially qualified to discover and establish the existence of facts, there will indeed be facts, and that facts can properly be the basis of profitable analysis. At one level, this is simply a truism. But it conceals a subtle danger of error. Critical history depends on verification, and is more interested in what can be verified; therefore, it is most concerned necessarily with concrete entities—rather than, or at least prior to, the organizing relationships which obtained among those entities. Facts are facts, delimited, separable, and whole. A battle is a battle, a manuscript is a manuscript, a statement of doctrine is there in a datable text. Either may have causes, or results, or both, and since we are a priori interested in causes and results, we will probably relate our facts in terms of them.[2] Thus, though we can record Laurence de Premierfait's statement that the *Divine Comedy,* like the *Romance of the Rose,* was a "vraye mappemond,"[3] we tend to be disqualified from following de Premierfait's example to make similar analogies between medieval books on our own. We need a new method which aims at classifying facts and discovering the structures which relate them meaningfully to one another.

As our starting point, then, we have assumed that all the materials which Chaucer left behind to be included in the *Canterbury Tales* must be taken seriously as functioning elements in his final design. Because they have played so small a part in previous explanations of the poem's structure, we have paid special attention to the tales. We have attempted to discover medieval literary theory, or practice, which might suggest the manner in which Chaucer expected all the various parts of the poem to work together. The search for medieval presumptions about how literary works were to be organized has led us to the age's assumptions about where the divisions and classifications of the world are to be made and what relations exist among those divisions once they are made.[4] The ordering principles which we will recommend attempt to take advantage of such medieval habits of mind as analogy and allegory, the *distinctio,* the use of *exempla,* and the willingness to consider important such questions as the reality of universals. Even though to do so feels at first as strange as repeating the classes of Borges's Chinese animals with a sincere attempt at conviction, we have attempted to follow medieval practice in trusting to the wholeness of the picture composed by the tales.

Previous efforts to explain the poem's unity are unsatisfactory for two reasons. First, they do not make all the pieces of Chaucer's grand project, particularly the tales, fit comfortably together; and, second, the unifying principles they propose are not well attuned to the medieval character of the work. Robert Jordan's proposal, which is the most rigorously medieval in its reference to "homologous parts and parts of parts," has been helpful in arguing against a dramatic reading of a linearly structured journey to Canterbury. But the nonorganic relationship among the parts of the poem he describes comes close to meaning nothing more than nonrelational.[5] Though he insists on the division of the text into parts, Jordan provides no convincing explanation for why these particular parts have been brought together into a single work. Other critics dealing with the subject have, in one way or another, begun by proposing a principle of unity they believe to be universally valid, under which they have tried to fit the *Canterbury Tales*.[6] Two such organizing principles have tended to dominate—the first is Aristotelian plot, and the second the drama of the human comedy, with its implied procedures of character analysis and the treatment of the tales as speeches. Neither of them is medieval;[7] nevertheless, because they are true of large tracts of human experience, they have given many helpful, if only partial, insights into Chaucer.

Some critics have found a plot for the poem in the action of the Canterbury journey; others have looked to the thematic significance of a spiritual pilgrimage in order to discover the plan of the poem.[8] On the one hand, the actual pilgrimage to Canterbury is seen as something which begins in London, goes along the way in the middle, and ends in Canterbury—or alternatively, and with more correctness, back in London again.[9] Such a plot is founded on the progress of the pilgrims, taking into account allusions to the familiar stopping points on the road to Canterbury; but the events outside the flow of time are more difficult to place inside the structure. They remain an unexplained middle suspended between the clear-cut beginning set forth in the General Prologue and the apparent conclusion provided by the Parson's Prologue.[10] The other, more popular plot joins the end of the pilgrimage in Canterbury with the thematic climax of the *Parson's Tale* and structures the plot in terms of a journey from London to, or toward, heaven. The most significant study of this spiritual pilgrimage is Ralph Baldwin's, whose initial presentation was taken up by many other critics.[11] Interpretations of the spiritual pilgrimage attempt to establish a structure which is worked out not only in the physical details of the journey but also in the thematic development of the alternative values for life expressed by the pilgrims, climaxing in the judgment of the Parson.

The axiom of these plot approaches to the *Canterbury Tales* is, of course, Aristotelian. The analysis of narratives in terms of beginnings, middles, and ends is a commonplace of modern criticism. In the Middle Ages, however, both theory and practice call this axiom of plot into question. The Averroistic version in which medieval critics knew Aristotle's *Poetics* makes it quite clear that the beginnings, middles, and ends of which poetry was to be composed were discursive or logical features, and not causally ordered narrative ones; and Chaucer's rhetorical strategy with the *Parson's Tale* in fact probably undercuts the sense of climax which its final place encourages us to see in it.[12] Medieval treatments of *dispositio* have a far better developed doctrine of beginnings than of endings,[13] and it is probably safe to presume that medieval sensibility would therefore expect the most important element in any writing to come first, rather than last.

The human comedy approach to the *Canterbury Tales* prizes the poem for its faithfulness to individualizing details of description and its accurate reflections of real life.[14] Homage to Chaucer's camera eye has even prompted researches into possible originals of the fictional pilgrims among the artist's acquaintances.[15] The modern impulse to empirical realism has led critics to suppose that the surface of Chaucer's poem glitters with the unadorned face of the poet's time; by logical extension, Chaucer becomes for many no more than the man who holds the mirror. His self-portrait as a well-meaning but innocent reporter of his age has been taken seriously. Within the last twenty years, students of medieval learning have offered valuable correctives to the excesses of this reverence for Chaucer's unsullied realism by showing how habitually medieval people saw in the real world forms and processes defined by traditional ideas rather than close personal observation.[16] For medieval art particular representational figures tended regularly to be exemplars of typical ideas or states; golden ribbons of written speech connected painted figures with their message; this connection with the typical or allegorical persisted, even heightened, as verisimilitude reached virtuoso levels in late medieval and Renaissance painting in Flanders. One may properly generalize from Averroes's remark about the poetry of praise to all art: "Tragedia etenim non est ars representativa ipsorummet hominum prout sunt individua cadentia in sensum, sed est representativa consuetudinum eorum honestarum et actionum laudabilium et credulitatum beatificantium ... et ars scientialis que montrat [*sic*] sive docet ex quibus et qualiter componuntur poemata principalior et perfectior est quam ipsa operatio poematum."[17] This is not of course to say that particulars occurring in medieval art should be reduced to, or dismissed in favor of, the general or the typical, after the fashion recommended by critics who allegorize in the manner of C. S. Lewis. It is to say that overtones of widely accepted definitions of the human condition are an element in all of Chaucer's very particular figures, such as the Wife of Bath or the Tabard's Host. Behind the concrete details of story always stood the *consuetudines* and *credulitates* whose truth or moral value remained of primary value and interest. Throughout the Middle Ages the fit relationship between such general truths and their physical, particular counterparts was discussed.

We shall return to these discussions when we consider Chaucer's attitudes on the authority of poetry; it is enough to say here that as a poet of the later Middle Ages, Chaucer's belief in these traditional associations was refined by his awareness of growing challenges, in an era not fully confident of analogy, to its philosophical validity.

Formulations of the marriage group are an important corollary of the human comedy view. It might be objected that Kittredge's proposal should not be grouped with human comedy readings because it is aimed at defining something typical in the poem, that is, the institution of marriage. But Kittredge's article, as well as most work of this kind, falls short precisely because of the same assumptions we characterized as basic to the human comedy approach.[18] These critics evaluate the pilgrims as realistically drawn characters, with limited points of view and personal prejudices interesting in themselves, and not existing as typical of anything. Critics of the marriage group are really claiming that the discussion is not so much of marriage as of marriages—of personal options open to real people, modern as well as medieval (with Archie Bunker's and Andy Capp's wives as reasonable modern analogues). Such common ground as critics find in the marriage group as a whole tends to be dramatic rather than typical— dictated by the interaction of the pilgrims more than by the interaction of themes. Because the critics are concerned above all with people, in all their bare forked variety, they tend to minimize the importance of what these people say as having any validity beyond the immediate and psychological. The marriage group is an important test case for our hypothesis that, for Chaucer as for the Middle Ages, particular figures were offered as exemplary of general truths. Medieval marriage evokes a wide-ranging series of associations with other relationships, including that of Christ and the church, of the higher and lower reason, of the mind and body, and of ruler and subjects.[19] Robertsonian formulations push this evocation too far, by tending to take the allegory and leave the letter.[20] But most critics who discuss the marriage group do so literally, and lose the full and proper medieval context by presuming that the stories involved are merely realistic in the nineteenth-century sense and contain nothing but the ordinary human behavior they recount. They ignore the allegorical dimension—admittedly in proper opposition to letting it displace, or replace, the story—but in so doing they fail to appreciate how the allegorical overtones of stories containing marriages satisfy the medieval fondness for the typical. A notable instance of this problem is in readings of the *Clerk's Tale*.[21] Efforts to explain the tale's plot in terms of dramatic and personal principles, such as Walter's hubris, cannot account for the complex game Chaucer plays with the literal and allegorical levels of this traditional exemplum of Christian patience. Without taking into account the extended senses of marriage, with which the Middle Ages was accustomed to invest its literal occurrence, Chaucer's manipulation of his source in order to heighten the issue of Griselda's obedience and his subsequent ironic commentary in the Envoi are lost, and the tale threatens to become, for the modern reader, a scandalous proof of the need for women's liberation. We will deal with these matters, in focus on the *Clerk's Tale*, later.[22] What is important here is that discussions of the marriage group, and other analogous discussions of Chaucer's characters as merely charming, real people, leave out half of what Chaucer wrote. What is lacking is awareness of the tendency of medieval particulars toward dependable associations[23]—which can be trusted as the ground of structure in which those particulars relate to meaning and to each other. This lack of interest, as we have implied, is axiomatically based; it results from too univocal an interest in something else—in this case, people, in all their simple humanity.

Recently, however, a growing number of critics seem to be seeing that no univocal approach will work with Chaucer; they have therefore been able to discover richer and richer ironies in his work. The basic ground of their work is still the presumption that the plot which leads to heaven and the people whose particular individuality seems so obvious actually exist, but now both instead of one, side by side in the *Canterbury Tales*. The point of their existence, however, is not ultimate but instrumental; Chaucer is not choosing between them or commenting on one by subtly preferring the other, but rather is indulging in a "double vision," which is the "ironical essence" of his art.[24] Arthur W. Hoffman puts the polarities involved in this fashion: "The Prologue begins, then, by presenting a double view of the Canterbury pilgrims: the pilgrimage is one tiny manifestation of a huge tide of life, but then, too, the tide of life ebbs and flows in response to the power which the pilgrimage acknowledges, the power symbolized by 'the hooly blisful martir.'"[25] An analogous doubleness, that between the typical and the individual, is proposed by Jill Mann as the basis for Chaucer's moral ambiguity.[26]

The doubleness is certainly there—between earth and heaven, between Chaucer the pilgrim and Chaucer the poet (though this one probably has been overdone), between the particular and the typical, between the literal and the allegorical, bet: een the thing and the word that names it.[27] To call this an ironic vision suggests to the modern reader that Chaucer has decided wisely not to choose between two aspects of life, but simply to hold them in suspension as both truly present in man.[28] But irony, for the Middle Ages, is simply one of the forms of allegory, that is, not a denial of meaning but an affirmation of it.[29] This double vision is structually persistent in Chaucer's collection because he proposes to gauge the relationship between these two components of life and establish from these elements a coherent picture of the human condition. The medieval strategy of *assimilatio* is an alternative to the crucial Aristotelian term *mimesis*.[30] The *Canterbury Tales* is constructed from contradictory materials of life, not in order to witness to a confusion beyond human understanding, but rather to draw the contradictions into a pattern revealing their true harmony.

We have said that the various unifying principles surveyed here are nonmedieval and have suggested briefly how they have obscured, or distorted, our understanding of what they were intended to explain. One aspect of the modern search for the poem's unity deserves special comment. With few exceptions, critics treat the tales and the links in different ways; the stories are read individually or in small groups, whereas the links are treated as if they constituted a dramatic whole, a continuous narrative of character development and interaction. The "real life" of the pilgrims is distinguished from the "fictions" they present. Modern readers interested in plot and characterization have found the links susceptible to analysis in such terms; they have presumed that Chaucer, too, was more interested in, or more willing to trust the reality of, the "real life" of the frame than the "fictions" it encloses. As a result, the stories are subordinated to their tellers, and in explanations of the poem's design, are treated either as "beautiful lies" which are exposed by the truth of life or as dramatic monologues in which the pilgrims expose their own psychological complexities.[31]

This dramatic principle is so powerful in the minds of modern critics that it operates, not just as a conscious tool of criticism, but as an unconscious axiom determining what the critic might expect as he begins his work. Because it is thus so insidious, it needs especially to be put down, lest in the rest of the book we be misunderstood as failing to say what we never intended to say, or as saying badly in dramatic terms what in fact we are saying well in medieval ones.

The most significant effect of post-Cartesian philosophy has been to focus attention on epistemology rather than metaphysics; by now this attention has generated a host of attitudes and cultural interests, all presuming, in one way or another, individual point of view as a point of departure for knowledge and action. The dramatic monologues of Browning, the subtle treatment of point of view by Henry James, the structuralist surrender to individual acts of reading, phenomenologist thinking, the theory of relativity, the Heisenberg principle of indeterminacy, and even opinion-poll evidence—all trace to the essentially modern conviction that statements are relative to their speakers, experiences to their sufferers or enjoyers. Nothing is except as it is witnessed or endured. Thus our modern critical interest in Chaucer's tales as dramatic utterances, and in him as a layered series of personae beneath which the "real" author–civil servant, himself a point of view, ironically hides himself, is ultimately more an interest in ourselves and our own phenomenological predicament than it is in anything authentically medieval or Chaucerian.

Both drama and testimony existed in the Middle Ages, of course, And considerable attention was paid to distinctions among roles. But these facts give no special support to the dramatic principle as modern critics of Chaucer have practiced it. Literary criticism produced in the Middle Ages provides us with slight evidence bearing on point of view; such as there is, when properly understood, leads us more toward a taxonomy of types than to an epistemology of individualized witnesses. Chaucer's northern dialect students in the *Reeve's Tale* are, according to John Fisher, the first in English literature;[32] as a kind of ethnic humor, this usage obviously shows no respect for an individual point of view, but just the reverse, as opponents of ethnic slurs have always known. It reduces the individual to something merely typical. A gloss on the speech of Tideus in book 2 of the *Thebiad* evaluates this kind of "realistic" writing with the proper medieval emphasis: "Nota Stacium valde rethoricum in hac oratione esse, cum non faciat Tideum loqui rethorice. Digna est enim persona tali locutione."[33] Statius, in making Tideus speak as Tideus should, underlines not Tideus but his own rhetorical presence as author. Ultimately, and by analogy, Chaucer is the only speaker in the *Canterbury Tales;* his rhetoric tells it all.[34] What makes even this persuasive, however, is not Chaucer's personal witness as author or speaker—not his speech as his—but his speech as speech. The dramatic principle does indeed hold for law oratory, but it is not properly exercised in poetry: "Argumentatio seu probatio rectitudinis credulitatis aut operationis non per sermonem persuasivum (hoc enim non pertinet huic arti neque est conveniens ei) sed per sermonem representativum . . . ideoque non utitur carmen laudativum arte gesticulationis neque vultuum acceptione sicut utitur hiis rethorica."[35] What this *sermo repre-sentativus* presents may indeed be personae, but they are made credible by it, and not it by them. Thus Thomas Waleys, commenting on Boethius's *Consolation,* says: "Causa autem formalis tractandi est modus agendi Boetii, et est dialogus, idest sermo duorum. Introducit enim Boetius in hoc libro duas personas, scilicet seipsum suam miseriam deplangentem, et philosophiam sibi condolentem, et ipsum super suam miseriam consolantem."[36] What is fundamental here is the form, dialogue. The personae are the result of the exis-tence of this genre, not its cause. Both philosophy and the persona of Boethius are aspects of that temporarily depressed instance of *humanitas* named Boethius, who must achieve his true selfhood in the knowledge of the highest good. There is nothing here that is even remotely phenomenological; the psychomachic dialogue does not constitute an individual so much as deliver a self from its improper individuality. What is true of these Platonist personifica-tions of Boethius is equally true, mutatis mutandis, of Chaucer's nominalist exempla. In fit array they may exemplify the truth, but their witness does not constitute it. The fact that Chaucer's collection is divisible into frame and stories was probably less vivid to Chaucer than it is to us. Commentaries on the *Metamorphoses* contemporary with Chaucer, for example, ignore distinctions between framelike stories and enclosed stories; instead, they allegorize them all alike, as a collection of morally instructive exemplary actions. Furthermore, when Chaucer introduces the question of the relative authority of art and life, or experience and authority, he comes to conclusions oppo-site to those most twentieth-century readers have attributed to him. Chaucer and his first audiences regarded the *Canterbury Tales* as at least as interesting and significant as the Canterbury journey during which they were told. With all this in mind, we are convinced that an avenue of approach to the text, via the tales rather than the links, remains unexplored. It is there that we propose to begin.

The most promising place to look in a piece of writing for clues to its unity, from the medieval point of view, is its beginning; if clues are not unambiguously clear at this level, then the second most promising place to look is in analogous cases—sources or models to which one's book can be unquestionably related. Of the many things we learn from Chaucer's beginning, the most emphatic is that the Knight and his tale have unusual authority. The Knight is the first pilgrim de-scribed; his tale is the first tale. Rank tells, and the dramatic device of submitting to the luck of the draw only reinforces the inevitability of the Knight's position. The easiest next step is to suppose that the General Prologue will define the order of all that is to follow—but this is not true. Neither the Host nor the Miller wants to hear the Squire speak after his father. In terms of ordering, then, the Prologue predicts only the Knight's Tale, and otherwise contributes to the wholeness of the poem in different ways, as we shall later suggest.

Empirically, and without recourse to theory, it is obvious that the tales of the first fragment are unified. They present a complex and witty interweaving of characters and ideas; they all treat the same basic love triangle; and they show a common concern for order and justice, even though each tale's action is more vulgar and disorderly than the one before.[37] One might therefore suppose that this kind of unity, defined by the precedent and example of the first and most carefully worked out fragment, might operate throughout the whole. Yet this promise of order also seems to break down, following the *Cook's Tale*, much as the arrangements the General Prologue seems to promise, whether in its list of pilgrims or in the casting of lots, collapse after the *Knight's Tale*. Discoveries of analogous interrelationships among other small groups of tales indicate that the unity of the first fragment may not be coincidental, but no overall scheme of this type has been expanded to include the entire collection.[38]

The only unambiguous certainty in Chaucer's beginning is the *Knight's Tale*. Given the Prologue and the Miller's interruption, which are structurally contradictory, we have in the emphatic and defining position as prescribed by medieval manuals only the *Knight's Tale*.[39] It is a tale weighty in matter and rich in "solaas," whose subject matter of young love and brotherly combat seems to echo throughout the remaining stories. As the first tale it is in this collection more determinative a prologue than all the mere transitions which come later and which, for medieval sensibilities, must be taken more as gloss than as determining frame. Therefore, both because of pride of place and because of significance of content, the *Knight's Tale* should be expected to forecast an orderly unity for the collection it introduces. In order to explain how the tale functions in this way, we must see it in terms of correctly medieval structuring principles. For these we need the guidance of Chaucer's models.

The search for a medieval precedent to explain Chaucer's method and interest in story collections has extended beyond Boccaccio and Sercambi, even as far as Mandeville and de Guileville, but with results that are at best unprofitable and often misleading.[40] In fact, the precedent for Chaucer's collection of tales in a frame is one which is most prominent in medieval culture, most widely known and respected, as itself a morally normative array of tales, that is, Ovid's *Metamorphoses*. Ovid's possible or probable influence on Chaucer in this regard has been often enough noticed.[41] But the investigation of Ovid, and even of Ovid as he was known in the Middle Ages, has lacked proper grounding in the medieval commentaries and has therefore failed to understand the *Metamorphoses* in a way which makes sense of Chaucer. This we propose to do.

In absolute terms, it might well be fair to say that we are not so much drawing a parallel between Chaucer's *Tales* and Ovid's *Metamorphoses* as between the tales and a body of medieval commentary on stories, which in the Middle Ages circulated with the *Metamorphoses* without saying anything much of permanent interest about Ovid's poem. We do indeed depend for our guidance in reading Chaucer as much on commentaries as on the Ovidian text itself, if not more. Since these commentaries are neither widely known nor indeed more than very partially published, we are very conscious that this relation which we intend to argue between Chaucer's *Canterbury Tales* and a very medievalized understanding of Ovid's *Metamorphoses* is far more self-evident to us than it is to readers who know both poems entirely or substantially by virtue of having read them for themselves, in modern editions and translations, as literature. We are not claiming that the medieval commentators were right about the *Metamorphoses*, but only that they wrote what they wrote, and that Chaucer read it and found it fitting. Obviously we are not claiming that sensitive readers of Ovid have been perversely blind for nearly five hundred years in failing to see that the *Canterbury Tales* and the *Metamorphoses* were identical to one another. Unless read through a certain medieval filter of commentary, they are not. A sensitive modern reader of Ovid might well find, as John Fyler does, that the greatest similarity between the two poets was a certain ironic tone.[42] In seeing this similarity, the modern reader has correctly noticed certain features of the experience of reading these poems. But it is crucial to realize that he is set up to do so—that he is also reading through a filter. Modern readers are interested in point of view. Because we are incorrigibly self-conscious, we are persistently curious about, and sensitive to, the self-consciousness of others. Further, we have learned from Wayne Booth, if not from Conrad's Marlow, to expect, and to appreciate with understanding, a certain irony as the ground of our relation with the authors we read.

We must put aside for the moment all these attitudes, if we are to appreciate, under the guidance of the medieval commentaries, that Ovid's *Metamorphoses* is the formal precedent for Chaucer's *Canterbury Tales*. The analogy which makes this precedent true is, admittedly, a difficult one—one in which the "alterity" of medieval literature is especially insistent.[43] The disappearance of the commentary of Peter Lavinius from editions of the *Metamorphoses* after about 1530 is evidence that this analogy might already have been less than obvious in the Renaissance. But what we are attempting in this book is historical criticism, against which no modern or merely synchronic attitude is privileged. In historical terms, the only Ovid that matters to Chaucer is the medieval Ovid, and for that one, given the passage of time, we must perforce trust the medieval commentators even more than our own reading of the book they glossed.

We have already mentioned Laurence de Premierfait's willingness to equate the *Romance of the Rose* and the *Divine Comedy* as examples of a "vraye mappemond"; his analogy is very much the kind we are making between Ovid and Chaucer. It is not an analogy based on style, tone, or plot; rather, it is an analogy based on a medieval sense of the logic, meaning, and application possible in a text which is an assembly of stories. It is an analogy which is only possible for us because the medieval text of Ovid survived with commentary.

There is not room in this book to include another book on the literary theory of the medieval commentators.[44] Some things must therefore be merely asserted here, in confidence that they have been proved elsewhere. As far as commentary on the *Metamorphoses* is concerned, the edited texts which we cite do fairly represent the character, if not all the variation of detail, of what manuscripts preserve.[45] With regard to the strategy of classification of metamorphoses, in terms of which Ovid commentary is specifically relevant to Chaucer, we are necessarily concerned with full detail, and so we quote from manuscripts as well as from edited commentary texts. To be convinced that this commentary material would have been unavoidable, one has only to look randomly at any dozen manuscripts of the *Metamorphoses* early enough to have been used by Chaucer. Fully blank margins and flyleaves are rare.

Once one is willing to trust the medieval commentators, including those whose texts are still unedited, one cannot avoid seeing that the *Metamorphoses* provides not only the obvious precedent for the genre of the framed story collection but also, and more important, the implicit explanation of the unity of any such collection. The commentaries make all this explicit. They preserve elaborate medieval analysis of structural and classificatory principles and categories which name parts and in so doing define wholes. These principles tend to occur most explicitly in the commentary *accessus* which circulated with the *Metamorphoses*. Of these commentaries, the one by Arnulf of Orleans, with its variants, was the most influential. But substantial evidence also comes from incidental glosses, *divisiones*, and allegories on specific tales. From this evidence several generalizations are possible.

First, the commentaries conventionally identify the material of the *Metamorphoses* as changes whose purpose is to exemplify the range of possibilities of moral action. Second, this material—changes—is classified into a few major types according to one or another of two complementary systems. Third, in the actual process of glossing, no distinction is made between frame and framed—the Minyades are allegorized in their turn, in a series with the stories they tell.

The ethical interpretation of the *Metamorphoses* is to be expected. Arnulf's language, however, deserves to be examined in some detail:

> Intencio est de mutacione dicere, ut non intelligamus de mutacione que fit extrinsecus tantum in rebus corporeis bonis vel malis sed etiam de mutacione que fit intrinsecus ut in anima, ut reducat nos ab errore ad cognitionem veri creatoris. Duo sunt motus in anima unus rationalis alter irrationalis: rationalis est qui imitatur motum firmamenti, qui fit ab oriente in occidentem, et e contrario irrationalis est qui imitatur motum planetarum qui moventur contra firmamentum. Dedit enim deus anime rationem per quam reprimeret sensualitatem, sicut motus irrationalis VII planetarum per motum firmamenti reprimitur. Nos vero rationabilem motum more planetarum negligentes contra creatorem nostrum rapimur. Quod Ovidius videns vult nobis ostendere per fabulosam narrationem motum anime qui fit intrinsecus. Ideo dicitur Yo mutata in vaccam quia corruit in vicia, ideo pristinam formam dicitur recepisse quod emersit a viciis. Vel intencio sua est nos ab amore temporalium immoderato revocare et adhortari ad unicum cultum nostri creatoris, ostendendo stabilitatem celestium et varietatem temporalium. Ethice supponitur quia docet nos ista temporalia, que transitoria et mutabilia, contempnere, quod pertinet ad moralitatem.[46]

The most significant feature of this piece of literary criticism, which continued to be copied into the fifteenth century, is its trust of analogical thinking. Stories of corporeal changes parallel cosmic motions, in two opposite ways. Both of the rival cosmic motions, and analogously both of the rival psychic motions, are part of the same system—one "reprimitur" by the other. Throughout, the critic's presumption that his material will be of some practical ethical use is obvious. Understanding, then, comes as a result of the fit perception of parallels and, when it is achieved, makes possible an improved state of the ethical self. The structure of parallelism internal to the work must also be understood to be rhetorical; it includes the reader, who is supposed to inform his own life by the experience of the book.

We know that this particular sense of the formal structure of ethical behavior is really intended because in another place the commentator specified the four kinds of *mutationes* as from animate to inanimate, from inanimate to animate, from animate to animate, and from inanimate to inanimate.[47] Since this same fourfold schema is also used from Donatus to John Balbus as the classification of the kinds of metaphor, it is obvious that for these critics the formalities of metaphor and the formalities of ethics were the same.[48] That is, the same relationship which obtains between tenor and vehicle, or between the two halves of a simile in the operation of *assimilatio*,[49] also obtains between *quidam homo* and the example, rule, divine command, or human counsel by which he orders his ethical behavior. Therefore, for this reason also, the reader of any given piece becomes, as we shall see in chapter 2 more fully, that piece's tropological level—parallel to it, its rhetorical object, and its ethical result.

This analysis in terms of changes from animate to inanimate, and so on, is one of the two systems the commentaries use. Its primary critical use, as far as we are concerned, is to demonstrate the real analogy that informs the operation of poetry and ethics as parallel systems. The second system, on the other hand, will prove of more use as we seek to rationalize the coherence and unity of specific medieval poems such as the *Canterbury Tales*.

This second system has been less than clear because the printed evidence is misleading. Ghisalberti's editions of the *accessus* of both Arnulf of Orleans and Giovanni del Virgilio present texts in which the kinds of metamorphoses are specified as natural, magical, and spiritual.[50] The commentary of William of Theigiis, preserved in MS Paris, B.M. lat. 8010, agrees; after listing and illustrating them, he says, "Istis tribus modis dicitur mutatio, et non pluribus" ("Change is defined in these three modes, and not in more"). But in the same *accessus* he also gives an alternate version: "Sciendum est quod quadruplex assignatur mutatio scilicet naturalis, moralis, spiritualis et magica. Naturalis quam actor innuit in divisione elementorum, moralis que attenditur in Lycaone mutato in lupum, et ideo dicitur quia prius benignus postea factus predo et improbus. Spiritualis sicut de Agave que primo discreta mutata fuit in insanam. Magica est de ymagine Pymalionis in virginem mutata, et est magica sicut apparet in Circe que per incantacionem mutabat homines in porcos."[51] Other manuscripts tend to confirm the tradition as one wavering between three and four changes. MS B.N. lat. 15136, a thirteenth-century book from St. Victor, specifies three, but a different set: "Videndum est quot sint modi mutationis tres scilicet. Est enim ethica mutatio et theorica et magica. Ethica de animali rationali ad irrationale [*sic*] ut mutatio licaonis in lupum. Theorica est spiritualis ut deificatio herculis. Magica ut de re inanimata ad rem inanimata [*sic*] sicut mutatio ymaginis quam fecit prometheus" (fol. 198r). ("What may be the modes of change must be specified—they are three. For there is ethical change and theoretical and magical. The ethical, from a rational animal to an irrational, such as the change of Lycaon into a wolf. The theoretical is spiritual, such as the deification of Hercules. The magical, from an inanimate thing to an animate [cod. inanimate], such as the change of the image which Prometheus made.") Still another set of three, the artificial, the natural, and the "mistica et magica," occurs in a fourteenth-century French manuscript, now MS Vat. lat. 1479.[52] Otherwise, in the Arnulf-Giovanni tradition, the three specified omit the ethical, even though in Giovanni's commentary interpretations for Hermaphroditus are specified as both "naturaliter" and "moraliter."[53] The *mutatio* of the person turned to stone in book 10 is similarly labeled in MS Vat. lat. 1598: "Item moralis est ista mutatio. Allegoria talis est. Philosophus quidam fuit qui cognita subtilitate herculis qui docuit terram esse tripartitam quam dedit intelligi per cerberum. Unde fingitur cerberum traxisse ab inferis desperavit post herculem nichil philosophicum dicere et stupore percussus destitit a sensu. Unde in lapidem fingitur esse mutatus" (fol. 101r). ("This change is moral. Its allegory is thus: he was a certain philosopher who understood the subtlety of Hercules (Hercules taught that the earth was tripartite and let this be understood by Cerberus, and so it is imagined that he dragged Cerberus out of Hell) and after Hercules despaired of saying anything philosophical and became depressed and out of touch with reality. When it is imagined that he was changed into a stone.") It is probably only natural, therefore, that the list triplex— natural, magical, and spiritual—should have often become the list quadruplex. The fullest explanation of this scheme we have encountered is in MS Vat. lat. 2781:

In nova fert animus: Notandum est quod quadruplex est mutatio, scilicet naturalis, moralis, magica et spiritualis. Naturalis est que fit per contexionem elementorum. Vel retexionem vel mediante semine vel sine. Per contexionem enim conveniunt elementa. Ut cum de spermate nascitur puer, et de ovo pullus, et de semine herba vel arbor et sic de similibus, et hec mediante semine. Per retexionem vero sicut fit dissolutio in quolibet corpore et hoc sine semine, et hec quantum ad elementa et ad yle. Yle est nature vultus antiquissimus generationis virtus indefessus formarum prima subiectio materia corporum substantie fundamentum. Elementa sicut fit quando terra rarescit in aquam, aqua levificatur in aera, aer subtiliatur in ignem. Item ignis spissatur in aera, aer grossificatur in aquam, aqua conglobatur in terra. Et hinc mutatio est naturalis de qua facit mentionem pictagoras dicens: quattuor etternus genitalia corpora mundus continet, etc. Moralis est illa mutatio que attenditur circa mores scilicet cum mores mutantur. Ut de licaone in lupum quidem dicere de benigne in asperum vel econtra et raptorem vel econtrario, et sic de similibus que attenduntur circa mores. Magica autem mutatio est que circa artem magicam attenditur. Et fit tandem (cod tm) in corpore quando videlicet magici aliquid alterius essentie quam sit per artem magicam faciunt apparere, ut de sociis ulixis a circe mutatis in porcos. Hec autem ars scilicet magicam olim extitit in valorem. Spiritualis mutatio est que attenditur in corpore et spiritu, scilicet quando corpus sanum efficitur morbidum, et inde vexatur spiritus et sic spiritus cum corpore pariter mutatur. Ut apparet in illis qui habent febres acutas, in spiritu quidem tandem ut de sano fit infirmus, scilicet insanus sicut de horeste legitur et de agave que proprium filium laceravit, sicut etiam quotidie videtur de patientibus frenesim qui mactarent patrem, matrem, et alios nisi libarentur. De quibus hominibus in hoc opere agit autor. [Fol. 186v–187r][54]

According to at least some authorities, therefore, the Ovidian changes which inform right human behavior are classified as natural, moral, magical, and spiritual. By medieval standards we should expect that this schema would have some rightness of its own, independent of or prior to an empirical examination of the *Metamorphoses;* medieval schemata of classification, of which the most famous is the four causes, tend to be imposed from authority rather than discovered in the course of investigation. This habit, of course, is natural to an age which believed seriously in the possibility of definition and therefore in practice tended to adapt existing forms and procedures rather than to invent new ones.

There are in fact other fourfold schemata which are closely analogous to this Ovidian one and inform it in ways which sharpen, refine, and make more effective its usefulness as an instrument of Chaucer criticism. These analogous systems occur in discussions of hell and classify the kinds of descent into hell, which, apparently, could cover all cases.[55] The schemata occur in the commentary of Bernardus Sylvestris on the *Aeneid,* the commentary of Dante's son on the *Commedia,* and the *De laboribus Herculis* of Coluccio Salutati. In these classifications terminology is not absolutely consistent, but the illustrations and definitions which go with the terms make it clear that all three authors are fundamentally talking about the same thing.

For Bernardus, "descensus autem ad inferos quadrifarius est: est autem unus naturae, alius virtutis, tertius vitii, quartus artificii" ("the descent into hell is fourfold, for there is one of nature, another of virtue, a third of vice, and a fourth of artifice"). One descends naturally by being born into a human condition which has hell as its possible future and vice its possible present. One descends virtuously by noticing how fragile and unworthy the things of this world are. One descends viciously by being totally preoccupied with "temporalia." One descends artificially by necromancy.[56] All of these descents are figurative, or symbolic. All of them are moral. For one of them, the virtuous, Bernardus's explanation repeats much the same medieval commonplace which Arnulf uses to justify attention to the material and temporal "changes" of the Ovidian story: "Est autem alius virtutis qui fit dum sapiens aliquis ad mundana per considerationem descendit, non ut in eis intentionem ponat sed ut eorum cognita fragilitate eis abiectis ad invisibilia penitus se convertat et creaturarum cognitione creatorem evidentius agnoscat."[57] The artificial, from Bernardus's comment, is obviously the same as the Ovidian "magical."

In the commentary of Dante's son, Pietro, the descent is also "quadruplex ... scilicet, naturalis, virtuosus, vitiosus, artificialis et nigromanticus" ("fourfold ... that is, natural, virtuous, vicious, artificial and black magical"). "Artificialis" and "nigromanticus" are apparently synonyms. Otherwise, the categories are the same as those of Bernardus. Pietro illustrates the descent of vice with the victims of Circe who were companions of Ulysses and Aeneas, and who in the Ovidian tradition were the subjects of magical change.[58]

Salutati's treatment is the longest and most elegant, but it amounts to much the same thing. The natural descent is "anime rationalis descensum in corpora" ("the descent of the rational soul into bodies"). The magical is accomplished by the invocation of spirits or demons, or by the shedding of human blood, or by diabolic arts. The descent of vice is made by those "qui relictis celestibus in terrena descenderint" ("who having left celestial things descend into earthly"). The moral and virtuous descent is made "cum ad mundana ista et ad ipsorum falsitatem contemplandam descendimus ... ut superiora melius per hec intelligenda cognoscat, et ad illa desideranda per hec animetur intellectus" ("when we descend into these worldly matters and into the contemplation of their falsity ... that by this understanding the intellect may better understand higher things, and be animated to desire them").[59] Richard Green explains this fourth descent in a most illuminating way: "It is the imaginary journey into the underworld to contemplate the consequences of vice in order to ascend again to the practice of virtue. Some variation of this mode of interpretation was applied to the fables of Orpheus, Theseus, Amphiarius, Hercules, and Aeneas. And it was used by Dante's commentators to explain the pilgrim's journey through hell as the necessary condition of his ascent to Paradise."[60]

Because this scheme defined by natural, magical, moral, and spiritual has four parts, and because we propose to use it to interpret the *Canterbury Tales*, it may seem obligatory that we relate it to that fourfold system of analysis by which medieval biblical interpretations were classified. Two parallels are obvious: the natural with the literal, and the moral with the tropological. We can easily go further, and say that anagogy is the category under which the earthly is interpreted as a way of understanding and loving the spiritual. Allegory, on the other hand, is not magical, since allegorical meanings of the Bible usually have to do with Christ, and magic is the category for false miracles, false appearances, and deceptions. If there is a relationship here, it is a relationship between opposites.

These relationships are far from perfect and consistent; we suspect they are merely accidental and insignificant.[61] If there is a significant relation, it arises out of the fact that the four-level system of biblical meaning defines, in general terms, a semiotic array of the ways in which a given text or deed or word may be meaningful. In practice the exegetes found meanings which were Christian in content, as of course they should. But if one analyzes the structure of their interpreting, one finds meaning in four, and only four, significant kinds, which as kinds define the medieval semiotic possibilities for texts which have no necessarily Christian meaning.[62] Thus a given story may illustrate some abstract universal, such as justice; it may inspire us to some specific moral act; or it may be, in addition to an actual report of an event, a text which we may receive epideictically as symbol or myth. These possibilities may, from time to time, occur for the natural, magical, moral, or spiritual metamorphoses of Ovid, or the tales of Chaucer; when they do, there is obviously a relation between the fact that some tale has a particular kind of meaning and the scheme of possible meanings, but this relation is neither mechanical nor dependent upon the fact that both the scheme for classifying tales and the scheme for classifying meanings have four parts.

The crucial difference between the fourfold method of the exegetes and the fourfold scheme of categories which we propose here is that in any given instance the exegete has only one text or story and up to four meanings for it, whereas we have many stories, all different from one another, which we classify into four categories in order to see that they present different aspects of some single subject.[63] Classifying the tales thus, we can define among them a unity of moral purpose and of general subject, which fits because it has, as such, a variety of parts, subtopics, and themes which corresponds to the tales as arrayed. Thus, a classification which names exhaustively the parts of a subject is transferred to a literary classification, which names kinds of stories treating of the subject in all its parts. For the *Metamorphoses,* the subject of the work is defined as changes, both in matter and in men, and the moral purpose is to reveal the varieties of ethical behavior which these changes exemplify. The four kinds of changes often used for classification are simple or natural actions; apparent changes in the natural order achieved by deception or magic; moral actions, in which man consciously attempts to live up to the truth which he should exemplify; and spiritual or anagogic or virtuous actions, by which the correct, heaven-centered sense of life is brought into contact with the world and the world below. These changes become the means of distinguishing between the various kinds of tales in the collection, as they treat the different kinds of changes possible. The value of such a method of discussing stories is that it enables the reader to relate them in a number of ways, through the moral lesson they teach or through the subject they have in common, while remaining sensitive to the differences which distinguish them from each other, especially details of situation and character, and to the individual contributions they make to the whole of the work's statement.

Such a classification enables the commentator to explain why the work's parts go together, in the sense that they relate to a common subject. But it does not specify an arrangement of the parts necessary to a proper exposition. In fact, medieval commentators on Ovid explain the parts of the work in two ways: one is the classification according to the parts of the work's subject which we have been discussing, and the other is in terms of organization, both into books and also as a progression in chronological order, from creation to Ovid's time.[64] Whereas modern readers seize on a familiar structural device for narrative, such as chronology, in order to explain the structure of the *Metamorphoses,* the medieval practice was to mention such a progression and then to concentrate, instead, on the stories as they related to their common subject, and the parts of that subject.[65] A similar logic is at work in biblical exegesis; the book is sacred history and encompasses a movement in time, but time is often ignored in explaining the true sense of an event. Time is drawn together in the single defining moment of Christ, and in him all events become repetitions of a single subject, salvation. The *Biblia Pauperum* is an example of a literary arrangement which accommodates, in its structure, both the principle of chronology and also a principle of arrangement, the grouping of New Testament events with their Old Testament parallels, dictated by the parts of the subject. We shall return in chapter 3 to consider medieval ideas of structure more thoroughly. Before discussing the organization of the *Knight's Tale*, in the terminology of changes we have derived from Ovidian commentary, however, it was necessary to make clear the important distinction between a unity by subject and a unity by arrangement.

The reading of the *Knight's Tale* which follows attempts to practice a medieval procedure for discovering the unity of a story, by defining, first, its subject, and then the parts of that subject. The classification into parts which we apply to the tale, and will go on to apply to the entire collection, is the division of changes into natural, magical, moral, and spiritual, the division we have analyzed at work in commentaries of the *Metamorphoses*. In following such a procedure, we are suggesting that Chaucer may have developed a method of composition from a medieval way of reading. There is, of course, no way of verifying this, nor do we intend to commit the intentional fallacy. The suggestion that a poet would learn how to write from the way he had learned how to read is not so strange, however, for an age whose commentators regularly did commit the intentional fallacy, claiming in every allegorization that they were presenting the author's true meaning.[66] The practice is certainly questionable, but it would lend itself readily to taking the commentaries as lessons in writing as well as in reading. By adapting the medieval methods of reading Ovid to reading Chaucer, however, we do not claim to find a uniformity of meaning or method between the two writers. The congruence between the parts of Ovid's subject and the parts of Chaucer's is not perfect; but the similarity is strong enough, we believe, to justify using the categories of Ovidian changes, natural, magical, moral, and spiritual, as a starting point for defining the unity of the tales in the Canterbury collection. Our test case is the tale in the defining first position, the *Knight's Tale*.

The *Knight's Tale* presents Theseus's successful efforts to maintain the peace of Athens. The disturbance which receives most attention is the tangled romantic triangle of the warring brothers-in-arms Palamon and Arcite and the unwilling Emelye. However, Theseus's part in this personal struggle, as the guardian of Emelye, and the emblematic significance of the three lovers' places of birth invest the love problem with implications for the order of family, society, and even man's place in creation. The many-layered significance of the tale's events has been noted often enough, but the weight that Chaucer gives the story, as a situation which encompasses the essential problem of human existence, merits further consideration. Leaving aside the particulars of the struggle for a moment, we find in the four parts of the poem four ways of attempting to deal with a problem. In part 1 Theseus's force of arms establishes order from chaos—included in that order, however, is the unhappy pair of former comrades, Palamon and Arcite, neither of whom has any hopes of winning Emelye; in the second part both young men, by changes in their situation caused by their love, are free in Athens and at the point of fighting to the death; in part 3 the lovers' requests to the gods lead to a solution of the dilemma that their contrary desires have established; and in part 4 the foregone conclusion is made visible to human eyes. The four parts, in some ways, answer to the modern sense of dramatic action, in that they follow a series of struggles for a particular goal, which is finally won. But they also isolate from the ongoing progress of seeking a goal four particular moments as especially significant; they are moments in which changes, created by force or love or prayer, have introduced new possibilities for action. The four kinds of changes into which Chaucer divides his subject have much in common with the four changes identified in Ovidian commentary.

The first kind of change, exemplified by part 1 of the tale, is the simple or natural action, controlled by human effort. The *Knight's Tale* begins with an achieved order. Theseus has married the Amazon Hippolyta, has made Emelye his ward, and is returning home in triumph. In his progress he meets the ladies of Thebes. The scene is very like the one in which Dante idealizes Trajan as an exemplum of royal humility,[67] and there is every likelihood that Chaucer meant the compliment, since the pagan Theseus is so perfectly a model ruler. In being presented with the problem of Thebes, Theseus meets the supreme test. Thebes is, for the Middle Ages, the generic bad city, as the Rome of Aeneas is the generic good city. Thebes is the city of patricide, bad marriage, fratricide, civil war, and sacrilege; from the example of Thebes mankind is instructed in every possible disorder. Theseus apparently meets the test, as he and his army conquer Thebes, permit the obsequies of the dead, and arrange for the custody of Palamon and Arcite. Thus, as ruler of Athens, husband of Hippolyta, and conqueror of Thebes, Theseus has ordered his world. His situation has been allegorized as the achievement of a fit relation between the rational soul (Theseus in Athens), the concupiscible soul (his marriage), and the irascible soul (Thebes).[68] As long as we do not lose Theseus himself, Athens, Thebes, or the two ladies in all this, such analogy-making is both permissible and informative; Plato's *Republic*, which the Middle Ages knew indirectly through the *Timaeus*, is powerfully based on just such an analogical instrument of analysis. Theseus is at peace in his family, in his kingdom, and in himself; such orders are properly mutual and mutually reinforcing; and as king, husband, and human being, Theseus has done as well as a mortal can be expected to do. Aegidius Romanus, in fact, in his *De regimine principum*, analyzes the nature and duty of the sovereign in terms of right rule of himself, his family, and his realm, and Chaucer, in including the elements of the story as he did, could not but underline the typical and definitional force of this king of Athens.

Both Emelye and the two Theban princes, however, are principles of disorder. Emelye is an unawarded virgin and an Amazon. Unmarried, she represents all those problems which Theseus solved, at another level, by conquering and marrying Hippolyta.[69] Even more, Palamon and Arcite are a problem, which Theseus recognizes by condemning them to eternal imprisonment. In a manner, all these people can be seen as emblematic and, as such, unavoidable. Every city, every civilization, faced the temptation to become a Thebes. John Lydgate saw this very clearly, when he inserted his story of Thebes as another, and final, Canterbury tale. He reminds us that Thebes will not go away but must be dealt with, even though, as Theseus finds, the children of its sisters must be imprisoned within one's own society. In his additional Canterbury tale, Lydgate analyzes troth, marriage, and true and false rule in a manner profoundly relevant to Chaucer's great themes. The whole matter deserves additional and separate study;[70] here it is sufficient to note that, in the Middle Ages, an addition to an inherited story is the profoundest kind of interpretation, and that the addition of Thebes confirms the focus on civil and familial strife with which Chaucer lets his Knight begin.

Although the complications of life may be unavoidable, for Theseus, the lesson must be learned. Under the appearance of his total victories—first, the wedding of Hippolyta, and second, the conquest of Thebes—there remain the disorderly elements of Amazonian independence and Theban fraternal discord which Theseus has taken into his kingdom, unreconstructed, in the persons of Emelye, Palamon, and Arcite. The three young people form a romantic triangle, whose sorting out promises to be no easy matter. A sworn virgin is the unknowing object of the fierce longing—rendered by Chaucer here, ironically, as courtly love—[71] of two young men, whose brotherly accord is turned by rivalry in love into a bitter hatred. Eventually the whole city will be concerned with the love affair's resolution. For Theseus the struggles faced in the external world of war must be faced again, in his own city and his own household.[72] Here in part 1, however, we see only the beginnings of this struggle with disorder. Emelye remains unaware of what her mere existence as an unawarded virgin is doing to the two aging young men; and their rivalry in love, though sufficiently bitter at one level fitly to evoke the rivalry of Eteocles and Polynices, is comically futile and completely harmless.[73] Even when Arcite is delivered from prison and sent home, exiled from a lady love whom he has presumably never once met, order is preserved, and Chaucer underlines the comic security of the situation by posing, in formal courtly fashion, the lovers' question, "Who hath the worse, Arcite or Palamoun?" (I [A] 1348).

In terms of the four-part *distinctio* of metamorphoses which Ovidian commentary defines for us, this first part of the *Knight's Tale* presents the order of the natural. In the Ovidian tradition, natural changes were those resulting "per contextionem elementorum." In the descent-into-hell tradition, the natural descent meant being involved in the normal human condition, whose possible future is hell and whose possible present is vice. Adapting and combining, we have the first part of the *Knight's Tale* as the level of the normally human—the best that can be done with the natural man. Order exists, but in the presence of potential for disorder; Theseus rules, but his subjects include Palamon, Arcite, and Emelye. Order exists, but it is an order which has not yet been tested by all the various changes which the world may bring against it.

The second part of the *Knight's Tale* begins with what can only be called a magical metamorphosis, in which a person changes his appearance but remains really the same, this time under the influence of love. The action is dictated by a reversal of the natural order of the human sexual hierarchy; while Theseus has achieved domestic order and civil peace in conquering Hippolyta, Palamon and Arcite remain in the disorderly chaos of allowing themselves to be ruled by Emelye. In this section the advice of women (as opposed to their supplication) is given and heeded, and on the key issue of allowing the knights to contend for Emelye—in the medieval tradition, of course, such advice traces to Eve and is frequently an invitation to disaster. The events of this section, in Theseus's own judgment, are the "myracles" of the god of love (I [A] 1788). As such, they obey no law but love's; they are, for the government of Theseus, intrusive chaos. The whole section is full of disguises, deceptions, changes of identity; the most persistent imagery of animals as descriptions of human actions is in part 2. This is the most disorderly section of the whole tale.[74]

The third section is the moral one—in terms of the descent-into-hell tradition, the descent into vice. Here devotion to the things of this world is most elaborately and devoutly professed, with all the trappings of shrines and pagan gods. Here, in ritual lists which underline their exemplary quality, are the deeds and fortunes of worldly men. The atmosphere throughout is one of calamity, framed by the sovereignties of rival and malevolent gods. The fact that Palamon, Arcite, and Emelye express, in this section and to these gods, what they desire of the world underlines the worldliness of their desire. Chaucer does not, like Lydgate, call these devotions pagan or devilish, but his presentation has similar overtones.[75] Most of the exempla—Ydelnesse, Narcissus, Salamon, Ercules, or, more impersonally, "the smylere with the knyf under the cloke" (I [A] 1099) or "the stranglyng and hangyng by the throte" (I [A] 2458)—are clear enough. One, however, deserves a pause, because it is an implicit evaluation of one of Chaucer's characters, and because it underlines the atmosphere of worldliness appropriate to the mode, which is merely moral.

Among other things, Saturn says, "I slow Sampsoun, shakynge the piler" (I [A] 2466), less than fifty lines after Arcite, praying to Mars, offers in exchange for victory the sacrifice of

> My beerd, myn heer, that hongeth long adoun,
> That nevere yet ne felte offensioun
> Of rasour nor of shere.
>
> (I [A] 2415-17)

In general, in the exegetes, the loss of Samson's hair figures a commitment to carnality. Bersuire's statement is the clearest, and the nearest to Chaucer:

> Hic habetur quod postquam Samson mediante mala muliere Dalila fuit caesarie tonsus, et per consequens fortitudine privatus, statim Philistaei

ipsum ceperunt, et captum excoecaverunt, et excoecatum in carcere posuerunt, et incarceratum molere, et coram se ludere fecerunt, sed tamen post hoc factum est, quod Samson a Philistaeis excoecatus qui ipsum excoecaverunt, simul in domo sui convivii ruina domicilii facta super eum, omnes perierunt. Sic vere quando Samson, idest aliquis fortis et virtuosus homo mediante mala muliere, scilicet carne propria, caesariem virtutum, et per consequens resistendi fortitudine [*sic*] perdit, statim a Philistaeis, idest a daemonibus per diversa peccata capitur, et oculis discretionis orbatur, et sic excoecatus, obstinatus, et hebetatus in carcere malae consuetudinis includitur, et tandem molere, idest ad mundi labores et negotia circumire compellitur, et sic coram Philistaeis, idest demonibus ipsarum voluntati obediens, ludere et ludos diversorum peccatorum facere comprobatur. Finaliter tamen in eorum convivio, scilicet in inferno, una cum ipsis moritur et damnatur, et sic homo per fraudulentiam mulieris qua[m] amabat, idest proprie carnis, non solum excoecatur, imo etiam vita spirituali et aeterna privatur.[76]

Arcite puts himself in Samson's place, and has by this time already paid Samson's allegorical penalty literally, to be compelled "ad mundi labores et negotia circumire." And his ultimate deprivation, of Emelye and of life, is as pathetic and hopeless as anything in Chaucer.

The last section of the *Knight's Tale* represents the spiritual mode. Explicitly, it corresponds most closely to the mode of the virtuous, as defined in the descent-into-hell tradition, which is made "cum ad mundana ista et ad ipsorum falsitatem contemplandam descendimus ... ut superiora melius per hec intelligenda cognoscat" ("when we descend into these worldly matters and into the contemplation of their falsity ... that by this understanding [the intellect] may better understand higher things"). But just as clearly it depends on the whole enterprise of Ovidian commentary, whose existence affirms that these stories are of use only if and as they are properly understood, by seeing in their real surfaces the *veritatem* which they contain and represent. As the third section treats human efforts to arrange their own destinies, in consort with the gods who symbolize the forces of merely human and natural energy and calamity—love, hate, selfish self-preoccupation, and chaos—so the fourth deals with what actually happens when those arrangements go awry. The unexpected irony involved in the fact that both combatants, Palamon and Arcite, actually get what they have prayed for only underscores the point that merely human wisdom is not enough, and that finally there must come a Boethian recognition that within and beneath the events which fortune brings to pass there is truth not of human making.

The action of the *Knight's Tale*, then, part by part as Chaucer has divided it for us, is structured in terms of four great modes of ordering: the initial achievement of merely natural order in the givenness of the human condition; the intrusion of disorder, deception, and chaos; the human attempt to achieve order in terms of private wishes and worldly struggles; and the final reassertion of order based on the right interpretation of such events as have, under Providence or Fortune, actually occurred. The tale is a moderately hopeful definition of human experience as the achievement of actions which are in harmony with the purposes of the universe, even if man's intentions for what he does prove to be in error. The parts of the tale divide human activity into four kinds; although the arrangement of these parts corresponds, in some ways, to the logic of a plot, the parts are also offered as a number of alternative activities simultaneously present and being done by men. The story's arrangement answers more than the needs of a dramatic action. In addition, the historical sequence is adorned and clarified by structuring the poem in order to reveal the parallelism and mutual completion achieved by the four parts. Charles Muscatine characterized the structure of the *Knight's Tale* as a pageant, ordered in symmetrical harmony, rather than as a linear plot.[77] The pattern uniting the four parts has been suggested in previous analyses of the poem's formal elements.[78] The four parts might be imagined as being arranged in a square, with parts 1 and 2 the upper quadrants and parts 3 and 4 placed below them. In this way, the various parallelisms established by similar events in different parts of the poem would be clarified: for example, parts 2 and 4 both end with combats for Emelye, which are concluded by surprising reversals, in part 2 by Theseus's promise that one of them may wed Emelye, and in part 4 by the overturning of the apparent decision of the combat. At the same time, parts 1 and 4 and parts 2 and 3 also share important actions: in part 1 a royal wedding is followed by a bloody combat involving Palamon and Arcite, and in part 4 their confrontation is followed by another royal wedding. The harmony of four parts, maintaining one another in a balance requiring the interaction of all the parts on each other, is a structural feature of the poem intimately related to the divisions of its subject matter. It is an echo of that "fair cheyne of love" which Theseus discerns as the sustainer of the universe and uses to bind up the confusion in his realm.[79]

The *Knight's Tale* begins the Canterbury collection by defining the kinds of human experience and promising that man may find among them a way of life which harmonizes with the providential order of creation. The tale's arrangement forecasts the relationships which Chaucer will use to bind together the many stories he tells; it is an arrangement which reflects the dual aspects of the order of history, both sequential and yet simultaneously present in the single event of Christ. But the *Knight's Tale* is only the beginning; like any one part of itself, it is not all the truth of the whole of which it is a part. The challenges which will assault the integrity of Theseus's discovery of universal harmony begin immediately. The happy ending of the struggle to wed is overturned, not only in the *Miller's Tale* but throughout the collection, with stories of unhappy marriage. Doing what comes naturally, the highest goal of the Golden Age in which Theseus lives, is suddenly revealed to be insufficient as, in the *Miller's Tale*, we enter the time after Christ. In order to understand how the *Knight's Tale* functions as one of the many parts of the story collection, and how that collection, together, presents a unified picture of the human condition, it will be necessary to inquire, first, how the Middle Ages understood the category "fiction" and, second, how medieval poets adapted from their materials the techniques of arrangement which unified their works. Once these questions of the nature of fiction and the proper disposition of its parts are answered, we can begin to read the *Canterbury Tales*.

1. Michel Foucault, *The Order of Things* (New York, 1973), p. xv.

2. Medieval historians, of course, organized their books quite differently. Cf. William J. Brandt, *The Shape of Medieval History: Studies in Modes of Perception* (New Haven, 1966).

3. Cited by John V. Fleming, *The "Roman de la Rose": A Study in Allegory and Iconography* (Princeton, 1969), p. 18.

4. We acknowledge a similar interest in Foucault's *The Order of Things*. See the discussion of medieval language theory, pp. 17–42.

5. Robert Jordan, *Chaucer and the Shape of Creation* (Cambridge, Mass., 1967). Jordan's analysis of medieval aesthetics and his analysis of Chaucer's poetry fall into two parts, whose congruity is not always perfect. He finds the turning point of the stories in the juxtaposition of the "truth," stated in the *Parson's Tale*, with the "lie" of the limited truths presented in the "fictional" tales. See below for further discussion of the truth value of fiction. Cf. Jordan, pp. 240–41.

6. The Ellesmere Order continues to be used by many scholars as the most authoritative sequence for the tales and, therefore, the logical starting place for studying the relationships among the parts of the poem. For recent discussions of the order, see Donald Howard, *The Idea of the Canterbury Tales* (Berkeley and Los Angeles, 1976), pp. 210–16; and E. Talbot Donaldson, "The Ordering of the *Canterbury Tales*," in *Medieval Literature and Folklore*

Studies in Honor of Francis Lee Utley, ed. Jerome Mandel and Bruce A. Rosenberg (New Brunswick, 1970), pp. 193–204.

7. The Middle Ages read Aristotle's *Poetics* in the version of Averroes, which substituted for Aristotle's doctrine of beginning, middle, and end a doctrine of rhetorical length. See W. F. Boggess, "Averrois Cordubensis Commentarium Medium in Aristotelis Poetriam" (Ph.D. diss., University of North Carolina, 1965), pp. 24–26. The medieval parameters within which it is possible to continue to believe in the human comedy have been brilliantly defined by Jill Mann in *Chaucer and Medieval Estates Satire* (Cambridge, 1973), though her conclusion permits more individuality to survive the Chaucerian irony than we think her evidence really allows. The reader reactions to which she permits the perceptions of individuals rather than types are those of modern readers, whose attitudes to apparent moral ambivalence would be far more nominalist, or relativist, than any in a medieval audience.

8. Judson Allen must here recant having presumed the axiom of plot himself; he used the fact that the pilgrimage is planned to end in London, with "a banquet in Harry Bailey's public house," to defend the human comedy view, and thus committed both axiomatic sins at once. See his *The Friar as Critic: Literary Attitudes in the Later Middle Ages* (Nashville, 1971), p. 129.

9. At the most literal level, the pilgrimage plot results in geography-based recommendations of an order for the tales, most notably the Bradshaw Shift. See Robert A. Pratt, "The Order of the Canterbury Tales," *PMLA* 66 (1951): 1141–67. The Six-Text Edition follows the proposal that the tales from the Shipman through the Nun's Priest, group B², move to a position immediately after the *Man of Law's Tale.* See below in chapter 3 for a discussion of the appropriateness of trusting to the geographical signposts given in the links as key evidence for Chaucer's final design. Proposals for reconstructing a two-way journey from the tales have been made by several scholars, most recently by Charles A. Owen, Jr., *Pilgrimage and Storytelling in the Canterbury Tales: The Dialectic of "Ernest" and "Game"* (Norman, Okla., 1977). This study includes a bibliography of other writings in which Owen proposed and defended his scheme for the two-way journey.

10. Some scholars have attempted to treat the stories as literary objects by classifying them according to genre, style, or tone. Paul Ruggiers distinguishes between "prevailingly comic" and "prevailingly romantic" tales, suspended between the principal tales of the Knight and the Parson, in *The Art of the Canterbury Tales* (Madison, 1965), p. 10. Charles Muscatine, *Chaucer and the French Tradition* (Berkeley and Los Angeles, 1966), also classifies the tales in literary terms (p. 171).

11. Ralph Baldwin, *The Unity of the Canterbury Tales* (Copenhagen, 1955). Other critics in substantial agreement with Baldwin include Robert Jordan, *Chaucer and the Shape of Creation;* D. W. Robertson, *A Preface to Chaucer* (Princeton, 1962); and Ruggiers, *The Art of the Canterbury Tales.* An excellent survey of the various approaches to unity is provided by Charles A. Owen, Jr., "The Design of the *Canterbury Tales,*" in *Companion to Chaucer Studies,* ed. Beryl Rowland (Oxford, 1968), pp. 192–207.

12. For an extended presentation of the evidence on which these generalizations are based, see Judson B. Allen, "The Old Way and the Parson's Way:

An Ironic Reading of the Parson's Tale," *Journal of Medieval and Renaissance Studies* 3 (1973): 255-71.

13. Baldwin notes these doctrines of the manuals but is still fundamentally dominated by modern notions of narrative; in the same paragraph he says that the conclusion "should summarize or reflect aphoristically the word at hand," and that "it is fitting for Chaucer in this climactic place in the story, in the pilgrimage, to make the Parson the spokesman, the mediator, the scourge, and the ender of it all" (*The Unity of the Canterbury Tales*, pp. 89-90).

14. The psychological authenticity of Chaucer's creation is vital to many studies; perhaps the most elaborate working out of the theory of the tales as character revelation is in R. M. Lumiansky, *Of Sondry Folk: The Dramatic Principle in the Canterbury Tales* (Austin, 1955).

15. In this tradition are John M. Manly's *Some New Light on Chaucer* (New York, 1926) and Muriel Bowden's *A Commentary on the General Prologue of the Canterbury Tales* (New York, 1948).

16. The spiritual pilgrimage approach is a result of the growing appreciation of the importance in medieval art of its Christian cultural values. As we shall see in discussing the faults of a dramatically constituted Marriage Group, the allegorical dimensions of marriage, which contemporary evidence suggests would have been in Chaucer's mind when writing a tale like the Clerk's, are lost in the psychological combat proposed by G. L. Kittredge. Martin Stevens, in "Chaucer and Modernism: An Essay in Criticism," published in *Chaucer at Albany*, ed. Rossell Hope Robbins (Albany, 1975), pp. 193-216, argues that D. W. Robertson's allegorical method was formulated in opposition to critical "realism." Stevens goes on to question the relevance of Robertson's position to contemporary criticism. On Robertson, see n. 20 below.

17. Boggess, "Averrois Cordubensis," pp. 20, 23. "Tragedy indeed [and by extension poetry] is not an art representative of men themselves, just as they are, as individual things falling into perception, but it is the art representative of virtuous customs and praiseworthy actions and beliefs of holy people . . . and the art of understanding, which shows or teaches from which things and how poems are composed, is more important and more perfect than the composition of poems itself." This and all other translations from Latin are our own.

18. G. L. Kittredge, "Chaucer's Discussion of Marriage," in *Chaucer: Modern Essays in Criticism*, ed. Edward Wagenknecht (New York, 1959), pp. 188-215. This essay has spawned numerous progeny, of which one of the latest and most medieval is R. E. Kaske, "Chaucer's Marriage Group," in *Chaucer the Love Poet*, ed. Jerome Mitchell and William Provost (Athens, Ga., 1973), pp. 45-65, who reads the four tales as a chiastic analysis of the relation between authority and sexuality, with marriage as the context.

19. The medieval understanding of marriage as a background for Chaucer's tales has been discussed by Robertson, *A Preface to Chaucer;* Henry Ansgar Kelly, *Love and Marriage in the Age of Chaucer* (Ithaca, 1975); and Patricia M. Kean, *Chaucer and the Making of English Poetry* (London and Boston, 1972), among others.

20. Robertson offers as proof that marriage is the theme of all the tales that the allegorical dimensions of marriage were in fact the subject, whether the

story itself treated real human marriage, the Christian's relationship with God, or the priest's particular status as bride of Christ. Robertson's work has been an immense contribution to literary medieval studies, but more in spite of than because of the creedal orthodoxy which he attempts to impose. Both the exegetical tradition and the related analogizing through which physical and moral facts were viewed have left for us a body of evidence whose importance he rightly defends, and about which he has published much pioneering and useful information. However, since our use of some of this evidence may suggest the too hasty conclusion that we are "Robertsonian," we would like to state bluntly and categorically that we are not. The enterprise of this book is to value Chaucer's literal sense, his fictions themselves, and in them the sublimely lively and subtly moral facts which idealists might label "merely" human. Chaucer knew about allegory and commentaries and glossing with a comfortable familiarity which permitted him to play games with them and use them for his own ironic high comedy. If we follow his ironies for the moment into Latin, even the *glosa,* it is only in order to return more convinced than ever that it is the fiction that is true, the act that generates the definition.

21. Many critics have faulted Chaucer or his age for the tale, on the grounds that to accept Griselda's submission and Walter's domination is impossible for modern readers. Cf. Bertrand H. Bronson, *In Search of Chaucer* (Toronto, 1960), pp. 103–12; Jordan, *Chaucer and the Shape of Creation,* p. 200; Raymond Preston, *Chaucer* (London and New York, 1952). The defense of Chaucer's manipulation of the tension between the allegorical and literal dimensions of his story comes from James Sledd, "The *Clerk's Tale:* The Monsters and the Critics," in *Chaucer Criticism,* ed. R. J. Schoeck and J. Taylor (Notre Dame, 1960), 1:160–74.

22. See below, in chapter 6's treatment of the tale.

23. Eventually we wish to use, instead of the word *association,* an array of the medieval words associated with allegory—especially typology. But these words are still widely misunderstood and will be used only after they have been properly defined.

24. E. Talbot Donaldson, "Chaucer the Pilgrim," *PMLA* 69 (1954): 933. We must here acknowledge a very great debt to Professor Donaldson, even though we disagree with a few of his conclusions and more of his emphases, because in his wit and in the affectionate irony which he addresses to his subject, he more resembles Chaucer than does any other practicing critic. One of the things that makes our new critical enterprise necessary is that he has in many areas, such as "Chaucer the Pilgrim," said so well the last word.

25. Arthur W. Hoffman, "Chaucer's Prologue to Pilgrimage: The Two Voices," *ELH* 21 (1954): 4.

26. Mann, *Chaucer and Medieval Estates Satire,* pp. 187–202.

27. A preliminary theoretical working out of this understanding can be found in Judson B. Allen and Patrick Gallacher, "Alisoun through the Looking Glass: or Every Man His Own Midas," *Chaucer Review* 4 (1970): 99–105.

28. In such a modern view, Chaucer becomes a sympathetic admirer of all the ways of life represented by his pilgrims. See Donaldson, "Chaucer the Pilgrim," p. 933, and Hoffman, "Chaucer's Prologue," pp. 4, 14.

29. Isidore of Seville *Etymologiarum* 1. 37. 22. It is more than coincidental, we think, that Wayne C. Booth's theory of irony, whose fundamental focus is with much more modern literature, recognizes as one of the chief features of irony that it presumes, and creates, sympathies and, ideally, unities between properly disparate elements. That is, when irony is properly understood, an intimacy is created between the ironist and his audience which overcomes the otherwise literal meaning of the communication. This sympathy or unity is in modern times largely a feature of subjectivity; the relationship between medieval irony and medieval allegory implies that then it was more largely influential and related things and events as well as subjectivities. Cf. Wayne C. Booth, *The Rhetoric of Irony* (Chicago, 1974).

30. This point will be discussed more elaborately below. See also Judson B. Allen, "Hermann the German's Averroistic Aristotle and Medieval Poetic Theory," *Mosaic* 9 (Spring 1976): 67–81.

31. Frederick Tupper's classification of tales and tellers by means of the seven deadly sins has the flavor of Jordan's juxtaposition of the *Parson's Tale* to the remainder of the poem and has been taken into the construct of the spiritual pilgrimage as an expression of the doctrinal answer to the pilgrims' excesses, which may cure their failings. See his "Chaucer and the Seven Deadly Sins," *PMLA* 29 (1914): pp. 93–128. Interest in the tales as psychological self-revelations is best exemplified by the scholarship of the *Pardoner's Tale.* See the summary offered in John Halverson, "Chaucer's Pardoner and the Progress of Criticism," *Chaucer Review* 4 (1970): 184–202.

32. John H. Fisher, ed., *The Complete Poetry and Prose of Geoffrey Chaucer* (New York, 1977), p. 8.

33. Oxford University, Magdalen College Library MS lat. 18, fol. 16v. "Note that Statius is very rhetorical in this speech, when he lets Tideus speak without using rhetoric. Such speech is appropriate to his character."

34. This rhetorical principle does not deny, of course, that legitimate insight may be gained from comparing or contrasting the character of any given Canterbury pilgrim with an associated tale, or with any other pilgrim or tale. Whether positively or ironically, such an analogy can have a good deal of medieval force and significance; many such analogies will be dealt with in part 2. The undoubted practical success of some modern criticism which presumes the dramatic principle traces to this medieval practice of multiple exemplification; comparisons between teller and tale are informative as comparisons, even when our motivation for making them is nonmedieval.

35. Boggess, "Averrois cordubensis," p. 23. "Argument or proof of the correctness of belief or practice is not [achieved] by persuasive speech (for this kind of speech does not pertain to the art of poetry nor does it suit it) but by description ... and therefore poetry does not use the art of gestures nor of facial expressiveness as rhetoric does." This passage is a part of Averroes's definition of *consideratio*, a term which displaces, but is not equivalent to, the genuine Aristotelian "spectacle." It is an extremely complex concept, for which the best single English equivalent is probably "credibility." For a discussion of this important text, and a justification of less literal elements of this translation, see Judson B. Allen, "Hermann the German's Averroistic Aristotle."

36. *Boetius de consolatione . . . novissime cum Sancti Thomae philosophi profundis-simi commentariis* (Venice, 1524), fol. bb5v. "The formal cause of the treatment is Boethius's manner of doing [i.e. genre], and this is dialogue, that is, the speech of two. For Boethius introduces in this book two characters, himself complaining of his misery, and Philosophy sympathizing with him, and by consolation helping him overcome his misery." The attribution of this commentary to Thomas Aquinas is mistaken.

37. William C. Stokoe, Jr., "Structure and Intention in the First Fragment of the Canterbury Tales," *University of Toronto Quarterly* 21 (1952): 120-27. Cf., also, William Frost, "An Interpretation of Chaucer's *Knight's Tale*," in *Chaucer Criticism*, 1:112-15; Gerhard Joseph, "Chaucerian 'Game'—'Earnest' and the 'Argument of Herbergage' in the *Canterbury Tales*," *Chaucer Review* 5 (1970): 83-96; and John Leyerle, "The Heart and the Chain," in *The Learned and the Lewed: Studies in Chaucer and Medieval Literature*, ed. Larry D. Benson, Harvard English Studies, no. 5 (1974), pp. 113-45.

38. Organizations of other schemes are proposed by Paull F. Baum, *Chaucer: A Critical Appreciation* (Durham, N.C., 1958), who defines group B^2 as a "surprise group" (p. 74). Bruce Rosenberg, "The Contrary Tales of the Second Nun and the Canon's Yeoman," *Chaucer Review* 2 (1967): 278-91, and Penn R. Szittya, "The Green Yeoman as Loathly Lady: The Friar's Parody of the Wife of Bath's Tale," *PMLA* 90 (1975): 386-94, suggest that patterns of contrast function to relate the tales in group H and group D, respectively. Alan T. Gaylord, "*Sentence* and *Solaas* in Fragment VII of the *Canterbury Tales*: Harry Bailly as Horseback Editor," *PMLA* 82 (1967): 226-35, and several other authors, who will be mentioned in part 2 of this study, have examined the themes and imagery uniting the tales in specific fragments, as well. Cf. Howard, *The Idea of the Canterbury Tales*, chap. 5, pp. 210-36. Kean, *Chaucer and the Making of English Poetry*, 2:75, voices the common reservation, however, that such a method of interrelationships would have been too constricting.

39. Geoffrey of Vinsauf, in the *Poetria Nova*, describes the first place in a composition as the "apex operis . . . dignior hospes et tanquam dominus." Cf. the edition of Edmond Faral, *Les Arts poétiques du XIIe et du XIIIe siècle* (Paris, 1923), pp. 200-201, lines 112-20. See also the helpful translation of the text by Margaret F. Nims, *Poetria Nova of Geoffrey of Vinsauf* (Toronto, 1967), pp. 19-20.

40. This is not to say that among these authors there are not helpful indications of the tradition of framing story collections which might have influenced Chaucer's design of the *Canterbury Tales*. Robert A. Pratt and Karl Young attach much importance in their article "The Literary Framework of the Canterbury Tales," in *Sources and Analogues of Chaucer's Canterbury Tales*, ed. W. F. Bryan and Germaine Dempster (London, 1941; reissued 1958), pp. 1-81, to the similarity between Chaucer's frame and the frame journey in Sercambi's collection. Kean presents an excellent summary of sources for the frame journey; she rightly expands the search for sources beyond story collections whose frame is a journey of a large group of storytellers to consider the possible influence of such allegorical journeys as are found in de Guileville

and Mandeville, as well as in Dante. See *Chaucer and the Making of English Poetry*, 2:72. But the fact that Chaucer resembles Sercambi does not of itself explain the unity of either work, and the journey motif inevitably makes the frame too important at the expense of the tales themselves.

41. Most elaborately by Richard L. Hoffman, *Ovid and the Canterbury Tales* (Philadelphia, 1966), pp. 3–20, who limits his analysis of the relationship to facts at the "sources and analogues" level. More typical is Charles Muscatine's remark, "There is in literature, besides the framed collection, a tradition of the intercalation of short tales in longer works, evidenced for instance by Ovid's *Metamorphoses, The Romance of the Rose,* etc." (*Chaucer and the French Tradition*, p. 167).

42. John M. Fyler, *Chaucer and Ovid* (New Haven, 1979).

43. For the latest brief statement of H. R. Jauss's position, see his "The Alterity and Modernity of Medieval Literature," *New Literary History* 10 (Winter 1979): 181–229.

44. For full treatment of this theory, see Judson B. Allen, *The Ethical Poetic of the Later Middle Ages: A Decorum of Convenient Distinction* (forthcoming).

45. For fuller bibliography, see Judson B. Allen, *The Friar as Critic*, pp. 162–63.

46. Arnulf of Orleans, in Fausto Ghisalberti, "Arnolfo d'Orléans, un cultore di Ovidio nel secolo XII," *Memorie del Reale Istituto Lombardo di Scienze e Lettere,* Classe di Lettere, science morali et storiche, vol. 24 (15 of series 3), fasc. 4 (Milan, 1932), p. 181. "Ovid's intention is to deal with change, not chiefly that we might understand the extrinsic changes which affect physical things, good or bad, but more importantly that we might understand intrinsic changes, such as those which affect the soul, so that he might lead us from error toward knowledge of the true creator. There are two motions in the soul, one rational, the other irrational. Rational is that which imitates the motion of the heavens, which go from east to west, and on the other hand the irrational is that which imitates the motion of the planets, which move against the heavens. For God gave the soul reason through which it might restrain sensuality, just as the irrational motion of the seven planets is restrained through the motion of the firmament. But we, neglecting rational motion in the manner of the planets, are led away from our creator. Ovid, seeing this, wishes to show us through the narration of the fables the motion of the soul, which is within. Therefore it is said that Io was changed into a cow because she fell into vice, and that she regained her lovely human form because she put away vice. Or, Ovid's intention is to call us back from an immoderate love of temporal things and to urge us to the single devotion of our creator, by showing the stability of the heavens and the variation of temporal things. It is classified as ethics because it teaches us to hate those temporal things, which are passing and changing, because this belongs to morality."

47. Ibid.

48. Judson B. Allen, "Commentary as Criticism: Formal Cause, Discursive Form, and the Later Medieval Accessus," *Acta Conventus Neo-Latini Lovaniensis,* ed. J. Ijsewijn and E. Kessler (Munich, 1973), pp. 33–39.

49. For a further discussion of this extremely rich term, Averroes's substitution of Aristotle's term *mimesis*, see Judson B. Allen, "Hermann the German's Averroistic Aristotle," pp. 75-79.

50. Ghisalberti, "Arnolfo," p. 181: "de mutacione enim agit tripliciter scilicet de naturali, de magica, et de spirituali" ("he treats change as threefold, that is, natural, magical, and spiritual"). Giovanni says: "triplex est transmutatio, naturalis, spiritualis, et magica" ("transformation is triple: natural, spiritual, and magical"), in Ghisalberti, "Giovanni del Virgilio, espositore delle 'Metamorfosi,'" *Il Giornale Dantesco* 34 (1933): 17.

51. William is quoted by Fausto Ghisalberti, in "Medieval Biographies of Ovid," *Journal of the Warburg and Courtauld Institutes* 9 (1946): 55. "It should be known that change is considered fourfold, that is, natural, moral, spiritual, and magical. The natural change is implied when the author discusses the division of the elements [in Creation]; the moral change is the one we see when Lycaon is changed into a wolf—it is a moral change because Lycaon, who was at first a gracious man, became a robber and a scoundrel. Spiritual—as in the case of Agave, who was at first dignified and then went insane. The magical change happened to the statue of Pygmalion, which was changed into a maiden; another example of magical change occurs in connection with Circe, who by spells changed men into pigs." Ghisalberti prints two more *accessus* bearing on this problem. From the fourteenth-century MS Paris B.M. lat. 8253: "Plures enim mutationes esse assignantur. Est autem mutatio naturalis sicut illa de elementis.... Et est mutatio spiritualis sicuti fuit de Agave que facta est insana. Et est mutatio moralis et magica mutatio sicuti de Pigmalione qui fecit virginem" (p. 52). "Several changes are to be marked out, for there is natural change such as that having to do with elements.... And there is spiritual change such as happened to Agave who became insane. And there is moral change and magical change such as of Pygmalion who made a virgin."

52. The text is printed in B. Nogara, "Di alcune vite e commenti mediovali di Ovidio," *Miscellanea Ceriani* (Milan, 1910), p. 417.

53. Ghisalberti, "Giovanni," pp. 56-57.

54. "*My mind is turned to new forms:* It should be noted that change is fourfold, that is, natural, moral, magic and spiritual. That change is natural which happens through the combination of the elements. Or the dissolution, either with seed bringing the change about or without. For the elements come together through combination. As when a boy is born from sperm, and a chicken from an egg, or plants or a tree from seed and thus various things from similar sources, with seed bringing the change about. But dissolution happens through separation as in any body, in this without seed, and these things happen for the elements and for hyle. Hyle is the most ancient face of nature, the untiring power of generation, the first laying under of forms, the matter of bodies, the foundation of substance. It makes the elements as when earth thins into water, water lightens into air, air is dispersed into the ether. Then the ether is thickened into air, air is made heavier into water, and water is formed into earth. And thus it is natural change concerning which Pythagoras makes mention: 'The eternal world contains four elemental substances, etc.' That change is moral which takes notice concerning customs or

morals, that is, when customs are changed. As indeed they say from Lycaon into a wolf, from good into harsh or in the other way, and into a plunderer or in the other way, and thus concerning similar things which concern customs. Then, the magic change is the one which concerns the magic art. And it occurs in the body when magicians make something appear of a different essence than it is through magic art, as in the case of the companions of Ulysses changed into pigs by Circe. However, this art occurred once in magic power. Spiritual change is that which is observed in the spirit and the body, that is when a healthy body is made ill, and thus the spirit is troubled, so that the spirit, equally with the body, is changed. And this appears in those who have acute fevers, indeed as he becomes infirm from healthy, thus insane in the spirit, just as it is read concerning Orestes and concerning Agave who maimed her own son, so also it seems daily in those suffering people who would slay father, mother, and others unless they be freed from their sickness. The author writes concerning such men in this work." The list quadruplex also occurs in MS Ambrosiana 18 inf. (ca. 1420), fol. (iii)v.

55. The value of the descent is attested to by William of St. Thierry in his *Golden Epistle,* written to the Carthusians. See *Un Traité de la vie solitaire: Epistola ad Fratres de Monte-Dei par Guillaume de Saint-Thierry,* ed. M.-M. Davy (Paris, 1940), p. 79; PL 184, col. 314; *The Golden Epistle: A Letter to the Brethren at Mont Dieu,* trans. Theodore Berkeley (Spencer, Mass., 1971), p. 21.

56. *Commentum Bernardi Silvestris super sex libros Eneidos Virgilii,* ed. William Riedel (Gryphiswald, 1824), p. 30.

57. Ibid., p. 30. "Another is the descent of virtue, which happens when someone wise descends to earthly things through thought, not so that he may place his intention in them but so that, with their fragility known and earthly things put aside, he may convert himself inwardly to invisible things and may know the creator more fully through the knowledge of creatures."

58. *Petri Allegherii super Dantis ipsius genitoris comoediam commentarium,* ed. Vincentio Mannucci (Florence, 1845), pp. 11–17.

59. *Colucii Salutati de laboribus Herculis,* ed. B. L. Ullman (Zurich, n.d.), 2:483–86.

60. R. H. Green, "Classical Fable and English Poetry in the Fourteenth Century," in *Critical Approaches to Medieval Literature,* ed. Dorothy Bethurum (New York, 1960), p. 127.

61. More work remains to be done both on the historical development of the exegetical method and of its relationship to secular schemata resembling it, such as those we have singled out here for comment. On the history of biblical exegesis, see Beryl Smalley, *The Study of the Bible in the Middle Ages,* 2d ed. (Notre Dame, 1964), pp. 1–36; on the background of the four-part explication of the descent into hell, see Green, "Classical Fable and English Poetry in the Fourteenth Century," p. 127. Because we ourselves are singling out one particular pattern of explication, a four-part schema, from a tradition which included other patterns as well, it is worthwhile to note that the four-part allegorization of Scripture, although widespread, was by no means the only system of allegorical levels in use during the Middle Ages, nor was its use in the hands of all commentators uniform. See Smalley, *The Study of the Bible in the Middle Ages,* pp. 97–105, on Hugh of St. Victor.

62. For a fuller discussion of this semiotic understanding of the fourfold procedure of the medieval exegetes, see Judson B. Allen, "The *Grand Chant Courtois* and the Wholeness of the Poem: The Medieval *Assimilatio* of Text, Audience, and Commentary," *L'Esprit Créateur* 18 (Fall 1978): 5-17, esp. pp. 8-10.

63. Cf. above, notes 46, 51, 54, for instances of medieval commentaries on Ovid. Allegorizations of Scripture took many forms, of course, ranging from the verse-by-verse gloss, in which each line of the text might be given a four-level reading, to sermons or expositions developing particular levels for a brief text. See Smalley, *The Study of the Bible in the Middle Ages,* pp. 281-307.

64. Medieval commentators conventionally relate a work's division into books and parts to its *forma tractatus.* Giovanni del Virgilio, commenting on the *forma tractatus* of the *Metamorphoses,* says, "Forma tractatus est compositio et ordinatio 15 librorum in hoc volumine et capitulorum in dictos libros et partium in capitulis descendendo usque ad partes minutas que per se sententiam aliquam important" (Ghisalberti, "Giovanni," p. 18). "The *forma tractatus* is the composition and ordering of the fifteen books in this volume, and of the chapters in the said books, and of the parts in the chapters, descending to the smallest parts which contain distinct meanings." "Ordinatio" is corrected from Oxford, Bodleian MS 457, fol. 2r. Another commentator on Ovid, whose work is preserved in a thirteenth-century French manuscript, makes the chronological point: "Videndum est qualiter agat. Agit enim heroyco metro colligens mutationes diversas a prima creacione mundi usque ad suum tempus, quod signat sua invocatio ubi dicit *primaque ab origine mundi*" (Leiden University Library, MS BPL 95, fol. 1v). "We must see what is the genre of the book. Generically, it is in the heroic meter; it is a collection of diverse changes from the first creation of the world up to its own time. This its invocation indicates where it says 'and first from the origin of the world.'"

65. Brooks Otis, in *Ovid as an Epic Poet* (Cambridge, 1970), acknowledges the presence in the poem of a chronological motion but finds the fundamental principle operating in the poem's structure to be not chronology but rather the grouping of stories according to thematic links. For a fuller discussion, see chapter 3 below.

66. The medieval formula for talking about the meaning of a passage in the *Metamorphoses* is, apparently, "vult Ovidius." For a discussion, see Allen, *The Friar as Critic,* pp. 59-60.

67. The *House of Fame* is sufficient witness that Chaucer knew the *Commedia;* the story also occurs in the *Legenda Aurea,* in the life of St. Gregory. Such resemblances as this between Theseus and Trajan, both of whom stop in the midst of triumph to deal with suppliants, the medieval critics would have taken most seriously.

68. See Robert S. Haller, "The *Knight's Tale* and the Epic Tradition," *Chaucer Review* 1 (1966): 80-81.

69. Chaucer makes no special point of the fact that Emelye is an Amazon, and he permits her desire to remain unmarried an overtone of virtue which his own very different Christian world had to be alert to see as ironic. But the ironies are unavoidable, and they lead us to the conclusion that, in a manner, Theseus has brought his troubles on himself. The problem of Emelye is

perhaps the most striking image in the collection of the observation, developed at length below, that the events of married life grow directly from the manner in which marriage is first constituted. This element of irony has, however, gone largely unnoticed among the critics; for reasons different from ours, Frederick Turner has seen that Emelye is a problem. See his "A Structural Analysis of the *Knight's Tale*," *Chaucer Review* 8 (1973): 279-96.

70. Lydgate's Canterbury story might be analyzed profitably for information on a variety of questions: his testimony on the plan of the Canterbury journey, which he assumes to have reached Canterbury and to be on the point of return, has rarely been taken into account by modern critics of the poem's geography (on this point, the *Tale of Beryn* might also be consulted); his poem is a major document on the medieval understanding of Thebes and suggests that Lydgate saw the theme of this disorderly city as central to the Canterbury material; and his reintroduction of the Theban history points to the poem's beginning, rather than its pietistic ending, as the core of its statement.

71. For the latest debunkings of courtly love, see the papers of the Binghamton Conference of 1967, and especially the paper of John F. Benton, "Clio and Venus: An Historical View of Medieval Love," in *The Meaning of Courtly Love*, ed. F. X. Newman (Albany, N.Y., 1968), pp. 19-42.

72. Chaucer begins his story with Theseus's principal, personal victory already achieved; he stands as the conqueror of the Amazons and the husband of their queen. Yet, paradoxically, his troubles have only just begun. John Halverson, "Aspects of Order in the *Knight's Tale*," *Studies in Philology* 57 (1960): 620, describes the tale as a "progress from disorder to order," the disorder stemming from Theseus's admission into his home of the refugees from the Amazons and from Thebes.

73. Hermann the German defines comedy as the "ars vituperandi" and tragedy as the "ars laudandi." What he has done, of course, is to mistake Aristotle's higher and lower than ourselves as designations of moral quality, rather than of status, but his connection of blame with comedy is, for Chaucer, precisely right in all senses. The fit condition of evil is to be futile, helpless, inferior, and laughable; comic distance for Chaucer is far more often a moral posture than an existential refuge. Cf. Boggess, "Averrois Cordubensis," pp. 19-20.

74. F. N. Robinson, ed. *The Works of Geoffrey Chaucer*, 2d ed. (Boston, 1957), p. 675, notes that in introducing the queen's request to spare the lovers, Chaucer has departed from his source in Boccaccio. The rule of woman as a symbol of social disorder is echoed in the dominance of Emelye and, more closely in the court of Arthur, described in the *Wife of Bath's Tale*, when the ladies arrange for the knight-rapist's quest (III [D] 894-97).

75. The prayers of Oedipus, in the *Siege of Thebes*, are to a statue of Apollo, which had "with-In a spirit / ful unclene" and which answered questions "be fraude only / and fals collusioun." It spoke to Oedipus as "the fend anon / with-Innen Invisyble, with a vois dredful and horrible" (Lydgate's *Siege of Thebes*, ed. Axel Erdmann, *Early English Text Society*, ES 108 [London, 1911], pp. 24-25 [lines 532-54]).

76. Pierre Bersuire, *Reductorium morale super totam Bibliam*, in *Opera Omnia totam sacrae scripturae, morum, naturae historiam complectentia* (Cologne, 1631),

p. 90. "Thus it happened that after Samson, through the bad woman Dalilah, was deprived of his hair, and as a result deprived of his strength, immediately the Philistines captured him, and blinded the captive, and put the blind man in jail, and made the jailed man to work in the mill and to play the fool before them, but nevertheless, after this happened, Samson, blinded by the Philistines who blinded him, all at once in the palace made a ruin of their dwelling, over himself, and all perished. Thus truly when Samson, some strong and virtuous man, through a bad woman—that is, his own flesh—lost his hair—his virtue—and as a result his strength against temptation, immediately, he was captured by the Philistines, that is, by devils through diverse sins, and was deprived of the eyes of discretion, and so blinded, held, and made weak, he is placed in the prison of bad habit, and further compelled to work the mill, that is, to go about on the works and businesses of the world, and he is forced to play the fool and to make games of various sins before the Philistines, that is, forced to obey the will of demons. Finally, in their gathering, that is, in hell, one with them he dies and is damned. Thus a man through the evil of a woman whom he loved, that is his own flesh, is not only blinded, but also deprived of eternal and spiritual life."

77. Muscatine, *Chaucer and the French Tradition*, p. 181.

78. See, for example, Jordan, *Chaucer and the Shape of Creation*, pp. 169-78; and Turner, "A Structuralist Analysis," passim.

79. We have suggested already, and will consider in the next chapter, a variety of classification systems for things, both literary and natural, which are grouped in fours. Some of these systems bear directly on the four-part structure which we find underlying Chaucer's selection and distribution of his stories. Others are only peripherally related. An example of such peripheral connection would be the plan of fourfold biblical exegesis, which may represent a parallel phenomenon to the system of Ovidian classification but does not seem to bear directly on Chaucer's selection of a four-part structure. We have shown, on the other hand, that the classification of changes in Ovid probably influenced Chaucer's schema. Another group of four parts which seems to bear directly on the form and the meaning of the Canterbury collection is suggested in Theseus's speech: "For with that faire cheyne of love he bond / The fyr, the eyr, the water, and the lond / In certeyn boundes, that they may nat flee" (I [A] 2991-93). The harmony of the elements, bound up in a golden chain, which held in perfect balance the tensions and oppositions among the four members of the group, was an image of the natural order of the universe. By winding this golden chain of order about his tales, Chaucer identifies his subject as the world and its proper functioning; he directs his attention to "natural man" in his day-to-day existence, rather than to his heavenly destiny. For the Middle Ages the most significant treatment of number theory, and consequently of the golden chain of the elements as a harmony of four, was Macrobius (*Commentary on the Dream of Scipio*, trans. William Harris Stahl [New York, 1952], pp. 104-6). For a treatment of the golden chain and its significance for medieval understandings of the world's order, see Bernard McGinn, *The Golden Chain: A Study in the Theological Anthropology of Isaac of Stella* (Washington, D.C., 1972), pp. 61-102. The importance of four, and its centrality to enumerations of the world's parts, is

perhaps most evident in the works of John Scotus Eriugena, whose desire to discover the world's shape led him to postulate a wide range of classifications for its elements, especially in groups of four. For a treatment of the number as a basis for both imagery and narrative organization, see Alastair Fowler, *Spenser and the Numbers of Time* (London, 1964), pp. 24-33. Fowler's study is an excellent example of a properly balanced evaluation of the place of number theory in poetry; his work on Renaissance poets, especially Spenser, might be profitably adapted to medieval writers. By placing such special emphasis on the range of meanings associated with the number four, we are not suggesting that every group of things in the tales must number four, nor that Chaucer had forced an artificial scheme on his material; further, we believe that the evidence of Chaucer's poem shows that we are not forcing an artificial scheme on his material, either. Rather, it is helpful to consider the backgrounds of such ordering schemes as the four elements in analyzing the art of an era such as the Middle Ages, whose belief in world order caused men to place greater trust than our own times might in such systems of classification.

2

Medieval Notions
of Story

In the most obvious and literal sense, the *Canterbury Tales* is the record of a storytelling contest. The question which the work intends to pose and answer is not any question of salvation after Canterbury. Rather, a judgment is promised, which will specify the best story and honor its teller at a feast. Chaucer never dramatizes the expected judgment, because his own project is not to single out one story but to use many. Rather he uses this contest, within the drama of his competing pilgrim raconteurs, to conduct a serious and quite conclusive discussion of the nature and value of story—of the quality of exemplary fiction which makes it for him a trustworthy and significant medium for expressing his ideas.

Chaucer's discussion of his art of story is complicated both by the fact that it is dramatic—that is, its text consists of an array of speeches—and by the fact that it consists both logically and by rubrication of prologues. Its dramatic character requires us to read through it to its definition with a certain allowance for irony and dramatic relativity; its quality as prologue material requires us to read it with a confident expectation of logical procedure in discursive statement, and further requires us to take it as introductory to the stories, and therefore as dependent on them rather than as the enclosure on which they depend. These qualities might seem to contradict one another, in that on the one hand there is the uncertainty of shifting points of view and the dramatic possession of tale by teller, and on the other both the ultimate certainty and the discursive organization of extended statements whose essential character is logical and expository. But both, as we shall see, are proper parts of that strategy of exemplification which Chaucer achieves.

In taking the frame of the *Canterbury Tales* as Chaucer's discussion of the art of story, we do not in any sense intend to claim that Chaucer is, after the modern fashion, merely writing poetry about poetry. The text which he makes is an expository text, a discursive text. It is formally and rhetorically very complex, but its complexity is not what its author substitutes for meaning; rather, it is the strategy which permits him to be both clear and definite. Chaucer is, of course, an artist, as his work attests, and one may find in many places in his work expression of quite conscious concern for the craft of words as such, the value of literary precedent, the strategy of symbol.[1] But there is a difference between discussion of verbal art and discussion of some valid result of its use. What we intend in this chapter is an exposition of Chaucer's sense of proper use—specifically, of Chaucer's notion of the relation between telling a story and telling the truth.[2] Our discussion deals with two complementary kinds of evidence: Chaucer's own explanation of storytelling, conducted in the prologues which his pilgrims speak, and the definitions stated in, and implied by, the literary commentaries and manuals known in his time. On the basis of these two kinds of evidence, we can know clearly the theoretical possibilities within which Chaucer's stories exist.

We begin by examining Chaucer's prologues as his dramatization of the human difficulties with which storytellers must cope as they try to understand and appreciate the fiction they present. At the same time, we admit the logical and rhetorical force of the word *prologue* and argue that the drama does not exist for its own sake, but merely as an unusually subtle expression of something discursive. Essentially, the prologue material is Chaucer's introduction to his discourse in story; seen as such, the prologue material tells us what kind of discourse to expect, as well as what material will be discussed, and thus defines for us Chaucer's doctrine of story.

We then go to external evidence—to medieval literary commentary and to manuals related to poetry—and find there both confirmation and elaboration of the definitions which Chaucer implies for himself. In all this we establish clearly Chaucer's sense of priorities. We establish, as it were, the logic of a discourse which takes the form of general prologue, prologues, and tales. On the basis of this logical expectation, we then know what to read first, what to take most literally, and what to take as properly conclusive. Reading thus, we see that logical discourse and storytelling are for Chaucer the same thing, under an identity which in no way compromises either the validity of discourse or the art of fiction. Then we can see that his doctrine of story is a vital, indeed a fundamental, element in his description of a perfected way of life, in which honest speech and properly made promises form the basis of a good human society.

Once again we must enter the historian's caveat. Chaucer's doctrine of story is a medieval doctrine, not the modern Aristotelian one rooted in notions of plot. As we shall show, Chaucer's doctrine is one under which his tales have, as a collection, both moral and architectonic beauty—under which, in fact, his tales have with even greater clarity and attractiveness most of the beauties which we have seen in some fashion in the light of other theories and other approaches. If we seem to be getting to these beauties by a strange route—that is, by means of a doctrine of story as something exemplary, expository, and discursive rather than as something plotted—it is because only by such medieval means will some values be reached at all.

Both in Chaucer's *Canterbury Tales* and in the larger presumptions of the medieval critics in general, the distinction between prologue and what follows is partly logical and partly rhetorical—logical in that prologues introduce or summarize, often, what the subsequent treatise discusses at length; and rhetorical in that prologues are supposed to get readers, or hearers, in a mood to be persuaded by what follows. Prologues are not, to modern taste, literary at all—one of the first rules of modern fiction is that necessary exposition must be sugarcoated by action, so that right from the beginning one is showing rather than telling. But for Chaucer prologues are logical, rhetorical, and literary.[3] They serve the usual discursive purposes, and in addition they demarcate the preliminary ground which the reader must pass through in order to enter the world of fiction from that world of fiction proper. Given the modern sensibility, it is curious that the word *prologue,* which is constantly on the lips of Chaucer teachers and in the running heads of their editions, should have been repeated so often without giving offense for its blatantly logical and rhetorical, or in a sense antiliterary, connotations. We have indeed correctly labeled our material. But we have been quick to go off and talk of other things—of characterization, of dramatic interest or propriety, or of geographical allusions on the London-Canterbury road. Chaucer's transformation of the framing events from an artificial excuse for storytelling, its conventional use in the medieval genre, to a vital element in his poem has convinced many readers that the prologues, as a representation of reality, interest Chaucer more than the tales, even to the extreme that the Parson's condemnation of all storytelling is taken seriously.

All the materials from which readers of the poem have tended to build a realistic portrayal of Chaucer's time—the descriptions of the pilgrims and their "condiciouns"—along with the exemplary anecdotes and proverbs which introduce particular tales are, in medieval terms, prologues. That is, they introduce the tales to which they are attached. Their relationship to the stories and to each other is determined by the rhetoric of fiction, rather than by the logic of real life. Chaucer ironically invites his readers, and has convinced many of them, to read this relationship between story and life backwards, both by the vividness of the prologue action and also by allowing his storytellers to suggest and demonstrate many wrong ways to present and interpret fiction. Guided by the dramatic principle, modern readers have concluded that the uses to which the pilgrims put their stories, as escape or insult or weapon, are for Chaucer either legitimate or, as the Parson suggests, the best that can be expected of fiction, and, further, that such uses exhaust the significance of the tales.

The classification of the *Canterbury Tales* into prologues and tales, on the other hand, unifies the poem in the service of the tales; it enables us to preserve and appreciate the real charm of the prologues while we discover in the frame of the stories a preparation for reading which praises, rather than discredits, fiction. A reevaluation of the prologue material, beginning with the assumption that the prologues serve the tales as helpful introductions, will affect both our understanding of the general concerns which unite all the prologues—that is, the idea of pilgrimage, the storytelling contest, the debates and rivalries of the pilgrims—and also our analysis of specific prologue-tale pairs. Guided by the example of Ovidian commentary, we intend to read the prologues in series with the tales they introduce, as exemplary units in Chaucer's story collection, rather than relating the prologues primarily to one another, as if they composed together a continuous narrative action. Not only what the storyteller actually says about his tale but also what the prologue says, whether discursively or dramatically, prepares the way for the tale. An example for this procedure, which we will follow in our reading of the tales below, may be seen in the Miller's Prologue and *Tale*. What are they about? Literally, and also sententiously, the prologue is about a drunken man who disobeys the rules to take another man's place and to perform another man's function. From the Miller-Reeve controversy, we might conclude that the usurpation is punished, but not very severely, and certainly not in terms which relate the punishment to the intrusion. Considered in the same general terms, the *Miller's Tale* is about a clever man who disobeys the rules to take another man's place and to perform another man's function and who, because he is not alone in this wicked kind of disobedience, is punished for what he does.[4] In the prologue the rules being violated are the Host's rules for a storytelling contest, and in the tale they are the rules of matrimony, but this is a difference at the level of the merely particular. Both the exemplum of the prologue, in which the Miller intrudes himself as storyteller, and the exemplum of the tale, in which "hende" Nicholas intrudes himself as bedpartner, illustrate the typical or sententious pattern of action which can be labeled intrusion against the rule. We shall define this sort of pattern later in the chapter by using the medieval term *consuetudo;* both Chaucer's prologues and his fictions define such *consuetudines.* In the Miller's Prologue and *Tale,* the same *consuetudo* is presented twice—once as an introduction, within the rules of an ad hoc and temporary social cosmos constituted in order to organize storytelling; once substantially, within the rules of a real social cosmos whose rules define marriage. The prologue is an unresolved illustration, in that it does not answer the moral question of the proper punishment of intruders against the rule; both the tale and the array of material which follows provide resolution of the question and thus fulfill the promise of the prologue.

The prologues are related not only to their specific tales but also to each other. They define the framing situation in which the stories are told, they share a group of characters, and they treat a number of general subjects. First, as Jill Mann has shown, they are a satire on the estates of society, presented with a rhetorical ambivalence which casts real doubts upon the proper moral response of the audience. Second, they are frequently preoccupied with sex, and with estimates of sexual potency. The first of these subjects is not limited to the prologues, but rather is to be found in links and tales alike. The prologue combat among representatives of rival occupations and ways of life exemplifies Chaucer's pervasive concern with the typical features of the human condition, and with the relations which can, in his array of fictions, construct between human particulars and typical principles which, in medieval terms, grant particulars true existence. The second subject, sexuality, is at one level too obvious to require comment—there has rarely been great art which did not reflect this aspect of life, from the Canticle of Canticles to Freud. But the sexual preoccupations of Chaucer's pilgrims specifically function to relate their conversations to their tales, which, following the example of the *Knight's Tale,* treat courtship and marriage more than any other subjects. The pilgrims' exuberant interest in sex probably also echoes the complex symbolism of sexual fecundity that reached Chaucer from Alanus de Insulis, by way of a wonderful detour through the *Romance of the Rose,* and so faults them for their failure to perceive behind the natural goodness of sexuality its spiritual dimensions, particularly as a visible symbol of productivity in virtue and good works.

A third subject the prologues share is the nature and proper use of fiction. Although the links say many specific things directed to the reasons for telling stories and the ways to appreciate them, the nature of fiction has not been identified as the focus of these remarks, because they have been either treated as locally dramatic events involving pilgrims' personality clashes or dismissed as morally empty because of the Parson's attack on fiction. It is certainly true that most of what the pilgrims say about stories is wrong, limited, harmful; but the doctrines they present ironically direct us to a proper respect for the materials of fiction. Once the errors of storytelling are defined, the reason for Chaucer's juxtaposition of the pilgrimage with his story collection may be reconsidered, in order to show how the idea of the journey, expressed in the links, functions, along with all the prologue material, to introduce and prepare us properly for the stories.

The ways of telling and interpreting stories offered in the links may be categorized according to whether they treat stories as "ernest" or "game," a proverbial contrast mentioned frequently by the pilgrims.[5] The Host's definition of the prize-winning tale, as "of best sentence and moost solaas," assigns stories to neither category, as earnest or game alone, but suggests that the best stories partake of both moral seriousness and delight. Throughout his administration of the storytelling contest, the Host remains the champion of the game and a searcher after moral lessons in the tales which he can apply to his personal life. Still his principles fail him continually: he neither maintains the peace and good humor of the game against drunkards and quiters nor allegorizes very acutely. More than this, he sets the storytelling contest against the pilgrimage journey, characterizing the stories as fun and the pilgrimage as spiritually efficacious but dull.

> Ye goon to Caunterbury—God yow speede,
> The blisful martir quite yow youre meede!
> And wel I woot, as ye goon by the weye,
> Ye shapen yow to talen and to pleye;

For trewely, confort ne myrthe is noon
To ride by the weye doumb as a stoon;
And therfore wol I maken yow disport,
As I sayde erst, and doon yow som confort.
And if yow liketh alle by oon assent
For to stonden at my juggement,
And for to werken as I shal yow seye,
To-morwe, whan ye riden by the weye,
Now, by my fader soule that is deed,
But ye be myrie, I wol yeve yow myn heed!

(I [A] 769–82)

Although he demands stories of "best sentence" and often finds moral truths in the tales, as they are presented, still he perceives no connection between this earnest dimension of the tales and the earnest significance of the pilgrimage. He establishes a distinction between the spiritual goals of the pilgrims, an earnest intent, and the immediate desire for entertainment of the contest, a game. In doing this he prepares the way for the Parson's attack on fiction, Chaucer's Retraction, and the modern conviction that the stories are morally inferior. We believe that the Host has committed an error in critical judgment, which functions, along with all the other critical errors in the links, ironically to place stories beyond the control of men too foolish to perceive their integrity and to reveal the power of fiction, even if we see this power wasted by the pilgrims. To suggest that the Retraction and the Parson's Prologue share the shortcomings of the prologue material is a controversial proposal which requires careful explanation; as a preparation for this, we will consider more clear-cut examples of faulty literary judgment in the links.

Most of the pilgrims fail to appreciate stories because they cannot preserve the game in their desire to discover an "earnest" value in fiction which they may use for their own purposes. The most striking example of such a misappropriation of story is the Pardoner. The Pardoner's intention for his story is to deceive—he conceals his own avaricious reasons for preaching behind an attack on the avarice of his listeners. He is so confident in his control over the story that he reveals the apparatus of his illusion to the other pilgrims:

Thus kan I preche agayn that same vice
Which that I use, and that is avarice.
But though myself be gilty in that synne,
Yet kan I maken oother folk to twynne
From avarice, and soore to repente.

(VI [C] 427–31)

The Pardoner fails to impress his pilgrim audience[6]—and Chaucer, by the dramatic interplay between the Host and the Pardoner, underlines this failure. Yet the pilgrims outsmart themselves by supposing that when they see through the Pardoner's trick, they also understand the story; modern audiences outsmart themselves in much the same way, by supposing that the story is important only as the tool of the Pardoner's intended deception and, dramatically, the occasion of his self-revelation. What pilgrims and many readers fail to realize is that the story, no matter what the Pardoner thinks of it, is a consummate production and a powerful teacher of the dangers of avarice. The Knight's suggestion that the game of the pilgrimage be restored reproves the Pardoner's effort to manipulate his fellow travelers and the Host's rude objections to being duped:

> Namoore of this, for it is right ynough!
> Sire Pardoner, be glad and myrie of cheere;
> And ye, sire Hoost, that been to me so deere,
> I prey yow that ye kisse the Pardoner.
> And Pardoner, I prey thee, drawe thee neer,
> And, as we diden, lat us laughe and pleye.
>
> (VI [C] 962–67)

But it also directs us back to the storytelling contest, the game in search of tales "of best sentence and moost solaas," in which the *Pardoner's Tale* is one of the most distinguished entries. The controversy between the Pardoner and the Host, and his plan to dupe the pilgrims, is an important element of the poem, but it is more properly read, when we realize that it ironically calls attention to the story's particular power and significance, by showing how the pilgrims fail to benefit from it.

Many pilgrims lose the stories in their pursuit of other pleasures, including drink and exchange of insults. Their uses of stories, as dirty jokes or character assassinations, do not exhaust the significance of the stories, although this fact is sometimes lost in the appreciation of the quarrels in the links. The *Miller's Tale,* and the *Reeve's,* for that matter, are respected as literary creations, with their own internal logic, when they are read independently; this respect for them often is forgotten, however, when the relationship between the tales and their tellers is discussed, because of the long-standing fascination with the drama of the pilgrims. Jordan rightly says of the quiting storytellers: "The Reeve's impulse and violent protest against what he takes to be public charges of cuckoldry and adultery reveals his own churlish inability to distinguish between actual instance and fictional generalization. In this exchange the Miller gains superiority not through his knowledge of the Reeve's past experience of matrimony—as maintained by dramatically oriented criticism—but by the immediate demonstration of a higher quality of mind."[7] Even the Host, who on most occasions objects to the disruptions of the quiters—he asks the Friar, for example, not to insult the Summoner (III [D] 1286-89)—yields to the temptation to make cruel fun, within the relaxation of formality permitted by the contest, and receives, in return, a quiting tale from the Cook about an innkeeper. Chaucer phrases the Host's defense of such insults in the terms of earnest and game, for the Host excuses his ridicule of the Cook by saying that even the truth is permitted, when stated playfully. "But yet I pray thee, be nat wroth for game;/A man may seye ful sooth in game and pley" (I [A] 4354-55). By naming this kind of speech "sooth," Chaucer calls to mind other sorts of truth that tales may tell and underscores the inadequacy of the pilgrims' expectations for their game of stories.

Chaucer's attitude toward the drunkards and the quiters is expressed through the Host's invocation to Bacchus as an appropriate god for the pilgrimage; the Host's optimistic assertion that drink will bind the wounds of the pilgrims' disputes is disappointed in the conduct of the pilgrims who disrupt the contest while they are drunk. In the Manciple's Prologue the Host praises Bacchus: "O thou Bacus, yblessed be thy name,/That so kanst turnen ernest into game!" (IX [H] 99-100). Previously he has said,

> "I se wel it is necessarie,
> Where that we goon, good drynke with us carie;
> For that wol turne rancour and disese
> T'acord and love, and many a wrong apese."
>
> (IX [H] 95-98)

He makes this statement at the end of a scene in which the Cook's drunkenness has made him unfit for storytelling, the game which is, after all, the focus of the Host's efforts; the Cook and Manciple have quarreled over the Cook's incapacity; and the Host himself pronounces on the debilitating effects of drink. The praise of drink here, as necessary to the good-humored conduct of the journey, is contradicted by the Host's angry reaction to the Miller's drunken interruption of the contest in order to tell his story. Of course, the pilgrims have also raised friendly glasses together. The journey begins with a toast to confirm the Host as leader of the contest.[8] The Host's invocation of "merry" Bacchus implicitly rebukes the pilgrims who allow drink to turn the contest into an earnest argument.

Chaucer's allusion to Bacchus, especially because it appears in the prologue of the tale he borrows from the *Metamorphoses,* calls to mind another aspect of the god's activity, relevant not only to those who drink but also to those who tell stories. The Host invokes a friendly god of mirth, but Bacchus, in book 4 of the *Metamorphoses,* is the "new" god of madness and violence, who punishes all those who will not accept his authority. Among these are the Minyades, who reject the new festival of Bacchus and stay at their work. Like the Canterbury pilgrims, they agree to tell stories as a diversion:

> utile opus manuum vario sermone levemus
> perque vices aliquid, quod tempora longa videri
> non sinat, in medium vacuas referamus ad aures.
>
> (4. 39–41)[9]

For their irreverence Bacchus transforms their weaving into vine and ivy, and the sisters themselves into bats. With this punishment of stories which insult his dignity, Bacchus becomes the god of all quiters. Bacchus's anger is repeated in the fury of the Reeve and the Summoner, who forget the pleasure of the storytelling because they think it is somehow directed against their dignity. According to Arnulf of Orleans, these storytelling defiers of the powers of Bacchus are alcoholics, whose wasteful indulgence finally ruins them.[10] The *Ovide moralisé* repeats this interpretation and adds two more, which complicate our response to the Ovidian context in just the right ways. *In malo,* the three sisters are "trois diversitez de pechiez,"[11] specifically, "charnel concupissance," "concupissance d'ieulz," and "orgeulz de vie" (4. 2532–44). *In bono,* they are "trois estas de perfection," "continence," "l'ordre de mariage," and "l'estas de prelacion" (4. 2634–2703). The storytellers of Ovid are allegorized in formulas which comprehend the human condition: sin is divided according to the domains in which it may occur—lust of the flesh, lust of the eyes, and pride of life—and perfection is named not by virtues but by conditions within which virtuous behavior is possible. Chaucer's evocation of the Minyades' disastrous storytelling contest is intended, in the case of the angry, spiteful, or drunken storytellers, to link them with the destructive, and undesirable, aspects of Bacchus. More generally, because the pilgrims resemble the Minyades in many ways— both groups are telling stories in a context of religious observance, which they put aside for the sake of other interests—they may be identified with the sort of treatment the Minyades received in commentaries. That is, they are characters who exist, *in bono* and *in malo*, to exemplify the sins and states which constitute society. They become, in sum, humanity, sponsoring stories which, although their value is complex and often ambivalent, are socially exemplary.

Thus, the stories exist separate from the uses the pilgrims would make of them and tend to rebuke the foolishness of selfish preachers, crude drunkards, and spiteful rivals, who suppose they control the tales that they hurl at one another. The errors of the pilgrims are often interpreted as allowing themselves to have too much morally irresponsible fun in the contest; in fact, they are not having the game that the stories themselves would have provided them at all. Their willingness to take a meaning, or reason, for the story as its significance, and to let the story go, is also the fundamental attitude of Chaucer the pilgrim—not only in the Retraction, but also throughout the book. The Retraction is read by many critics, as we shall see, as Chaucer's literal last word as author; Chaucer is supposed to be retracting all those stories which do not actually enforce a good moral. It would be more precisely accurate to say that Chaucer is really retracting those stories which are really about some sinful or bawdy action, or which contain gross language, and that in so doing he falls into the eternally persisting error of taking content for meaning. It is true, after all, that some of Chaucer's bawdiest stories do punish the guilty parties and so suggest the danger of their errors. Though they sound like sin, they actually reprove it.

To take the Retraction seriously, as the last word of Chaucer the civil servant, moralist, and human being with a soul to save, violates the integrity of the work in which it is dramatically integral and ignores the fact that Chaucer the pilgrim has been making statements of a similar character throughout his work. Chaucer the pilgrim is concerned for the actual content of his stories. He defends himself from charges of immorality or poor writing on the grounds that he is reporting accurately what really happened:

> For this ye knowen al so wel as I,
> Whoso shal telle a tale after a man,
> He moot reherce as ny as evere he kan
> Everich a word,[12] if it be in his charge,
> Al speke he never so rudeliche and large,
> Or ellis he moot telle his tale untrewe,
> Of feyne thyng, or fynde wordes newe.
> He may nat spare, althogh he were his brother;

> He moot as wel seye o word as another.
> Crist spak hymself ful brode in hooly writ,
> And wel ye woot no vileyne is it.
> Eek Plato seith, whoso that kan hym rede,
> The wordes moote be cosyn to the dede.
> Also I prey yow to foryeve it me,
> Al have I nat set folk in hir degree
> Heere in this tale, as that they sholde stonde.
> My wit is short, ye may wel understonde.
>
> (I [A] 730–46)

Chaucer the pilgrim finds the same virtue of accuracy a sufficient defense for any immorality or bad language his tales report, in the Miller's Prologue.

> For Goddes love, demeth nat that I seye
> Of yvel entente, but for I moot reherce
> Hir tales alle, be they bettre or werse,
> Or elles falsen som of my mateere.
> And therfore, whoso list it nat yheere,
> Turne over the leef and chese another tale;
> For he shal fynde ynowe, grete and smale,
> Of storial thyng that toucheth gentillesse,
> And eek moralitee and hoolynesse.
> Blameth nat me if that ye chese amys.
> The Millere is a cherl, ye knowe wel this;
> So was the Reve eek and othere mo,
> And harlotrie they tolden bothe two.
> Avyseth yow, and put me out of blame;
> And eek men shal nat maken ernest of game.
>
> (I [A] 3172–86)

The Retraction's advice to disregard all the tales that "sownen into synne," for the sake of those with holy subjects, resembles the Miller's Prologue passage closely. Both manuscript and internal evidence demand that we take the Retraction as an integral part of the whole, and not as a death bed testament.[13]

When the Retraction is drawn firmly into the remainder of the poem and identified as the statement of a character in that poem, it becomes possible to explain its puzzling aspects—the apparent contradiction it offers to the remainder of the poem, and its curiously ambiguous explanation of why Chaucer decided to take back as many of his works as he says he must. Olive Sayce, in an article on the medieval literary tradition of closing apologies, demonstrates that

Chaucer's Retraction, as an avowal of sinfulness and a request to be excused for scandalous works, draws on the traditional vocabulary of medieval conclusions. This is "the part of the work when apparently autobiographical statements are most likely to occur. It must be remembered, however, that the reason for their introduction is not personal but aesthetic."[14] Sayce convincingly argues that the personal note struck in the Retraction does not require that Chaucer the author be speaking in his own voice. The conventionality of the terms used, the faithfulness to medieval formulas, suggest, rather, that the passage should be attributed to Chaucer the pilgrim.

The Retraction is ambiguous, as well. Chaucer first seems to argue that all he wrote was written to a good end; he echoes Saint Paul's statement that "al that is writen is writen for oure doctrine"[15] and explicitly assures us that he has followed this rule. Then he decides that some things could not have been written "to oure doctrine," because they literally "sownen into synne." The error that the Retraction makes resembles the mistaken defenses of art that Chaucer the pilgrim offers both in the General Prologue and the Miller's Prologue. There, Chaucer the pilgrim has defined the truth of stories to be the accuracy with which they report an actual event; the artist is excused from moral responsibility because he did not commit the sins he reports, but only records them. The Retraction does not permit this defense; Chaucer the pilgrim, undoubtedly swayed by the Parson's grim rejection of the redeeming "solaas" of stories, decides that the record of an immorality is an immorality. Again, an "earnest" value of story, which does not perceive fiction as "game," fails to distinguish between life and its representation in fiction, and so loses the aspect of story which gives it authority to teach. The Averroistic poetics of Aristotle speaks to this point when it repeats the commonplace that "homo inter cetera animalia delectatur in assimilatione rerum quas iam in sensu percepit et in earum representatione seu imitatione. Et signum huius scilicet quod homo naturaliter letatur et gaudet ex assimilatione est quod delectamur et gaudemus in representatione aliquarum rerum in quarum sensu non delectamur."[16] In fact, the moral nature of poetry requires that its material "assumitur interdum ad ostensionem decentie valde exprimendo ipsam et interdum permutatur ad ostensionem alicuius turpitudinis similiter valde exprimendo illam."[17] Consonant with this doctrine, Sayce concludes about Chaucer that the ambiguity of the Retraction does permit one to value poetry, but only by recognizing the shallowness of the pilgrim's apologies.[18] The ethical measure of a story is not to be taken solely from the incidence of words or actions that would be called good or bad when performed in real life; rather, the stories that do not "sownen into synne" do so precisely because whether describing good men or bad they draw ethically appropriate conclusions about human life and exercise their rhetorical power toward convincing men to behave well.

But these two critical positions—that stories can be reduced to dramatic insults, and that their moral value equals the moral character of the specific incidents they contain—are not the only positions that Chaucer defines and defends in his prologue material. More important than these explicit mistakes is the pervasive implicit attitude that fiction is different from experience in some way, that it is game, that it is "solaas." This attitude is clear in a number of passing comments, concentrated in the prologue material, in which several of the pilgrims affirm the value and importance of fiction and recognize its place in the cultural tradition of the Middle Ages.

The majority of the pilgrims are concerned that they may not be equal to the task of telling a story well. In the dialectic of the work as such, they are of course right, because, as pilgrim storytellers, they are not stories but prologues. Their own lives are a boring pilgrimage, which they agree must be enlivened with stories. In other terms, the pilgrims are lesser fictions who frame further and greater fictions, which are rhetorically, as things framed, more fictional than the pilgrims. They achieve story by telling stories, more than by enacting one; thus they are outside story, and therefore by definition inadequate to story.[19] Their game with story too often reduces itself to a too easy and too trivial earnest; their morality oscillates between an impossible penitential rejection of the world they are (for the nonce) given and a too easy acceptance of its simply drunken aspects.

First of all, then, the pilgrims confess various insecurities in the face of fiction. The Man of Law rehearses Chaucer's work, saying that there is no story remaining for him to tell, and incidentally betraying his ignorance of the medieval fact that stories are to be repeated, or recelebrated, rather than invented ex nihilo. He says that he fears the fate of the Pierides, the sisters of the *Metamorphoses* who challenge the Muses to a singing contest and lose, becoming magpies because of their impudence and impiety:

> "Me were looth be likned, doutelees,
> To Muses that men clepe Pierides—
> *Methamorphosios* woot what I mene;
> ....

I speke in prose, and lat him rymes make."

(II [B¹] 91–93, 96)

The Franklin apologizes for his lack of rhetorical skill:

> But, sires, by cause I am a burel man,
> At my bigynnyng first I yow biseche,
> Have me excused of my rude speche.

(V [F] 716–18)

The Prioress fears that she will be unequal to her task of telling a holy story, and prays:

> My konnyng is so wayk, o blisful Queene,
> For to declare thy grete worthynesse
> That I ne may the weighte nat susteene.

(VII 481–83 [B² 1671–73])

The Monk apologizes for his problems of organization:

> "Though I by ordre telle nat thise thynges,
> . . . .
> But tellen hem som bifore and som bihynde,
> As it now comth unto my remembraunce,
> Have me escused of myn ignoraunce."

(VII 1985, 1988–90 [B² 3175, 3178–80])

Others, by referring to the tradition and learning of the Middle Ages, establish the fundamental importance for fiction of its ties to authorities. Even the Wife of Bath, who claims that experience is a sufficient teacher, trusts a good deal to biblical authorities as she tries to prove her skill as an exegete. The Clerk offers a story he learned from

> Fraunceys Petrak, the lauriat poete,
> Highte this clerk, whos rethorike sweete
> Enlumyned al Ytaille of poetrie,

(IV [E] 31–33)

and Chaucer the pilgrim likens his own efforts in telling a new story of the Melibeus to the work of the Evangelists:

> For somme of hem seyn moore, and somme seyn lesse,
> Whan they his pitous passioun expresse—
> I meene of Mark, Mathew, Luc, and John—
> But doutelees hir sentence is al oon.

(VII 949–52 [B² 2139–42])

The Pardoner's sincerest reverence is for the technique of performance and practical rhetoric:

> I peyne me to han an hauteyn speche,
> And rynge it out as round as gooth a belle,
> For I kan al by rote that I telle.

(VI [C] 330-32)

Still others, with timely interruptions, bring telling commentary to bear on tales that are disorderly, dreary, or bumbling. The Franklin interrupts the Squire with flattery, saying

> "In feith, Squier, thow hast thee wel yquit
> And gentilly. I preise wel thy wit,
> . . . .
> So feelyngly thou spekest, sire, I allow the!"

(V [F] 673-74, 676)

The Host interrupts the tale of Sir Thopas:

> . . . thou makest me
> So wery of thy verray lewednesse
> That, also wisly God my soule blesse,
> Myne eres aken of thy drasty speche.

(VII 920-23 [B² 2110-13])

The continually repeated emphasis here is on learning and skill—the faults are those of rudeness, uncunning, drastiness of speech, ignorance. Three principles of criticism emerge here, all calculated to affirm the importance and value of the stories which the pilgrims introduce. First, the storyteller is necessarily humble before his material, which requires excellence in presentation to fulfill its potential. Second, it is recognized that stories participate in the tradition of learning which the Middle Ages so much respected—they are *auctoritates*. Third, it is dramatically affirmed that bad stories should be challenged or stopped. It is important to notice that nothing in these principles depends either on the good intentions of the pilgrims or on the moral weight of the events in their stories. Rather, there is "rethorike sweete." The respect of the pilgrims points to the integrity of stories. Chaucer effectively cuts off the possibility of valuing his fictions as jokes, insults, or sermons only, and yet leaves us with the stories, somehow both instructive and entertaining, standing solidly in the realm of truth and high seriousness and yet in sympathy with the world of mistake and error which men inhabit.

Of all the members of the party, the Knight comes closest to read-

ing a story correctly. The Knight, who is the character most in harmony with the poem's largest patterns of meaning and who, throughout the links, defends the principle of the contest as a game, is given
the task of questioning the Monk's array of tragedies as being out of
harmony with fiction, not because it is too serious for the "game" of
stories, which is the Host's objection, but because it has not fulfilled its
serious obligations to make sense and order from life.[20] The Host
rejects a repetition of these tragic instances, because the task is of no
use:

> ... and pardee, no remedie
> It is for to biwaille ne compleyne
> That that is doon.
>
> (VII 2784-86 [B² 3974-76])

Ironically he opposes here the medieval reverence for exempla, particularly the tragic tales of falls from fortune, as valued teachers of
man's true place in creation. The Knight recognizes the exemplary
tone of the Monk's tragedies, because he sees that their force is directed at his own particular experience.

> I seye for me, it is a greet disese,
> Whereas men han been in greet welthe and ese,
> To heeren of hire sodeyn fal, allas!
> And the contrarie is joye and greet solas,
> As whan a man hath been in povre estaat,
> And clymbeth up and wexeth fortunat,
> And there abideth in prosperitee.
>
> (VII 2771-77 [B² 3961-67])

The Knight reveals his own limitation as a critic, a dislike for sad
endings, especially ones that come close to home, but he has read the
story in appreciation of its sententious character and with the courage
to apply its lesson to himself.[21] Among the pilgrims, who tend either
to the quiters' error of reacting angrily to tales they imagine insult
them or to the Host's smug application of moralizations to the faults
of others, the Knight reads the story for what it may teach him.

Chaucer permits such a careful reading of the *Monk's Tale*, perhaps,
because it is, like his own *Tales*, a collection rather than a single story.
He suggests that for life to be captured in a manner suited to his own
age a poem must encompass the multiplicity of experience; the *Monk's
Tale* does so and is the tale whose separate treatment may come closest
to the type of reading which Chaucer finds appropriate to poetry.

In sum, the prologues portray the pilgrims as storytellers,

Chaucer's *auctoritates*, whose comments on fiction present an elaborate *sic et non* on the validity of fictional communication. The answers they come up with are faulty, but their stories are not. The "earnest" and "game" they find in the journey's events, and in the uses they have for their tales, are not the "best sentence and moost solaas" the Host promises the best stories will provide. This is intentional, we think, because Chaucer places the true blending of earnest and game where he believes it to exist, in the stories themselves. And our appreciation for the individual tales is proof that the stories do have validity and impact beyond the distortions the pilgrims attempt to practice on them.

The relationship between the ideal of pilgrimage and the storytelling contest is not the easy distinction between earnest and game which the Host or the Parson would make, because the stories demonstrate throughout a capacity for speaking the true, the "best sentence," even while they entertain and delight. Chaucer's framing definitions of the stories, the pilgrimage, and the contest rather function together: the *Canterbury Tales* is both Chaucer's truth about life and the entertainment he offers to his readers. By turning attention away from the journey's end to its progress along the way, Chaucer identifies the subject of his work as this life, and the morality appropriate to its conduct. The Host is fit patron and guide for such a journey, because he is the director of the homeless, men in a state of transition. The pilgrims' decision to accept his direction affirms their concern for this life. The Host is the *viaticum* of this community,[22] but he conducts the pilgrims along no heavenly way. Yet the stories, to which he would direct our attention, are Chaucer's Eucharist, in which the flesh of life is transfigured by the truth which it should exemplify. This life, by means of the tales, makes contact with other times and even with eternity, not only as an eventual end but also as a saving grace continually present. The transcendent truth, which the Parson presumes to hold in his sermon, and which the repentant Chaucer the pilgrim thinks about only in the shadow of Canterbury, Chaucer places in our hands, in his story of the tales told on the way.

In all this we have attempted to establish that the prologues, and all the linking material, are to be considered as prologues in fact as well as in name, and that they depend on, and logically derive from, the fictions they introduce. We have offered an approximate definition of story, as a combination of "ernest" and "game," derived from Chaucer's prologues. But since Chaucer's introductory techniques involve elements of irony, and since the traditions of Chaucer criticism with which our work must exist have not put the stories first, we cannot presume too easily that we know what stories are. There have been radical changes in literary definition since the Middle Ages—changes which the critic is often, axiomatically and unconsciously, tempted to ignore by dealing with "literature" in the absolute sense. We must therefore be very careful in this enterprise of definition, first by seeing that we do not presume about the Middle Ages anything which in fact is not there, and second by coming to terms with the external evidence surviving from the Middle Ages, other than stories themselves, which points to definition.

At the outset we are faced with the puzzling problem of classification. As modern critics, we tend to value very much the distinction between art and experience, and to make of art something very special and unique. Such a distinction is puzzlingly unimportant, as we shall see, to medieval critics. We know perfectly well what we mean when we make a category that includes the *Divine Comedy,* the *Canterbury Tales,* the *Beowulf,* a number of canonical lyrics and romances, and perhaps the *Consolation of Philosophy.* We are equally clear in presuming that this category does not include the *Summa Theologiae,* the *Historica Scholastica,* the *Etymologies* of Isidore, or (except for utterly unreconstructed philologists) the *Ancrene Riwle.* Medieval critics would probably not understand these presumptions—the precise category which we mean by literature, or belles lettres, did not exist for them. The Middle Ages did have classes for such verbal things as *auctores,*[23] or the tripartite *historia, fabula, argumentum,* mentioned in various commentaries,[24] but none of these exactly corresponds. It simply will not do, in any critically responsible historical sense, to import and impose the modern word *literature,* without very careful qualification, on the array of material constituted by the books medieval people read. But it is no real loss to give up the word *literature.* Dante's *Divine Comedy,* no matter what word we use to name its category, continues to have a self-authenticating power which we gratefully acknowledge and to which we submit in reading it, and Chaucer remains as wise an observer of human nature as he ever was. In giving up, for the moment, the word *literature,* we indulge the expectation that the medieval categories and definitions, once we understand them, will enhance and enrich our appropriation of these texts in ways beyond the power of our modern category.

The word *literature,* in modern usage, presumes for poetry two characteristics which we must be very careful not to impose on medieval literature—careful primarily because they are characteristics so deeply rooted in our axiom system as to be almost unavoidable. The first of these has to do with the definition of poetic sentences; the second with epistemology. The debate over the fit definition of poetic sentences has vexed medieval studies primarily since the advent of D. W. Robertson's "historical" criticism, which, though it suggests quite properly that a number of formerly neglected medieval Latin texts were obligatory scholarly reading, seeks to impose on medieval poems a far from medieval structure of symbolic sentence construction. There has, thus, been much controversy over whether or not Beowulf "is" Christ, or the Wife of Bath "is" a grotesque figure of Luxuria, or the Pearl-maiden "is" spiritual dryness, or Jean de Meun's Rose "is" "le bien infini et vraye gloire celeste."[25] All the arguments, it seems, seek to establish whether or not the term on the left-hand side of these phrases in fact does or does not symbolize the term on the right-hand side. Common to all debaters is the presumption that such sentences are symbolic, and so describe mental operations seeking insight.[26] The sentence "Beowulf is Christ" is clearly not empirical or tautologous; it must be symbolic. Some critics find it of no use at all in understanding Beowulf, or satisfy themselves that the Beowulf poet was discussing Beowulf only, and not Christ in a cryptic manner. Others, for what they consider good reasons, find that using Beowulf as a symbolic word referring to Christ is a fit thing to do, and call the sentence true.

What has gone wrong here is that critics on both sides of the argument share, at the level of uncritical presumption, an essentially eighteenth-century theory of language, utterly alien to the etymology-trusting, Logos-and-creation-based theory of language of the Middle Ages. Allegorical statements in the Middle Ages were not, in our terms, either referential or symbolic, even though the forms of the sentences in which they expressed their allegories are the same as those which we now understand as symbolic. Therefore the array of terms, usually religious, which tended frequently to appear on the right-hand side of their allegorical statements were not by their location endorsed as "right meanings." Much more than this, these statements were simple descriptions, all participating hierarchically in a class of statements whose highest members were probably "This is my body" and "The Father, and the Son, and the Holy Spirit are one." The whole class of statements depended, as descriptions, on the presumption of a relationship of analogous parallelism between the level of reality to which the left-hand term belonged and that to which the right-hand term belonged. Allegorical statements in the Middle Ages were not so much referential, or even linguistic, as cosmological. They presumed and reflected and constituted by their existence a particular classification and relational arrangement of all that was. Further, because medieval language regularly presumed so, the cosmos which it described was presumed literally to include realities which we would now call mental, and therefore by our terms positivistically unreal.[27] Our importing of modern presumptions about language into our discussion of medieval sentences and possible sentences has, in short, gone wrong about what the Middle Ages meant because we forgot to begin by asking how they meant—or whether meaning as such was a category appropriate to the medieval sensibility at all.

A further presumption which we must avoid is rooted in the very method of historical criticism itself. It traces to our quite valid suspicion that medieval people were not quite like ourselves—the axiom of cultural relativism is the axiom which makes critical historical studies both necessary and possible. But to be interested in defining the point of view of people of the past tempts us to presume that naturally they had a point of view, and then by natural leaps to presume that they were therefore capable of mental states which we define by such terms as *phenomenology* and *subject-object relationship*. A world which could take the notion of the unity of the intellect seriously,[28] however, or which continued to debate the question of nominalism and by its very debating admitted that there could be two sides to the question, would have great difficulties conceiving the phenomenological and existential relativisms which ground our sense of point of view and impel us to allow for it by being critical of our histories. Thus, when we analyze the confession of the Pardoner or the persona of Chaucer the poet, we must take care to recognize that the first is more akin to the Vices of Prudentius than to Holden Caulfield and Jean Genet, and the second more in keeping with the fit behavior of a bishop than with the poses of a modern actor. There are indeed ironies in Chaucer, and they are based, as are all ironies, on the disparity between appearance and reality, but appearance is not necessarily the same as pose, nor reality the same as sincerity. A "sincere" human being may well be, in medieval terms, a mere pose or parody of truth, and reality is always something grounded in philosophical or theological, rather than personalist, definition.

The starting point of our investigation must be, then, a new way of framing the question of the nature of story, or, begging no questions, poetry, which would be acceptable to medieval commentators, writers, and readers. Medieval critics put the question by asking, To what part of philosophy does the text under discussion belong? The answer, with a few exceptions which only prove the rule, is, uniformly, ethics.[29] The formula of the commentaries is, "Ethica subponitur quia de moribus tractat."[30] What this formula means, we think, is not that medieval critics had a merely pedestrian and moralizing use for poetry, but rather that the category they called ethics and the category we call literature are remarkably similar, indeed congruent. Life becomes ethical as it rises to decorums which one finds most clearly in story; story therefore is naturally and necessarily ethics.[31]

If literature is to be classified as a part of ethics, then its own parts and features must obviously be ones which can fitly constitute, or reflect, an ethical system. The medieval analysis in which this fitness is most clearly and elaborately expressed is the Averroistic *Poetics* of Aristotle, as translated into Latin by Hermann the German.[32] A full treatment of the doctrine of this treatise, and its substantial agreement with what is otherwise known about late medieval literary theory, is beyond the scope of this book.[33] In the first place, Averroes defines poetry not as making, nor tragedy (and comedy) as imitations of action. Rather, tragedy is *ars laudandi*, and comedy is *ars vituperandi*. In the second place, Averroes substitutes for Aristotle's plot and character, in the six parts of tragedy, much more abstract entities, which he designates *credulitates* and *consuetudines*. Praise and blame, obviously, are activities which lead to essentially ethical conclusions; *credulitates* and *consuetudines* are abstractions to which individual persons are referred in ethical descriptions.

Averroes's discussion of the six parts of tragedy is quite complex. There are two lists of the parts in his own text, which do not absolutely correspond with each other and correspond even less clearly to the authentic Aristotelian six. It is clear at least that Averroes's fundamental distinction is between matter and means: three of the six parts— customs, beliefs, and meanings—are represented by the other three—description, verbal formalism, and expressive power. This distinction reflects the customary medieval procedure, in rhetoric, of assuming a material to be treated, and an array of rhetorical resources by means of which treatment can be accomplished.[34]

The material to be treated is ethical—in Averroes's terms, it is *credulitates* and *consuetudines*. An *accessus* on Ovid's *Heroides*, probably from the fourteenth century, puts the matter more concretely: "Materia libri sunt mores et vicia dominarum"; it then goes on to say that one of the features which makes the book worth reading is the "pulchritudo conditionum que sunt in hoc libro."[35] *Conditio* is a reasonable equivalent of the sum of *consuetudo* and *credulitas*. It is also the fundamental and initial concern of Chaucer's art, in his picture gallery of pilgrims:

> Me thynketh it acordaunt to resoun
> To telle yow al the condicioun
> Of ech of hem, so as it semed me.

(I [A] 37–39)

That it is *conditiones*, and not pilgrims as existential individuals merely, from which Chaucer derives this prologue, Jill Mann has demonstrated with great learning and convincing detail. Moreover, she accounts for Chaucer's apparent realism in moral terms which precisely reflect Averroes's concern for the *artes laudandi vituperandique:* "Chaucer's general aim of complicating the reader's emotional responses . . . is more comprehensive as a development from *descriptio* when described in medieval terms 'for praise or blame' than when it is anachronistically analysed in terms of the 'artificial' and the 'real.'"[36] The same concern for the general or universal instead of the particular also appears in Dante's theory of language, as Dragonetti explains it in connection with a discussion of the myth of Babel.[37] By the time of Malory this polarity between the typical and the individual had become a conscious moral problem, instead of an epistemological one, and received explicit thematic emphasis.[38] Averroes's emphasis on *consuetudo* and *credulitas*, thus, finds reflection in the implicit and explicit concerns of both commentators and poets.

Of what, then, does medieval poetry consist? According to Averroes it consists of manners and customs, presented in mannered verbal descriptions which have the power to move and convince the hearer. In any given poem, therefore, we must expect an array of examples of behavior and concomitant belief, which can be taken in sum as a normative array corresponding to some "signatio rationis Universalis"[39] in the reader or hearer who is the appropriate audience. Poetry, that is, is "about" exempla of ethical existence: its rhetorical effect is achieved by its being taken as analogous to its audience, and the unity and coherence of its particulars, that is, its exempla, both among themselves and in their rhetorical effect, are based on those relationships that exist between the individual and the typical.

The full meaning of these abstract statements will only be made clear by the elaborate practical analysis of the *Canterbury Tales* which follows. Here, however, it may help to pause for the sake of contrasting this medieval Aristotelian (and, to some extent, nominalist) definition of the content of poetry with the Platonist definition current in the twelfth century and before. Winthrop Wetherbee, in his definitive study of this theory, distinguishes between a rationalist and a symbolist use of the concrete particulars of this world, but in both cases the object and ultimate content of poetry are God, transcendence, and (particularly for the symbolist) a reality ultimately and essentially ineffable and beyond poetry altogether.[40] There is therefore in twelfth-century poetry much use of figures of prosopopoeia, of descriptions of astronomical ascent, of discussion of ideas and ideals whose existence is philosophical or theological.[41] By contrast, in later poetry we find La Vielle, the Wife of Bath, and the "faire feeld ful of folke." But this is no transition from dull allegory to the predecessors of Hemingway. The central philosophical problem of the Middle Ages, whether one was realist, conceptualist, or nominalist, was the problem of universals, and the central theological problem, after such obviously crucial personal matters as sin and salvation had been seen to, was the nature of valid language purporting to describe the deity. It is possible to speculate that the difference between the poetry of Alanus de Insulis and the poetry of Chaucer, to which we now refer by talking about Chaucer's "realism," is simply the difference between a philosophically realist willingness to reify theological universals by means of prosopopoeia and a nominalist desire to exemplify ethical ones by means of particulars. Until we know more about the writings of late medieval nominalists, and particularly about those among their casual and practical writings which might especially betray their philosophical posture, as distinguished from their philosophical doctrine, such speculation must remain unverified. But it should at least be beyond question that Averroes's emphasis on manners and customs, on the one hand, and on language which is explicitly both mannered and rhetorically effective, on the other, betrays a focus of interest on a kind of poetry different both in manner and in ultimate content from that of the twelfth century. It is therefore inappropriate to expect, in late medieval poetry, the same kind of referential energy, requiring allegorical readings in terms of divine truths, which is normal in the twelfth century. The energy of late medieval poetry is exerted, not between the letter of the poem and the transcendent to which it, and the reader, aspire, but rather within the narrower world of ethics, which encompasses an array of particulars, including the reader or hearer, who relate to each other in terms of some typical but still human set of definitions. Thus the actual words of Dante's *Comedy* describe heaven, but this anagogy is *about* "homo prout merendo et demerendo per arbitrii libertatem iustitiae praemiandi et puniendi obnoxius est."[42] And the referential energy of his poem, which in Alanus would be exerted toward pointing to the ineffable transcendent, is in Dante directed to the architectonic relationships of parallel incident which compose the poem. Thus the *Canterbury Tales* is about the *conditiones* of men; as an array, the poem contains "God's plenty" and is sufficient. The effect of this dialectic between the particular and the typical, however, is just the opposite of what we perceive in the eighteenth-century comedy of manners. There, the manners ironically collapse when confronted by some incorruptibly true particular—in the presence of the finally revealed innocence and purity of the ingenue, all mere rakes, fops, and sophisticates stand convicted of having been mannered rather than real. In Chaucer, on the other hand, failed particulars, in sum, exist themselves ironically, and the cumulative power of the ironies, operating in the sum, deposits a definition around which, as failed or fallible or mortal, they cluster.

Particular *exempla* of *consuetudines* and *credulitates,* then, are the matter of late medieval poetry: they and ethics, in sum, are what late medieval poetry is about. Already, in talking of normative arrays of *exempla,* we have implied in this discussion of the nature and content of story certain formal definitions. An array has a form, or structure; its best presentation tends to be a series in parallel, and not something so linear and sequential as, in modern terms, a plot. The whole of the next chapter will be devoted to an analysis of those aspects of medieval doctrines of structure and ordering which particularly illuminate the *Canterbury Tales.* But, though form does mean arrangement, it also is defined by the whole constructed by the sum of an arranged set of parts. One may discuss form by discussing possible arrangements of parts, as we shall do in the next chapter. But one must also consider what whole, or wholes, certain kinds of formal procedures are capable of constructing. With this consideration we conclude our medieval definition of story.

Theorists such as Geoffrey of Vinsauf recommend a rhetorical organization for poetry, and commentators reflect this recommendation when they divide their poems into *prohemium* and *tractatus.* But organization is not quite the same as form; modern critics have been misled in trying to deduce formal principles of coherence and unity from recommendations of rhetorical organization, which presume a material already unified on its own formal grounds, and therefore capable of being presented artificially by means of beginnings in medias res and digressions to parts not in the natural order.[43] Organization is not, therefore, the same as form or unity, but often exists in counterpoint to it. Form itself medieval critics discussed in their commentary *accessus* under the topic of formal cause. The subject has been dealt with extensively elsewhere; here we summarize only as much material as will make clear the critical point.[44]

Medieval *accessus* occur in two primary forms: an earlier one, deriving from Servius, in which such subjects as title, author, purpose, and so on are discussed, and a later one in which most of the same subjects were included under schemata derived from the four Aristotelian causes. One Servian topic was the *modus agendi;* in the Aristotelian *accessus* the equivalent is the *forma tractandi,* one of the two subheads under formal cause. It is here that late medieval critics defined their doctrine of literary form. Conventionally, formal cause included two subtopics, the *forma tractatus* and the *forma tractandi,* sometimes explicitly equated with the *modus agendi.* The *forma tractatus* was usually explained as the formal divisions of the work under consideration—for Ovid's *Metamorphoses,* the *forma tractatus* would be the division of the work into fifteen books, and within them into the *mutationes* which were the concern of individual stories.[45] The *forma tractandi* was conventionally defined in terms of five *modi,* with which modern scholarship is chiefly familiar because of the listing of them in Dante's letter to Can Grande (along with another anomalous group of five). They are as follows: "definitivus, divisivus, probativus, improbativus, et exemplorum positivus."[46] This list of five *modi* occurs over and over again. Even where there is variation, it is often more terminological than substantial, as when *collectivus* or inferential is substituted for *probativus* and *improbativus*[47]

What this analysis means is that medieval commentators understood poetry in essentially discursive terms. The definition in terms of hypothetical verbal constructs with which modern criticism is familiar would not have made sense to them. The words of poetry, like all other words, conveyed information related to truth, and the formalities which defined their integrity were the same ones which defined the valid discourse of logic. The metaphors and comparisons and analogous or associative relationships which poetry has always asserted, therefore, must not have been seen as anything special, or foreign to the normal operations of reality; this terminology of the commentators makes clear that these features, which we would call the habits of poetry, were received, like everything else in what was read, as the conveyors of information, as descriptions of what was.

If poetry is a valid discursive description of the real world, capable of being received as proof, refutation, division,[48] definition, and example, then obviously the world which it describes is not the same as ours. The chief differences have been defined in many ways, all tending toward the same meaning—for our purposes here, we define them as, for the Middle Ages, a fundamental trust of analogy as an organizing principle for reality, and a willingness to believe that the material facts of things are ontologically implicated in the intentionalities of God and man, and therefore operate rhetorically as well as in themselves.

According to Sheila Delany, the medieval trust of analogy came under substantial attack in the fourteenth century.[49] This is certainly true, both from the standpoint of professional philosophy and as a characteristic of polemic, willing to use whatever weapon came to hand. Nevertheless, the presentation of an array of conflicting authorities, arguments, or examples is not necessarily an admission that there is no possibility of judgment among them. Taken ironically, such an array may well define by analogy profound and seriously held doctrine. Robert Holkot, certainly a skeptic[50] and by most accounts some kind of nominalist,[51] nevertheless depends constantly on the kind of analogizing which trusts exempla, and even allegorizes them, as a way of making a point both clear and admissible. In her analysis of the problem, Delany is dealing basically with professed doctrine, and rather advanced doctrine at that, whereas we are trying to deal with the more fundamental level of posture or habit of mind. Thus medieval philosophers who believe themselves opposed to analogical thinking—and indeed by twelfth-century standards believe so correctly—nevertheless still make analogies far more readily and trustingly than we do now.

This habit of mind can be broadly defined by an example. The *Vita Edwardi Secundi*, a typical aristocratic chronicle, ignores a clearly causal pattern of explanation for a historical event in favor of an analogy-based one: "Perhaps a hidden cause, not immediate but remote, punished the earl. The Earl of Lancaster at one time bore off the head of Peter of Gaveston, and now by the command of the king, the Earl of Lancaster has lost his head. Thus, perhaps not unjustly, the Earl received measure for measure, as it is written in Holy Scripture: 'For with the same measure that yet mete withal it shall be measured to you again.' Thus Abner killed Asahel, striking him under the fifth rib, but Abner did not escape, for he afterwards perished by a similar wound."[52] English history, in short, operates as it does in this case because there exists an ethical pattern, defining measures meted and received, which events can be expected to fit. One proves the fit by citing an analogous case, and such citing is a sufficient explanation of "causality." William J. Brandt explains the procedure in this way: "History, for the author of the *Vita*, provided not examples but analogies of a most elementary sort. The link between the historical incident and the one being commented upon was some sort of aphorism at loose in the world and prior to both of them. Hence meaning was not implicit in an action sequence, it was implicit in the *relationship* between one sort of incident and another."[53] Trust of analogies of this kind is obvious in Chaucer, as in his use of the Midas story as a comment on the Wife of Bath, Pygmalion and Jephthah as analogies to the predicament of Virginia, and Echo as conclusion to the *Clerk's Tale*. Chaucer's case is complicated by the frequent trust of medieval glosses to govern the full ironic significance of his analogizing exempla—we shall return to this feature of his work in some detail later. Here it is sufficient to note the simple fact of analogy itself—which persisted, of course, to validate the double plots of Renaissance drama.

A slightly more complex example is *Gawain and the Green Knight*, where the fact that Sir Bercilak and the Green Knight are the same person asserts within the poem a fundamental analogy, from which further analogies develop which interpret the poem's structure and meaning. Formally, the basic analogy is exactly like the complex resonating relationship established and defined by biblical exegesis; the only difference between its operation in exegesis and its operation in the *Gawain* is that the primary relational energy is contained within the poem itself, whereas in exegesis only the allegorical level, which focuses upon Christ, stays within Holy Writ, and the other two—the tropology and the anagogy—assert relationships outside the text, with its hearer and with his potential and proper spiritual destination.[54]

Exegesis, then, defines the sort of relationship which gives fundamental coherence to events and objects in the real universe, and therefore naturally to the parts and particulars of the fictional ones in poems. Generically, it is a relationship of analogy; specifically, as defined by the practice of medieval Bible study, it is a relationship operating on only certain kinds of particulars and within a certain classification of levels. Exegesis, and its derived structural principles, are not simply naively pious parallel-mongering, nor the result of the willingness to find religious meaning everywhere. The Middle Ages did so, and thus tempt those who read exegetical texts for their meanings instead of the forms of their procedure to find similar pieties over again. But the system as such requires no such results. In order to see it properly, as the general formal understanding which can permit us to find a medieval unity in the weltering and apparently incoherent parts of medieval poems, finished and unfinished, we must understand that, though medieval habits of reasoning from analogy often generated explicitly Christian meanings, they could generate other kinds of meanings as well. In the largest sense, analogical thinking simply presumes that full explanation of any given subject is accomplished in terms of an ordered array of parallel narratives and figures and propositions, each resonating in terms of all the others, and all properly dealt with and analyzed by a conscious elaboration of one-to-one parallels. Full explanation is achieved by assent to the asserted parallels. It is historically true, of course, that medieval thinkers elaborated these parallels most fully as they explained the Bible. But the same procedures worked in other contexts; none of the parallel narratives, propositions, or figures is required, formally, to be Christian. Structurally, it is the relationship which matters: structurally and formally, the relation between the Green Knight and Sir Bercilak, or between (for instance) the Wife of Bath and the loathly lady, or between Constance, Griselda, and May, can be best understood by knowing the form and character of the typological relation between David and Christ—not for the sake of Christ, but merely because this was the normal medieval illustration or defining example of the procedure. In other words, typology can generate relationships without also being required to generate pregiven meanings.

In summary, then, poetry is ethics, its parts are customs and beliefs and the examples which define them, its formal principles are the same as those of all valid discourse, and its relational principles are based on the great structural system of typology. This is a set of definitions which has no need for the validation of aesthetics, though it has a certain profound beauty of its own. It is a set of definitions which probably would yield interesting results if applied to any literature, and not just the medieval—its probable ability to make sense of such disparate writers as Faulkner, Joyce, and Durrell is a fascinating speculation.[55] But its best power lies in its own time, because it can define for us the coherence of works like the *Canterbury Tales,* which have no satisfactory unity except a medieval one.

It is in the light of these definitions that we are able to claim for Chaucer's stories, and for the doctrine of story which they exemplify, such a high place. The prologue and link material of the *Canterbury Tales* frames fiction with a discussion of stories—of their possible ethi-

cal application, of their rhetorical quality, of their sources and authority, of their local and universal fitness. This discussion, though it is
persistently ironic, and carried on by imperfect voices, invokes as a
whole the high doctrine of fiction as ethical exemplar, and, even
though ironic, permits an understanding of true doctrine. Behind it
all is the concept of spiritual pilgrimage, which is itself ironically misappropriated, but which nevertheless is necessary to the enterprise as
an informing presence, because it is ultimately that pilgrimage which
Chaucer's stories of human truth will constitute, define, and make
possible. Just as Dante's characters, in Hell, Purgatory, and Heaven,
get to be for all eternity what their stories on earth achieved of definition, so Chaucer's stories, in accumulating sum, define a human condition subject both to spiritual definition and to spiritual destiny. To
say this, however, is not in any sense to admit that we are trying to
reach Baldwin's conclusion by a different route. We do not insist on
the ethical character of stories, so that Chaucer's tales may serve as the
signposts of the Parson's journey to heaven. Rather, we note the
heavenly background, in order to add ultimate weight to our claim
that the stories themselves are important. Chaucer's purpose is not to
affirm the heavenly destination of mankind—rather, he assumes it,
and having done so, he turns to the enterprise of defining in ethical
and very specific terms his norms for the good human society.

To return to the *Knight's Tale,* which we have offered as Chaucer's
central statement both of structure and of subject, we find that the
central interest of the *Canterbury Tales* is defined there in human
terms. The *Knight's Tale* is outside the New Testament dispensation.
By choosing a story of pagan antiquity, Chaucer makes his purpose
clear: he is concerned above all with earthly conduct. Fundamentally,
the *Knight's Tale* is about three things: the efforts of Theseus to bring
order to Thebes, to settle the struggle between Palamon and Arcite by
the fit awarding of Emelye, and to reconcile himself through an act of
understanding to the ironic but orderly ending of his problem, which
is furnished him by the action of Saturn. In brief, the *Knight's Tale* is
about order—order in the kingdom, in the family, and in the person.
More than anything else, it is this ordering, on its parallel and mutually interpreting levels, which is the central subject and material of the
Canterbury Tales. The human condition as something at once personal
and social, and when social, both marital and civic, and under all
conditions as something capable of being blessed by definition—this is
Chaucer's subject. The *Knight's Tale* defines the climax of human
experience in Theseus's arrival at a human understanding of events;

by implication, we expect that the *Canterbury Tales* as well, in its final act, will infer God's truth, but from a position which is in this world and this world alone.

The subject of the *Canterbury Tales,* then, is not a theological subject, really. At any rate, it is certainly not the pious subject which the dramatic speaker of the Retraction had in mind. *The Canterbury Tales* is a worldly collection, in the best sense of that word—its tales focus the attention of a profound moralist upon the world in which morals and mores are enacted. As we shall see, Chaucer's view of society is one which bases itself on marriage—real marriage, and not the disposable verbal integument of Bernard's meditations, though the allegorical overtones of marriage are admitted to enrich, or comment upon, its literal existence as the central structure of society. When interpreted by the focus of attention of the stories told, the pilgrimage is not really on its way to heaven—even though some of its members will doubtless eventually get there. Even the Parson's recommendations are fundamentally a way of dealing with the events of this worldly life—his negations are pointed to and focused upon this life.[56]

If Chaucer's framing of ethical standards has overtones of theological terminology, it is because his culture provided only one context in which definitions of the human condition could be stated seriously, that is, a Christian one. The context of definition in which he places his tales draws on the assumptions about the order of the universe which Christian philosophy had taught him. The definition he achieves is not by overt statement, and above all not by some reductionist departure, on the wings of allegory, from any discardable letter of story or experience. Rather, he adopts the exemplary language of storytelling, in which the dialectic between ideal and real, definition and fact, role and person, intention and act, are embraced and appreciated, as well as resolved. The theological flavor of his ultimate reference points does not make him unusually pious, but rather a man of his own time. The evidence of his life and works really implies that he was happily skeptical, possessed of a faith which is partly worldly wisdom and partly the sophisticated invulnerability of one not easily committed or involved.

At the same time, he was a man who still held out hope that truth could be spoken with some exactness. Chaucer's strategy is nominalist, not Platonist, as would be expected of a person of his time and nation, but it is still capable of achieving reasonable certainty, and it certainly must not be mistaken for too open-ended a skepticism.[57] The irony of this life for Chaucer holds the promise of the ideal truth of the next;

the relentless exposure of the hollow promises and foolish actions which fail to organize men into proper hierarchies and orders suggests his belief that such hierarchies must be discovered and adopted. Moreover, the range and variety of his exempla of comic failure and occasional saintly or exemplary success suggest that behind these particulars there can be found the universal that is true. The discovery of that universal awaits, now, the principle on which his particular cases are to be related to one another. This is the subject of the next chapter.

1. Chaucer's medieval self-consciousness as an artist is obscured for us by our own various modern notions of art and the aesthetic, and especially by some critics' desire to read all poetry as essentially about poetry. These critics, in an atmosphere of uncertainty about the meaning and ground of discourse as such, take all poetry as in a sense only about itself, engaged ultimately in that deconstructive autonomy which is its only possible validation. Such thoroughgoing pessimism is not to be found in Chaucer, not even in the *House of Fame;* nor is it to be found in medieval nominalism. A failure to be Platonist is not necessarily a surrender to nihilism, nor even, in any radical sense, skepticism. Gabriel Josipovici's essay "Chaucer: The Teller and the Tale," in his *The World and the Book: A Study of Modern Fiction* (Stanford, 1971), pp. 52–99, is, we think, the most brilliant appropriation of Chaucer for the modern poetic that has been written to date; its instructiveness exists in a mode to which its historical incorrectness does not relate. But the possibility that such an essay can be written makes historically responsible description of Chaucer's medieval sense of himself as a poet extremely difficult. Aspects of this description are achieved by Eugene Vance in "Mervelous Signals: Poetics, Sign Theory, and Politics in Chaucer's *Troilus*," *New Literary History* 10 (Winter 1979): 293–337, paradoxically in the context of relating medieval literature to contemporary literary theory. The best full study of Chaucer's theoretical attitude toward poetry is a dissertation by R. A. Shoaf, *"Mutatio Amoris:* Revision and Penitence in Chaucer's *The Book of the Duchess*," (Cornell University, 1977), but it deals more with the poetic that Chaucer rejects than with the one he achieves.

2. Because our focus is on Chaucer and on the statement which his story collection achieves, we have no scope for treating any but the nearest of his antecedents. On the relation between fiction and truth we must at least cite Wesley Trimpi's closely reasoned and already classic studies "The Ancient Hypothesis of Fiction: An Essay on the Origins of Literary Theory," *Traditio* 27 (1971): 1–78, and "The Quality of Fiction: The Rhetorical Transmission of Literary Theory," *Traditio* 30 (1974): 1–118. Chaucer's literary attitudes fall near the end, but definitely within, the rhetorical tradition that Trimpi defines.

3. The strength of the medieval belief in prologues, as something as obviously a proper part of literary discourse as, today, lead paragraphs are of the writings of journalists, is proved by Chaucer's medieval editors. J. S. P. Tatlock, in "The *Canterbury Tales* in 1400," *PMLA* 50 (1935): 119, notes that the text is more complete in presenting prologues for the tales than in providing endlinks. The first editors of the poem, in providing spurious materials intended to disguise the incompleteness of Chaucer's work, regularly added prologues. Their practice with endings is less attentive and reflects medieval rhetorical manuals, whose doctrines of conclusion were brief and inconclusive—one finished a work by stopping.

4. Chaucer's own conclusion agrees with the consensus of criticism in finding the ending of the *Miller's Tale* an ostentatious example of poetic and real justice. Neither Chaucer nor modern critics seem disturbed by the fact Alisoun gets off scot free, though she has presumably been as much enveloped in sin as Nicholas. Alisoun functions more as occasion than person, as do the other "awardable" women in the first fragment; the failure of novelistic realism which this function enacts is concealed by Chaucer's exuberantly circumstantial narrative, but it is a failure nevertheless. We should probably take it as evidence that Chaucer was interested in something else—in this case, in rules and intrusions against them. His focus is therefore on the intrusive male and his supposedly sovereign adversary, and the story is, as an example, discursively complete, even if we have a character left over. Cf. Morton W. Bloomfield, "The Miller's Tale—An UnBoethian Interpretation," *Medieval Literature and Folklore Studies: Essays in Honor of Francis Lee Utley*, pp. 205-11.

5. Just what constitutes the "ernest" and the "game" of the pilgrimage and of the tales has been discussed recently by a number of scholars: Owen, *Pilgrimage and Storytelling in the Canterbury Tales*, pp. 3-6; Joseph, "Chaucerian 'Game'—'Earnest' and the 'Argument of Herbergage' in the *Canterbury Tales*," pp. 83-96; and William J. Brown, "Chaucer's Double Apology for the *Miller's Tale*," *University of Colorado Studies: Series in Language and Literature* 10 (1966): 15-22. The issue of earnest-game is related by Owen, in particular, to the general question of Chaucer's attitude toward poetry, as recorded in the *Parson's Tale* and Retraction; it is linked, as well, to the specific defense of poetry as accurate reporting, to be found in the General Prologue and the Miller's Prologue, by Brown.

6. But not his later scholarly ones, as all who have seen in him a "momentary conversion" betray. See the survey of criticism offered by Halverson, "Chaucer's Pardoner," pp. 184-202.

7. *Chaucer and the Shape of Creation*, p. 127.

8. "...and thus by oon assent/We been acorded to his juggement./And thereupon the wyn was fet anon;/We dronken, and to reste went echon" (I [A] 817-20). The Host also confirms his authority by a kind of oath on drink: "As evere mote I drynke wyn or ale,/Whoso be rebel to my juggement" (I [A] 832-33).

9. "Let us lighten the useful work of our hands by varied speech and let us in turn say something for our empty ears, in order that the time does not seem long."

10. "re vera fuerunt [Mineides] optime potatrices, que spernebant Bachum dicentes Bachum minime posse nocere. Unde Bachus contemptus telas earum in vineas id est pro vino et vineis vendi fecit. Vel quia hedere ad modum vinearum serpunt, dicuntur mutate esse in hederas. Ipse vero in aves, quia venditis omnibus que habebant, a patria sua exulantes auffugerunt. Sed in vespertiliones pocius quam in alias aves mutate sunt quia de nocte pocius quam de die vacatur potationi, sicut et aves ille pocius de nocte quam de die volant" (Ghisalberti, "Arnolfo," p. 211). "Truly the Minyades were above all drunkards, who spurned Bacchus, saying Bacchus was wholly powerless to be harmful. Wherefore Bacchus, contemptuous, made their weaving into vines, that is, to be sold for wine and vines. Or since ivy creeps in the manner of vines, the Minyades are said to be changed into ivy. But they, changed into birds, since all the things they had were sold, and exiled from their own country, fled. But they were changed into bats rather than other birds because in the night rather than the day they are given up to drink, so also those birds fly in the night rather than in the day." Bersuire and Giovanni del Virgilio have substantially the same interpretation.

11. "Selonc que la fable devise / M'est avis que Bacchus desprise / Cil qui vins boit outre mesure / Et cil qui dou boivre n'a cure. / Ces trois serours le desprisoient. / Quar a outrage le buvoient" (4. 2488–53) (*Ovide moralisé*, ed. C. De Boer, [rpt., Wiesbaden, 1966], 2:63–69).

12. This obligation to verbatim reporting of one's *materia*, of course, is not to be found in medieval manuals of poetic, nor in Chaucer's handling of his own known sources. To profess it is merely one more profession of dependence on individualized exempla, whose eventual complex interrelationships, and not their actual language or intentions, will define the truth. Cf. Brown, "Chaucer's Double Apology for the *Miller's Tale*," pp. 15–19, which links the appeal to accuracy with the statements on poetry's value in the Retraction, particularly with the phrase, "al that is writen is writen for oure doctrine," from St. Paul. See below, note 15. Chaucer makes use of this argument from verbatim reporting in the *Manciple's Tale*, as well; the place of the question in the tale is discussed by Britton J. Harwood, "Language and the Real: Chaucer's Manciple," *Chaucer Review* 6 (1972): 268–79.

13. Robinson, *Works*, p. 772.

14. Olive Sayce, "Chaucer's 'Retracciouns': The Conclusion of the *Canterbury Tales* and Its Place in Literary Tradition," *Medium Aevum* 40 (1971): 235. Judson B. Allen, in "The Old Way and the Parson's Way," pp. 255–71, also suggests the Retraction's conventionality and the necessity for its dramatic inclusion in the *Tales*, and further undercuts the Baldwin position by suggesting that Chaucer intended ironic overtones for the Parson's suggestion of penance as the right end of pilgrimage. R. K. Root, in "Chaucer and the Decameron," *English Studies* 44 (1912): 1–7, rightly notes that both Boccaccio and Chaucer offer comparable apologies for coarse tales, while justifying them on the grounds of their admissibility in a game. Most important, however, Root identifies the Retraction and the prologue of the *Miller's Tale* as two presentations of the same "formal apology." See also W. H. Clawson, "The Framework of the Canterbury Tales," in Wagenknecht, ed., *Chaucer*, pp. 3–23; and Hubertis M. Cummings, *The Indebtedness of Chaucer's Works to the*

Italian Works of Boccaccio (1916; rpt., New York, 1965), pp. 177–178. Of course, the argument that the Retraction is an integral part of the *Canterbury Tales* does not end in itself the controversy over the rejection of Chaucer's art which the brief conclusion provides. Some scholars have argued that it is, indeed, conceived as an integral part of the *Canterbury Tales*, and a judgment offered on its artistic merits. This is true of Owen, *Pilgrimage and Storytelling in the Canterbury Tales*, p. 6; Alfred David, *The Strumpet Muse: Art and Morals in Chaucer's Poetry* (Bloomington, 1976), p. 240; and others.

15. Caxton, one of Chaucer's first editors, echoes this phrase, in a reference to a specifically literary product, in his preface to Malory's *Le Morte Darthur*. See *The Works of Thomas Malory*, ed. Eugene Vinaver (London, New York, Toronto, 1954), p. xvii: "But al is wryton for our doctryne, and for to beware that we falle not to vice . . . " We find the phrase as well, of course, in the *Nun's Priest's Tale* (VII 3442 [B² 4632]). For a discussion of Chaucer's understanding of the phrase, see Brown, "Chaucer's Double Apology for the *Miller's Tale*," pp. 21–22; and Paul Ruggiers, "Some Theoretical Considerations of Comedy in the Middle Ages," in his *Versions of Medieval Comedy* (Norman, Okla., 1977), p. 15.

16. Boggess, "Averrois Cordubensis," p. 11. "Man among the other animals is delighted in the understanding of things which he perceives now in the senses and also in their representation or imitation. And the sign of this, that is, that man is naturally pleased and delights in this understanding, is that we are delighted and we rejoice in the representation of some things in whose sense impression we are not delighted."

17. Ibid., p. 9. ". . . is sometimes chosen to present the decent, expressing it strongly, and sometimes it is changed so as to present something shameful, similarly expressing it strongly."

18. Sayce, "Chaucer's 'Retracciouns,'" p. 245.

19. This is the reason why the "dramatic principle" yields limited and misleading results. The dramatic principle makes the stories relative to the speakers, rather than the speakers relative to the stories, less real than the stories and under the judgment of the stories. Thus the dramatic principle reads the *Canterbury Tales* backwards, as one might do who relished ice cream cones but threw the ice cream away.

20. The best full presentation of this point of view is R. E. Kaske, "The Knight's Interruption of the *Monk's Tale*," ELH 24 (1957): 249–68. He pairs the knight and the monk, and shows how the *Monk's Tale* is " philosophically incomplete" (p. 261) in the light of a proper understanding of Boethian fortune. In comparing the *Canterbury Tales* with the *Monk's Tale* as tale collections, we presume substantially the incompleteness which Kaske argues.

21. The Knight seems to have a taste for comedy, that is, stories of rising fortune that end in success and happiness; it is a taste appropriate, of course, to the *Canterbury Tales*. On the medieval categories of comedy and tragedy, see Ruggiers, "Some Theoretical Considerations of Comedy in the Middle Ages," pp. 2–5; and the discussion that follows below, in this chapter.

22. We are happy to thank John Leyerle for this notion, as developed in a seminar meeting at Yale University, and later presented in a paper, "Some

'Subtile Knyttynges' in the *Canterbury Tales,*" at the Chaucer session of the Medieval Academy, 11 May 1974. The Eucharistic overtones that this identification gives to the supper that the pilgrims eat together, in preparation for pilgrimage, suggest that Chaucer may have had in mind a parallel between his pilgrimage and one of the most important pilgrimage paradigms in medieval art, the story of the disciples traveling to Emmaus. For the history of the story and its impact on medieval religious drama, see F. C. Gardiner, *The Pilgrimage of Desire: A Study of Theme and Genre in Medieval Literature* (Leiden, 1971).

23. For the Middle Ages the *auctores* were the books of pagan antiquity recognized as culturally valid and, by derivation, medieval books other than the Bible and theology, narrowly conceived, which had authority. They are not the equivalent of what we call literature because, though most of them are by our terms literary, their medieval validation is different from the aesthetic one we would recognize and validates, in sum, a different array of books.

24. The classical source is probably Servius: "Et sciendum est, inter fabulam et argumentum, hoc est historiam, hoc interesse, quod fabula est dicta res contra naturam, sive facta sive non facta, ut de Pasiphae, historia est quicquid secundum naturam dicitur, sive factum sive non factum, ut de Phaedra," commenting on *Aen.* 1. 235; see G. Thilo and H. Hagen, eds., *Servii Grammatici qui feruntur in Vergilii Carmina Commentarii* (Leipzig, 1881), 1:89. "It must be understood that the difference between fable and argument, that is, history, is that fable is called a thing contrary to nature, whether it happened or not, such as the story of Pasiphae, [and] history is anything according to nature, whether it happened or not, such as the story of Phaedra." A French fourteenth-century commentary on the *Metamorphoses* elaborates: "Differentia est inter argumentum et historiam, fabulam et comediam. Argumentum est quando nos loquimur de veritate sub specie falsitatis ut apparet in denominatione athenarum, fabula quando nos loquimur de falsitate sub specie falsitatis ut per totum hunc librum apparet. Hystoria de veritate sub specie veritatis ut per evangelia et ecclesiasticum. Comedia de falsitate sub specie veritatis ut de mutatione nabugudonosor et Yo" (Bibliotheca Apostolica Vaticana MS Vat. lat. 1479, fol. 96). "There is a difference among argument and history, fable and comedy. Argument exists when we speak of truth under the appearance of the false, as appears in the naming of Athens; fable, when we speak of the false under the appearance of the false, as appears in this whole book. History [presents] the true under the appearance of the true, as in the Gospels and Ecclesiasticus. Comedy [presents] the false under the appearance of the true, as in the transformation of Nebuchadnezzar and Io."

25. Clement Marot, *Le Roman de la Rose* (Milan, 1957), 1:92.

26. Cf. Foucault, *The Order of Things,* pp. 294–322.

27. In making this generalization, we mean in no way to slight or ignore the late medieval development of nominalism, which denies, in various ways, the real existence of these mental "things." At the same time, it is most important to note that, in the whole history of philosophy, the playing field does not always remain in the same place. In a period such as our own, when metaphysics has been seriously out of fashion for some time, it helps to remember that we are not covering the whole field, and that therefore the

whole range of medieval argument, realist or nominalist, exists from our point of view in an area of philosophy more "realist" than ours. In a word, the modern existentialist is far more nominalist than any medieval nominalist. Robert Holkot would consider himself very far from being a Platonist, in his own times and terms, but he would almost certainly find himself saying rather Platonist things if he were called upon to deal with Jean-Paul Sartre.

28. This was one of the Averroistic doctrines condemned by Bishop Stephen Tempier in 1270. The fact that it was eventually judged heretical should not mislead us; it is not the conclusion, but the more fundamental fact that the question was debated, that betrays the parameters within which the medieval point of view must be defined.

29. For illustrations of this commonplace, see Allen, *The Friar as Critic,* pp. 40–41.

30. "It is put under ethics because it deals with behavior." R. B. C. Huygens, ed., *Accessus ad auctores, Bernard d'Utrecht, Conrad d'Hirsau, Dialogus super auctores* (Leiden, 1970), p. 25; see also pp. 20, 21, 22, 26, 27, 33 and others.

31. The classic description of this life of high-style decorum is, of course, John Huizinga, *The Waning of the Middle Ages* (London, 1924).

32. For discussion of the importance and influence of this work, see O. B. Hardison, "The Place of Averroes' Commentary on the *Poetics* in the History of Medieval Criticism," in *Medieval and Renaissance Studies: Proceedings of the Southeastern Institute of Medieval and Renaissance Studies,* Summer 1968, ed. John L. Lievsay (Durham, N.C., 1970), pp. 57–81; and William F. Boggess, "Aristotle's Poetics in the Fourteenth Century," *Studies in Philology* 67 (1970): 278–94.

33. Such a study is presently in progress. For a preliminary treatment, see Allen, "Hermann the German's Averroistic Aristotle," pp. 67–81.

34. Geoffrey assumes that a poet's *materia* will have its own order, which the artist may rearrange. Cf. Faral, *Les arts poétiques,* lines 87–100, p. 200; and Nims, *Poetria Nova,* pp. 18–19.

35. Assisi Bib. Com. MS 302, fol. 138v. "The behavior and vices of ladies are the material of the book"; "the beauty of the conditions [of humanity] which are in the book." For the full text of this *accessus,* with more extended analysis, see Allen, "Hermann the German's Averroistic Aristotle."

36. Jill Mann, *Chaucer and Medieval Estates Satire,* p. 184. That "science deals with the universal and the necessary" is an Aristotelian commonplace (Etienne Gilson, *History of Christian Philosophy in the Middle Ages* [New York, 1955], p. 502); the significance of this commonplace for poetic theory needs emphasis, lest it be ignored by modernists on the one hand and abused by allegorical reductionists on the other.

37. R. Dragonetti, "Aux frontières du langage poétique," *Romanica gandensia* 9 (Ghent, 1961): 23 ff.

38. This point is made with a correctly nuanced allowance for medieval sensibility by Elizabeth T. Pochoda in *Arthurian Propaganda: "Le Mort Darthur" as an Historical Ideal of Life* (Chapel Hill, 1971), pp. 28–29 and passim.

39. This phrase is from Aegidius Romanus, who uses it to account for the possibility of having *scientia* from the particulars treated in the Bible. See his *In epistolam B. Pauli Apostoli ad Romanos commentarii* (Rome, 1555), fol. lr.

40. Winthrop Wetherbee, *Platonism and Poetry in the Twelfth Century: The Literary Influence of the School of Chartres* (Princeton, 1972).

41. It is therefore most appropriate that one of the very few commentaries which assigns a medieval poem to some part of philosophy other than ethics should be that made by Robert of Sorbona on the *Anticlaudianus* of Alanus de Insulis: "Nota quod liber iste supponitur toti philosophie et non alicui parti per se quia communiter agit de septem artibus liberalibus. Modus agendi triplex est: aliquando procedit rationaliter scilicet quantum ad naturalem proprie dictam et trivium, quandoque disciplinaliter quantum ad quadrivium, quandoque intelligibiliter quantum ad metaphysicam" (Bibliothèque Nationale, MS lat. 8300, fol. 9v). "Note that this book is classified under all philosophy and not under any part as such, because it deals commonly with the seven liberal arts. Its mode of procedure is threefold: sometimes it proceeds rationally with regard to the natural properly so called and the trivium, sometimes in terms of the disciplines in dealing with the quadrivium, and sometimes cognitively with regard to metaphysics."

42. Epistola X (to Can Grande) in *Dantis Alagherii Epistolae,* ed. Paget Toynbee with C. G. Hardie, 2d ed. (Oxford, 1966), p. 174 ("man, according as he is liable to the reward and punishment of justice through free will in deserving and being guilty").

43. The question is discussed by Robert Jordan, both in the book-length study *Chaucer and the Shape of Creation,* mentioned above, and in "The Question of Genre: Five Chaucerian Romances," in *Chaucer at Albany,* pp. 77–79; and by Donald Howard, *The Idea of the Canterbury Tales,* especially pp. 1–20 and 210–26. We would distinguish between their comments and our own discussion primarily by our efforts to go outside the area of specifically "formal" or "technical" aspects of composition to search out principles of artistic organization and unity drawn from the artist's perception of the coherence of his subject matter.

44. The classic treatment of the *accessus* in its late classical and earlier medieval forms is E. A. Quain, S.J., "The Medieval Accessus ad Auctores," *Traditio* 3 (1945): 215–64. For Dante in particular (his own letter to Can Grande is a conventional *accessus* plus a dictamenal exordium) see Bruno Nardi, "Osservazioni sul medievale 'Accessus ad Auctores' in rapporto all'Epistola a Cangrande," in *Saggi Note di Critica Dantesca* (Milan, 1966), pp. 268–305; and Bruno Sandkühler, *Die frühen Dantekommentare und ihr Verhältnis zur mittelalterlichen Kommentartradition* (Munich, 1967). An analysis of *accessus* terminology as evidence for medieval literary theory is Allen, "Commentary as Criticism."

45. This is, in fact, the manner in which Ovidian commentators treated the poem, honoring the book divisions and then treating each separate *mutatio* in order.

46. Epistola X. *Dantis Alagherii Epistolae,* p. 175 ("defining, dividing, proving, disproving, and giving examples").

47. Where there is variation, the conventionality of the list is proved by the commentator's reference to it, as in an Ovid commentary in Florence: "Causa formalis est duplex, forma tractatus et forma tractandi. Est autem modus quintuplex, scilicet divisivus [*cod. divisius,* and similarly for the other schemata] diffinitivus, exemplorum positivus, probativus, et reprobativus et collectivus. In hoc libro triplex, scilicet divisivus, diffinitivus, et exemplativus" (Biblioteca Laurenziana MS Plut. 36.3, fol. 11r). "The formal cause is double, the form of the treatise and the form of the treatment. This is a fivefold mode: dividing, defining, giving examples, proving, reproving, and inferring. In this book it is threefold: dividing, defining, and giving examples." Thomas Waley's Boethius commentary is similar; after elaborately defining the form of the *Consolation* in terms of dialogue, Thomas says: "Vel potest dici secundum communiter loquentes, quod causa formalis tractandi est quintuplex: diffinitiva, divisiva, probativa, improbativa, exemplorum positiva, sicut videbitur in libro" (*Boetius de consolatione,* fol. bb5v). "Or one can say following convention that the formal cause of the treatment is fivefold: defining, dividing, proving, disproving, giving examples, as will be seen in the book."

48. Emphasis upon division betrays a medieval habit of mind which is often satisfied, for a definition of something, with the enumeration of its parts. This satisfaction even affects medieval usage—"dividere" may mean the same thing as "tractare," as when Bartholomew of Bruges, in his commentary on the Averroistic *Poetics,* says "primo *dividit* contextionem poeticam penes finem eius, secundo penes formam" (Paris, MS B.N. lat. 16089, fol. 146v; emphasis ours). "First he divides poetic composition with regard to its end, second with regard to its form."

49. Sheila Delany, "Undoing Substantial Connection: The Late Medieval Attack on Analogical Thought," *Mosaic* 5 (1972): 31-52. Se also her *Chaucer's House of Fame: The Poetics of Skeptical Fideism* (Chicago, 1972).

50. Beryl Smalley, *English Friars and Antiquity in the Early Fourteenth Century* (Oxford, 1960), p. 133.

51. Etienne Gilson, *History of Christian Philosophy in the Middle Ages,* pp. 500-502, treats Holkot in his connection with William of Ockham.

52. Quoted in Brandt, *The Shape of Medieval History,* pp. 102-3.

53. Ibid., p. 102.

54. This interpretation is worked out in some detail in Allen, *The Friar as Critic,* pp. 145-49.

55. For the opposite enterprise, rooted in structuralism and its continuings, see Gabriel Josipovici, *The World and the Book.*

56. For further discussion of this view of the *Parson's Tale,* see Allen, "The Old Way and the Parson's Way." On the pagan, worldly character of the *Knight's Tale,* cf. Joseph Westlund, "The *Knight's Tale* as an Impetus for Pilgrimage," *Philological Quarterly* 43 (1964): 526-27.

57. For a brief statement of the difference between Chaucer's nominalism and the skepticism which the modern critic is tempted to read into it, see the review of Robert Burlin's *Chaucerian Fiction* by Judson B. Allen, *Speculum* 54 (January 1979): 116-18.

3

Medieval Notions
of Structure

The manuscripts which Chaucer's medieval audiences read and collected were very different from our own books; they always lacked title pages, sometimes were without date and attribution, and frequently seem to us to have no coherence other than that of a very loose anthology. The rule would almost seem to be that whatever is put together, belongs together, even if its arrangement and organization seem to have been determined only by the availability of exemplars or by the changing interests of the man making or ordering the volume. The extreme situation is met in the manuscript in which one man or a group of men over a span of years recorded treatises, poems, documents, even personal notes which were important to them. Unless we recognize that medieval principles of organization are different from our own, however, some medieval works planned as unified and organized statements might look to us like such random collections of materials drawn together only by the author's interest. Treatises collecting exempla, word lists presenting the various scriptural uses of a particular image, bestiaries, letter collections, even romance cycles— all have rules of selection which may not be evident immediately to the modern reader schooled by novels and the scientific method. The medieval fondness for collections, of all sorts, must be examined and appreciated in dealing with Chaucer's collection of stories, because the *Canterbury Tales* has at least as much in common with a *distinctio* or the *Golden Legend* as it does with either novels or a modern book of travels.

Collections usually have, either stated explicitly or concealed in their preparation, an idea or theme that the author uses as his standard for selecting materials appropriate for the work. The medieval principle of typology, for example, permits a number of different things, such as historical events or saints' legends, to be collected in order to assert that in fact they resemble and interpret one central fact or idea. The normative array or *distinctio* is essentially the same, but procedurally just the opposite; under this principle a single idea or thing is examined by subdividing it into its kinds, or parts, presumably exhaustively. Both typology and the *distinctio* are associative in their logic, and each tends to generate the other. A group of typologically related things, once related and named, forms a *distinctio;* the parts of a *distinctio,* once assembled and listed, are very often typologically related. Whether we are furnished with the governing rule for the collection or must discover it by naming the common denominator for the materials collected, still the work itself is unified by the author's effort to gather a set of significant cases, exemplifying some general idea. The unity of such a work depends not only on structure or arrangement, but also on the principle of selection which guided the author's choice of materials.

Actual commentaries have very little to say about unity as such, not because no such thing existed, but rather because it was so obvious that it could be presumed. They are always quite able to name the *materia* of the work under discussion, and its end or purpose, as single or very closely related multiple things. The *materia* exists; what may vary is the treatment. The subject matter gives the work the unity which we have described above as relating, not to arrangement, but rather to the author's selection of his material. In his treatment of that material, a poet might introduce artificialities in the form of manipulated beginnings, fit digressions, and all the ornaments of grammar and rhetoric, but these artificialities are not the essence of the piece; instead they are strategies with a rhetorical function, which can be used at all only because the material on which they are imposed is definite and clear enough to sustain a dialectic with them. The medieval poet's first technique for creating a unified work of art was to treat his *materia* fully, because, in this way, he ensured that the unity of the *materia* would be reproduced in his poem.

We shall see, in examining some medieval poems, that searching for the presumed unity brought to the work by its subject matter is very helpful. In itself, however, this sort of unity does not explain the relationship of the work's parts to one another, either in terms of arrangement or in the sense of logical connections between them. On the first point, arrangement, medieval poetic manuals are not very helpful. They provide us with the principle of beginning, middle, and end, but in a conventional and rhetorically oriented manner with expectations far different from modern concerns for dramatic exposition. One may begin at the beginning, in the middle, or at the end, and one may in addition do any of these things in combination with a proverb or exemplum—altogether, there are nine ways to begin, eight of which are artificial and therefore preferable.[1] Past this point one is left rather on one's own—one may condense or amplify, but the material itself is itself, and has its own natural coherence. From *dictamen*, and ultimately from the *Rhetorica ad Herennium*, we have the outline of *exordium, narratio, conclusio*.[2] But here, as well, we are thrown back upon the material itself, which, being a discursive thing,[3] constitutes the entire content of the work—thus, its *narratio*—and leaves the other two parts of the work only the task of introducing and summarizing, rather than treating some essential part of the work's content. Both these divisions, therefore, represent an artistic and rhetorical adornment directed at engaging and convincing an audience, of a material with its own parts and its own logic of connection between those parts.

Medieval commentaries usually mention the parts of a work in their analysis, but go on from the enumeration to discuss each part individually.[4] They seem to presume that the wholeness of the material is explained fully by their explanations of all the individual parts. The kinds of connections which we would call image patterns, relating and enriching the meaning of various details of the poem, exist and may be explained in terms of a variety of relational strategies, irony, or other conventional allegorical patterns of association.[5] In order to understand this process of association, we must examine it at work. Still, commentaries, in their discussion of introductory material, shed some light on the medieval sense of the way parts related to one another, although their primary focus was on the rhetoric of audience response.

The commentary analysis of beginnings is conventional. A particularly elaborate version of this convention occurs in a Venice commentary on Statius:

> Et notandum quod satis ydonee quasi quadam prefatione prescribitur breviter partiendo in tria, scilicet in propositionem, invocationem, et narrationem, prohemiorum officia eleganter exequendo. Nam lectores benivolos, dociles, et attentos facit. Proponit ubi dicit *Fraternas acies* et ibi reddit dociles. Invocat ubi dicit *Unde iubetis etc.* et tunc attentos facit. Narrat ibi *Impia iam merita* et ibi facit benivolos. Vel ibi proponit de qua re

dicturus est. Ibi attentos, ubi invocat, benivolos. Nam tunc quoddammodo manifestatur modus tractandi, et in modo tractandi sunt semper lectores benivoli. In narratione vero dociles.[6]

Giovanni del Virgilio says more simply: "Hiis visis veniamus breviter ad libri divisionem. Dico ergo quod liber iste more poetico dividitur in partes tres, quia primo proponit, secundo invocat, tercio narrat."[7] Another Statius commentary explicitly uses the word *prologue:*

> Unde sciendum est quod auctor iste more poetarum facit prologus in quo proponit et materiam dicendorum [*sic*]. Secundo invocat et auctor, primo in generali ibi *Unde iubetis ire dee,* secundo specialiter ibi *Quem prius heroum clio dabis.* In invocatione generali movet duas questiones sive interrogationes: prima est an debeat incipere a remotis antecesoribus [*sic*] Thebanorum et primis fundatoribus enumerando antiquas antiquitates que precesserant propositum quod intendit describere, et hanc solvit ibi *longa retro series.* Secunda questio est a quo debet incipere. Multi fuerunt proximi et confines huic materie an debeat incipere a pio an a crudeli et hanc solvens incipit ab impio scilicet Edipo idest a domo et familia Edipi.[8]

The invocation, as the commentator makes clear, is more than simply a request for aid of the inspiring gods; rather, it is a request for aid in a project which is explicitly defined, or (as here) for which alternative definitions are given. Thus the invocation functions as summary exposition and would naturally render the audience "attentos."

The prologue is further defined in a commentary on the *Poetria Nova* of Geoffrey of Vinsauf, now in Assisi.[9]

> Dividitur ergo liber iste prima divisione in duas partes, scilicet in prologum et tractatum, quia incipit *si quis habet fundare domum,* et quia in prologis solent poete invocare et proponere, in tractatu vero narrare quod intendunt. Ideo prologus iste dividitur in duas partes. Et nota proprie dixi in prologum et non in prohennium et tractatum quia sicut dicit Aristoteles 3o Rhetoricorum prohennium est principium orationis sicut in poesi prologus et in fistulationem preludium, ex quo patet quod cum autor iste determinet de poesi sive de arte poetica et utamur poemate pro illo quod premittit proprie debet dici prologus quamvis etiam communiter loquendo possit dici prohennium quia hec idem sunt substantia et non differunt nisi ratione.[10]

Generic distinctions, in other words, are not substantial but merely analytical. There is a terminology appropriate to each of the various kinds of act which relate performer or communicator to audience, but the kinds themselves are substantially the same. In each case there is a beginning, which introduces rather than causes; a middle, which treats or narrates or presents rather than continues; and a conclusion, which stops or summarizes rather than provides a climax. All this is implied in the rhetorical basis of medieval organizations of communication.

We have already seen that the links collectively are about story-telling and the proper and improper uses of fiction. In addition, of course, they are opinions, and therefore necessarily opinions of people. In order fully to understand what Chaucer means by giving us this kind of prologue for his *Tales,* and in what way he intends to render us attentive, docile, and benevolent, we must consider the General Prologue from the viewpoint of its rhetorical, rather than its sententious, function.

In 1970, at the Modern Language Association convention, Donald R. Howard made the brilliant suggestion that the General Prologue was a memory system in which the pilgrim portraits correspond to the grotesque images in places of classical theory, and the exemplary ones of medieval practice. In this light, the seemingly haphazard materials of the General Prologue make ordered sense:

> If you take the description of the Prioress and her followers and that of the Guildsmen and their cook as single descriptions (which they are), and if you count the description of the Host, the portraits of the General Prologue can then be seen arranged symmetrically into three groups of seven, each headed by an ideal portrait:
> Knight: Squire, Yeoman, Prioress, Monk, Friar, Merchant
> Clerk: Man of Law, Franklyn, Guildsmen, Shipman, Physician, Wife
> Parson & Plowman: Miller, Manciple, Reve, Summoner, Pardoner, Host[11]

Howard goes on to admire the "mixture of particularities and abstractions" in the General Prologue and relates these to the emblematic or typical significance of the characters, as well as to their individuality. The General Prologue then, "is not just the beginning of the work, but its heart or backbone."[12]

Howard does not develop the emblematic or abstraction-oriented implications of his insight. It is, however, both possible and instructive to do so, as a way of seeing just what the General Prologue is about, and therefore as a way of discovering just what and how it introduces. In the first place, all these people are estates, or types, even though their portraits are individualized into a certain moral ambiguity and the point of the usual satire is blunted. Second, the groups, which we think Howard has correctly identified, can be usefully distinguished. The three ideal types—Knight, Clerk, and Parson-Plowman—are ideal for slightly different reasons: the Knight for what he is, the Clerk for what he knows, and the Parson and Plowman for what they do. The same distinction can be applied to the groups these ideal types head. The first are, with the Knight, the classes of society, lacking only nobility and serf, top and bottom. The second group are all, in one way or another, characterized by their expertise—both because, in most cases, their trade or occupation is one defined by having knowledge and because Chaucer is careful to emphasize this aspect of their characters in his descriptions of them. The third group are people primarily characterized by what they do; further, what they do is in every case something done for, in the name of, or as a steward of another person or authority.

The effectiveness of Chaucer's catalogue of pilgrims used to be attributed to his keen "camera eye"; more recently we have praised his deftness in choosing descriptive details which conjure up, à la Dickens, the wealth of human types. But Chaucer's directory of pilgrims, both its individual entries and in its schema of categories, gains especially from Chaucer's evident skill in the medieval art of list-making. The multitude of lists that come down to us from the period include many that call to mind Borges's Chinese encyclopedia: they are offered to us as normative and complete, yet the principle of their coherence eludes us and they may appear simply arbitrary. There are the obvious seven sins and seven virtues, five joys, four levels of meaning—but far beyond this it is impossible to avoid noticing the habit, probably homiletic, of casting one's outlines and one's discussions into this form. In its most elaborate manifestation, which occurs in the context of allegorical exegesis, this habit of schematization through lists produces the *distinctio*.[13] The *distinctio,* most simply, is a list of the allegorical meanings of a thing. More elaborately, it is a list of the characteristics of a thing whose allegorical meanings all refer to the same object. Most broadly, in the use reflected in the practice of Hugh of St. Cher, the *distinctio* becomes any classification of kinds considered as a meaningful and normative array. Though of course most lists are never complete in the absolute sense, medieval *distinctiones* indulge a rhetoric of completeness. Things exist *in bono* three ways, *in malo* five. God rules in seven ways; there are five kinds of sleep, six fears, and three obediences.

It is by analogy with the *distinctio* that the list of pilgrims in Chaucer's Canterbury prologue can be understood most profitably. These people are a normative array, sufficient for the definition of the category "man." Men can be distinguished in three ways—according to their types, according to their learning, and according to their actions of stewardship. More simply and obviously, man is soul,[14] mind, and body. The types of men are seven: knight, squire, yeoman, and so forth. The types of learning are also seven: five *in bono* and two *in malo*. The good ones are logical, legal, manual, geographical, and medicinal; the bad ones are gluttony and lust. The men of action are more simply various; what makes them a normative array, sufficient for definition, is that each of them, whether honest or dishonest, does his work in stewardship, and thus by responsibility to other people implies the social interconnections which constitute human society in its wholeness. The list is framed, ironically enough, by the pastor of the church and the *viaticum* of the pilgrimage, the one responsible for the cure of souls and the other responsible for the care of bored souls.

It is this normative array of human beings, who are the *auctoritates* of Chaucer's *summa narrativa* and at the same time the prologue exempla, who, sometimes with and sometimes without proverbs as well, introduce Chaucer's tales individually and collectively. To call them this, and to classify them in terms of abstractions, should in no way imply that they are not particulars. In this nominalist world they must be that, of course. We mean merely to claim that additively they can constitute universals as well as exist in themselves. In this function they are different both from the poetic figures which preceded them, who tended to evoke universals by their individual power as constructed allegorical figures, and from later figures such as Hamlet and—at the other extreme—Gatsby, who claim universality by the very virtue of their particular concreteness.

Chaucer's own beginning, for the whole book, is a proverb, or rather, a variant of a proverb. In its usual form, it is "In the spring, a young man's fancy lightly turns to thoughts of love."[15] Chaucer's variant, in the spring "than longen folke to goon on pilgrimage," is complexly ironic. The Easter evocations which Baldwin finds in this passage are there, but only in absence. The fact is that these pilgrims are not penitential, not serious, not even very religious—pilgrimaging, more than Canterbury, is their goal. Proverb plus pilgrims gives us a world very much in medias res, and determined to stay that way. This world, as prologue, introduces a collection of stories which comment on, evaluate, and give ethical definition to those middle things, those things of this life, with which the estates satire types of the prologue have, as we first meet them, such a morally ambivalent relation. In a way, Chaucer gives us not six characters in search of an author but thirty plus in search of definition, fortunately at a time and place where story, as such, had the power to furnish such a definition, because both story and definition had been at that time and place so fortunately understood.

We have thus far explained how various medieval formal principles—the principle of prologue and narration, the principle of the *distinctio* or normative array, and the specific principle of fourfold classification (itself a kind of *distinctio*) defined by the usage of Ovid and descent-into-hell stories—are medieval principles of literary criticism suitable for application to Chaucer. It remains to try to define the connectedness itself. That is, once we know where, by medieval standards, to define the borders between the parts of Chaucer's work, and once we know how to classify these parts by fit medieval categories, it remains to define the principle by which these parts, as such, can be presumed to be related into a whole. That principle, in the broadest terms, is analogy. The parts of a whole signify their common and single theme by being, in some way, like that theme, and therefore also like one another. The most complex and most influential example of this analogical unity which the parts of a text may achieve is, of course, the unity for the Bible achieved by typological exegesis. By the end of the Middle Ages, typological exegesis had engendered habits of reading and writing which achieved this same kind of unity for most texts and even most events, even for materials which signified no explicitly Christian theme, or which had no actual Christ at their centers. We have already alluded to the suggestion that the relation between the Green Knight and Sir Bercilak, which we mean when we say that the one "is" the other, is a typological relationship—that is, an analogical, allegorically one-to-one relationship between two independently existing entities of the sort defined by a thousand years of biblical exegesis. The same analogizing relationship seems to obtain quite generally in late medieval structures.

Of literary examples, Dante's *Commedia* is the one most notably exegetical. In the letter to Can Grande, Dante himself claims for his poem a typological organization.[16] Much of the burden of Charles Singleton's great work on the *Commedia* has concerned itself with elucidating relationships and meanings which are typological,[17] and he himself argues specifically to this point in "The Irreducible Dove," claiming that the fiction of the poem is that it is not a fiction.[18] Robert Hollander, in *Allegory in Dante's Commedia,* not only defends the typological approach theoretically but, more important still, exemplifies it by showing how much of Dante's meaning is carried by patterns of recurring figures, whose relationship to another and to the contexts in which they occur is figural. He speaks, for instance, of the "extraordinary use of figural techniques that intertwine through the discussions of love, the dreams, and the encounters with Matelda and Beatrice in the *Purgatorio*."[19] He goes on to discuss the various voyage images which Dante draws together: "Historically, the images make an imposing string: the ill-fated ships in *Aeneid* I, which are answered by the shipwrecked but safe Aeneas; the damned voyage of Ulysses; the voyage that is Dante's poem; the pilgrim ship that arrives safely at the shores of Purgatory, an angel on its poop; and now also on a poop, Admiral Beatrice, who is Supreme Commander of the fleet of which Dante's bark is one."[20]

Ovid uses parallel stories and figures to construct, by simple analogy, a pattern of meaning which evaluates and relates the respective divinities and men; his patterns are of course not typological, though the medieval commentators eventually claimed that they were. For Dante, on the other hand, the long tradition of biblical exegesis gave rich definition to his method. Hollander puts it precisely: "The function of the allegorical sense [what we are calling typological] is to relate two historical events or things or persons, each of which has a discrete and particular historical reality in time, so that the relationship between them may express spiritual significance."[21] Hollander finds that Dante wishes the incidents of his poem to function in a similar way with other parts of the work. Thus, the various voyages he mentions above are all linked together, all sharing a spiritual significance. Noting that Dante's poem includes figures from both the mythological history of pagan antiquity and the biblical history of Chrisianity, Hollander argues that Dante may have believed both to operate on a historical plane, which the text of his own poem may also reach. "All that must be understood is that for Dante the events recorded in the literature of pagan antiquity have, for the purposes of his fiction, as much historical validity as do the events recorded in the Bible. The latter may be more "true" in his eyes, but the situations of Aeneas or Jason are as significant for Dante's theory of the "true lie" . . . Again Charles Singleton's phrase comes to mind: the fiction of the *Divine Comedy* is that it is not fiction. I believe Dante treats other poems, myths, and stories in the same way in the *Commedia*."[22]

Thus, the people and places mentioned in the *Commedia*, whether they come from myths, from the Bible or from Dante's own contemporary situation,[23] all share a unity as part of "universal history" and so are all interrelated, and meaningfully connected with one another. "Seen with the eye of historical figuralism, each act in universal history has its part or future counterparts in other facts. It allows a polysemous interpretation that is both multitudinous and precise."[24]

Dante's literary application of biblical typology, of course, is Christian. This is natural, since the desire to find ties which unite disparate parts relates naturally to the great providential desire which has already related all parts of creation, in ideal at least, to the fact of Incarnation, which is the center and consummation of creation. Thus writing about the world, and even the world of fiction, may be a celebration of God's plan, in a world already too well informed to need simple explanation. The fondness of the Middle Ages for elaborate and repetitious exempla is an implicit testimony of their belief in the unity grounded in the underlying presence of God. In Dante this testimony is explicit in his story, as well as implicit in the forms and structures by which he gave his multifarious story its divine unity.

But the same structures may be formally present without at the same time containing the explicitly Christian content. We have already analyzed the exegetical four levels as a purely formal principle; it remains here to see how this formal principle—the principle of unity through resonating parallelism between two or more already existing and organized things—may operate to unify books, and traditions of books, whose subject is something other than Christ or the creed or the Christian life as such. In order to make clear both this formal principle and the unity it achieves, we must conduct, under medieval rules, a thematic analysis. The rest of this chapter will be devoted primarily to setting up this analysis for the case of the *Canterbury Tales.* Before doing so, however, we think it instructive to mention briefly a few other examples.

Gower's *Confessio Amantis* is an obvious instance. The eight books are arrayed under the titles of the seven capital sins, to which is added, in seventh place, the education of the prince; in each book the collection of stories told is coherent because all the stories share a thematic likeness. It is not always easy to explain precisely and simply the relevance of a given story to its asserted theme, but this critical problem only proves that an analogy may be powerful without being univocal or simple.

A more complex example is the *Romance of the Rose,* whose unity is founded on both internal and external analogies.[25] The *Romance,* like the *Canterbury Tales* and the *Metamorphoses,* contains an assembly of storytellers who tell a great many tales, digressively strung on an inconsequential plot. Internally, tales actually repeated or repeatedly evoked, or tales placed in ostentatious parallel, are the key to the *Romance*'s thematic structure. Thus Narcissus parallels Pygmalion, and there is repeated reference to the Golden Age, the castration of Saturn, the birth of Venus, and the adultery of Mars and Venus.

Externally, and in a way which gives explicit thematic definition, the *Romance* mirrors, in combination, the *Consolation of Philosophy* and the *Complaint of Nature*.

The precise nature of the reflection has not been properly appreciated because it is negative and ironic. Thus critics have been misled into looking for things that the *Romance of the Rose* did say, which were clearly borrowed or adapted from the *Consolation* or the *Complaint,* rather than looking for the things which the *Romance* did *not* say, or got wrong, which one might expect Jean de Meun to correct had he wished to. Once we see that he must have made these errors and omissions deliberately, and that we therefore must expect the parallel between the *Romance* and its predecessors to explicate ironically or inversely, everything becomes much clearer.

Two facts are immediately obvious. One is that Jean de Meun has taken over all the sexuality of the *Complaint,* has made it the basis of his plot as well as the content of a good deal of discourse, and has at the same time explicitly denied to this sexuality the allegorical reference to ethical and philosophical truths which are, in the *Complaint,* its reason for being. The second point is that, though Jean includes in his poem the central character of the *Consolation,* Reason herself, and though in his part of the poem he discusses most of the various topics of the *Consolation,* from the goods of fortune analyzed by Reason to the problem of predestination and free will analyzed by Nature, he nowhere includes the great climactic doctrine of the meter, "O qui perpetua." For this crucial middle point, on which the whole doctrine of the *Consolation* depends, Jean substitutes the ironic middle of more and more cynical advice from Friend, False-Seeming, and the Vekke.

In order to begin to read the *Romance* correctly, we must trust this external analogy and see the poem as one which advertises itself as having omitted something—as having omitted the climactic doctrine which would make Reason worth listening to, and having omitted the allegorical reference which would make what the Lover does, in the end, worth doing. This seen, we know what the poem is—not a narrative of a love story wildly padded out with digressions, but a coherent series of six discourses, each containing an array of exemplary stories, delivered by Reason and Friend, False-Seeming and the Vekke, and Nature and Genius. The frame—the love story allegory—is not the cause or structure of these discourses, but rather their result. Amant takes all the advice given him (Reason, after all, sends him to Friend by defining her highest potential self as a friend) and, as a result, goes, not from good to bad, but from bad to worse.[26] His progress exemplifies what the discourses, with great subtlety and ironic clarity, define.

In order to appreciate this clarity, this coherence, and this definition, we must as it were invert the poem—put aside the plot, take the digressions as the essence, and read in obedience to the logic of analogically ordered discourse rather than the logic of causally ordered action. In just this way, we propose, one understands the *Canterbury Tales* by inverting it, by putting aside the plot in order to read an array of stories. Our reading is made easier because for Chaucer, as for the *Romance,* we have external evidence—we have an informing analogy. It is, as we have repeatedly said, Ovid's *Metamorphoses.*

The medieval critics clearly saw Ovid's work as a story collection which could be taken as coherent on the basis of precisely this analogizing, thematic anaylsis which we have been defining here. In our own day, their understanding has received powerful confirmation by the reading of Brooks Otis, who has made what can justly be called independent modern discovery of precisely the same character for the poem. Otis recognizes, of course, the pattern which the critical tradition has always found—that of a chronological *carmen perpetuum,* extending from creation to the emperor, offering a miscellany of stories intended to praise the emperor. But in addition to, and more important than, this pattern, Otis describes the *Metamorphoses* as just that: an intricate series of transformations, arranged into four great parts, each with a central panel story surrounded by other similar stories which repeat with significant variation what they frame. These parts move from an exclusive concern with the gods to an ever-increasing and finally almost exclusive concern with men; the transformations move from the arbitrary and often comically undignified tricks of the immortal gods to the tragic calamities of men, with the transformation often acting as a literally enacted metaphor. Between the first and second editions of his book, Otis changed his mind about the ultimate meaning of the *Metamorphoses* and decided that the praise of the emperor was ironic or satiric rather than serious. But his view of the method remained the same. The essence of the *Metamorphoses* is not chronology, or praise, or frame, but stories—stories of transformation. As a concatenated series, they accumulate a meaning which is a definition of the nobility of human nature, and of the relation between the gods, men, and nature. They do so by an intricate and long-sustained pattern of parallelism and repetition, with incremental variations, clustered around the four great stories which constitute the centers of the four great sections of the poem.[27]

What Brooks Otis does for our day the medieval commentators did for theirs. They properly said that the material of the *Metamorphoses* was changes (mutationes); they divided the poem for purposes of analysis into separate stories of changes, without regard for levels of frame story and included story; and they analyzed the whole in terms of large categories of changes, all directed at a definition of the human condition in relation to man's material circumstances and his divine destiny. We must not let differences in terminology obscure for us the similarity of method, intent, and content which marks these two critical enterprises, one medieval, one modern. Together they make it clear that Ovid's *Metamorphoses* must join the *Commedia*, the *Romance of the Rose*, and, as we shall see, the *Canterbury Tales* as a work whose unity the principle of stories in parallel best explains.

We have already begun our analysis of the *Canterbury Tales* along the lines of investigation we have been outlining in this chapter. First, we named the parts of the poem as stories, whose elaborate prologue framework defined the poem's subject as ethical standards of conduct, presented in a form accessible and intelligible to man. The stories have in common a limited number of narrative situations, more than half of them describing an intrusion by an outsider into the harmony of a marriage, and most of the rest devoted to brotherhoods among men, usually including a clergyman, and difficulties which threaten to destroy the fraternal relationship. From the *Knight's Tale* and the tradition of Ovidian commentary, we found a division into kinds of moral activity which was helpful in distinguishing the kinds of stories into categories smaller and more specific than a division based only on the marital status of the characters could offer. Our classification of four changes enables us to identify four groups of stories, with each group exemplifying a particular kind of change and a particular kind of moral activity. We have identified four sorts of stories in the *Canterbury Tales*—tales of natural changes, whose preoccupation is with the nature and exercise of human authority; tales of magic, which furnish a normative array of disorders, illusions, deceptions, and mistakes; tales of worldly moral struggle, in which merely human solutions to the problem of orderly living succeed and fail; and tales of spiritual interpretation, which furnish a normative array of human postures within which given events may be confronted, lived with, and understood.[28] Together the tales constitute a normative array of exempla, classified and defined according to their place in a fourfold *distinctio* of moral activity, whose common subject and final goal is a definition of just order in human affairs, and of the human acts and human communities which constitute that ordered way of life.

In order to show all this meaning at work in the *Canterbury Tales,* we must obviously deal with each tale. To do so, we must arrange for the tales to occur in some appropriate order. As a framework for reading the tales, we have reordered the accepted fragments of the poem in a sequence reflecting the four kinds of Ovidian change, so as to make four groups of stories. Our purpose in this reordering, and this classification of stories into four groups, is essentially logical. The sequence which we propose is one which makes the significance of Chaucer's stories for a definition of human society clearly obvious and permits us to make a seriatim reading of stories in which the various parts and aspects of Chaucer's definition are logical, ordered, and coherent.

Since, in making this reordering, we respect the integrity of established fragments, we take advantage of as much of Chaucer's intention for the ordering of his collection as can be known. In so doing we have obeyed the critic's obligation to read the text as history has given it to him. But beyond this obligation we have felt not only free but obliged to order our discussion of Chaucer's tales in a way permitting greatest possible clarity to our argument. For the ordering of tales, and their classification into four groups, which supports this discussion, we wish to make one major and utterly serious claim, and several much more speculative ones. Our major claim is that this ordering is heuristically correct. It works. It grounds our reading. It was, in fact, a considerable catalyst for it. We found, as we worked, that having the tales in juxtapositions different from those familiar from the Ellesmere often stimulated insight. The tales responded well to having been classified, under the four Ovidian categories, into four quite speculative groups, and illuminated one another under the logic of the whole in precisely the way which medieval literary theory predicted. Therefore, on the grounds both of our a priori medieval definitions and of an experience of successful critical reading, we claim that our proposed order for Chaucer's *Canterbury Tales* is true in the only way which ultimately matters: it helps to make the work clear, both as a whole and in its parts.

Beyond this claim, there are several more speculative ones which we should make, because the order of the *Canterbury Tales* has been a much discussed topic whose bearing on our own proposal we cannot legitimately ignore. We are well aware that our order is not just a new one, but a new kind of one, whose proposal does not really enter into previous discussion, but rather dismisses it as an enterprise wrongly grounded, and therefore unlikely to produce interesting results. The point at issue is basically this: one can order the surviving fragments of the *Canterbury Tales* in terms of some perception of the logical or thematic demands of the tales themselves, as we have done, or one can order the tales in such a way as to make as verisimilar as possible the plot of the Canterbury journey, including, of course, Chaucer's incidental geographical allusions. One can, in short, order by ordering the tales, or one can order by serving the frame. Given the condition of surviving manuscript evidence, one cannot really do both at once.

As it happens, we do not find arguments about the order of Chaucer's tales based on the map order of the towns between London and Canterbury very interesting. They are not medievally grounded, and they do not enrich our understanding of the tales.[29] But we do not intend to be merely negative. Rather, we wish to suggest that asking a new kind of question generates the possibility of a rich new array of answers—we wish to suggest that in proposing a new kind of ordering for Chaucer's tales, based on considerations that have nothing to do with English geography, we are in consequence permitted to see the surviving manuscripts of the *Canterbury Tales* in a new and fruitful light. Fifteenth-century scribes of these manuscripts ordered the tales in a variety of ways; we should take this variety as an opportunity to take seriously the work of a number of late medieval editors in reconstructing, as best they could, groupings of the tales in terms of which they would make a coherent whole. The standard presumption that the order must be geographical blinded scholars to the likelihood that these scribes were serious editors, because they manifestly took no interest in such evidence. Realizing that the tales, as exempla, may have a logical order permits us to realize that the scribes seemed to have operated under similar assumptions. Work based on such a realization has not even begun; surviving manuscripts must eventually be the basis of numbers of specialist studies, on the basis of whose accumulated speculations and analyses this whole question of ordering can be answered on much firmer medieval grounds. Meanwhile, our speculative leap forward to an experimental final answer will be, at worst, methodologically instructive and, at best, a possible achievement of what further study will confirm. We have not, ourselves made exhaustive study of the manuscripts, but we are encouraged to have found, for each of the joinings of two fragments which our reordering requires, at least one medieval editor who agrees.[30]

More important than these specific correspondences, however, is the fact, clearly proved by the manuscripts, that the medieval editors tried to present their material in coherent groups of tales. Modern scholarly discussion of these groupings and their rationale was conducted primarily at the time of the publication of Manly and Rickert's *Text of the Canterbury Tales* and tended to discount the importance of these groupings because of reservations about the editorial capabilities of the scribes preparing the manuscripts. Although we differ from their conclusions in many ways, we are indebted to Tatlock, Dempster, and other interpreters of the Manly and Rickert text for much valuable insight into the procedures of manuscript preparation. Although they disagree with the wisdom of medieval editors of the text, Demster and Tatlock acknowledge that the manuscripts were produced by men conscious of their responsibility to give the poem an arrangement.[31] Though the principles of editorial judgment at work in these manuscript orders are not approved of by either critic, still their analysis of the early history of text helps us to recover some medieval attitudes toward the poem, which we believe bear a different interpretation from that proposed by Dempster or by Tatlock. The scribes generally are interested in making their text as complete as possible and in giving the pieces they have the appearance of constituting the whole of the poem.[32] Before we condemn the principle, we should bear in mind that the same desire to discover an arrangement revealing the wholeness of the *Canterbury Tales* lies behind most of the critical enterprises devoted to the poem and is certainly an important element in the selection process which lies behind even the most exhaustive of critical editions. Robinson's *Chaucer,* for example, acknowledges the existence of contradictory evidence of arrangement and of prologue links, buy presents as a final text the best solution available to him to all the work's difficult passages. Another scribal practice that Dempster records, although she does not approve of it, is the conservatism with which scribes regard any testimony to manuscript arrangement they receive along with the tales.[33] Such conservatism may be suspect, if we demand that scribes care as much about the geography of the journey as modern readers often do, but it is in keeping with the desire to retain any vestiges of the author's intention, which, in the absence of absolute evidence to the contrary, is understandably sought in any version of the text closer in time to the author than the scribe is himself. The transmission of certain variations from Chaucer's clear intentions for the fragments, particularly in the order of fragments E and F, may seem culpable, when modern searches for manuscripts reveal that other lines of transmission knew E and F in their proper form. However, scribes appear to have been limited in their exemplars, a situation which they acknowledge in various ways and which often disappoints the hopes we see, preserved in spaces left for tales never received, to complete the whole text.[34] In the absence of better information, their decision to remain faithful to the orders they have is understandable and acceptable; Dempster's rejection of their editorial choices, by suggesting only their desire to publish quickly and to make a profit, does not do justice to the difficulties faced by scribal editors and their achievement in disseminating the *Canterbury Tales.*

If we return to the manuscript order, we find that some groupings of tales, which violate no final judgment of Chaucer except the doubtful case of geography, suggest patterns of associations at work in the text which are not evident in the familiar Ellesmere Order. For example, three of the four textual traditions identified by Manly and Rickert place group G, that is, the tales of the second Nun and the Canon's Yeoman, after the *Franklin's Tale* and before the *Physician's Tale.* Many manuscripts preserve a provisional ordering of the tales of groups E and F, that is, the tales of Squire, Franklin, Clerk, and Merchant, made in early manuscripts before the authoritative forms of the links became available. Without exhausting the subject, we may suggest here the valuable new perspectives on the Canterbury stories which these alternative combinations of tales, familiar to many fifteenth-century readers, provide.[35]

The position of the tales of Cecilia and the avaricious priest between the tales of Franklin and Physician provides a focus of theme and imagery which bridges the gap between, on the one hand, the tales of marriage commonly supposed to reach their culmination with the Franklin and, on the other, the tales on a variety of subjects comprising groups C and the lengthy B^2. The tales of group G juxtapose the pursuit of a virgin and the pursuit of gold, suggesting a contrast between the two activities. The same juxtaposition occurs in group C; the Physician narrates the sorrows of Virginia, the beset virgin child, and the Pardoner tells the story of the three gamblers in pursuit of gold. The two themes of winning a woman's love and pursuing wealth are combined in the next tale, the Shipman's account of a woman's success at equating the goods of marriage and the golden goods of buying and selling. Finally, the *Prioress's Tale* becomes the third tale of virgin children beset by public dangers in a series of six stories, with the alternating tales treating the theme of the avaricious pursuit of gold and its death-dealing power. The similarity between the stories of Cecilia and the little clergeoun, and the possible significance of Chaucer's inclusion of the two saints' legends, is obscured in the Ellesmere Order because they are separated by the lengthy group B². In sum, it seems probable that the placement of group G before the *Physician's Tale* was prompted by a recognition on the manuscript editor's part that such positioning revealed the thematic unity drawing these tales together. It may be noted, as well, that a juxtapositional connection between the amorous pursuits of women and the avaricious pursuit of gold, suggested by group G, might be helpful in explaining the appearance of the tales of the Friar and Summoner among the tales of marriage in groups D and E.

Another very frequent variation from the familiar Ellesmere Order occurs with the splitting and rearrangement of groups E and F around group D. The order of the tales becomes Man of Law, Squire, Merchant, Wife of Bath, Friar, Summoner, Clerk, and Franklin. One benefit of this rearrangement is that the *Wife of Bath's Tale*, rather than her prologue, is given new prominence as the third story in which magical occurrences surround courtship and marriage. The magical tools of perception in the *Squire's Tale* give the heroine the means of learning the tercelet's sad lesson of trusting too much to a lover's promises; both in the fairyland atmosphere and in its theme of being able to see rightly the true desires and intentions of the opposite sex, the *Squire's Tale* is closely related to the *Wife of Bath's*, a connection hidden by the Ellesmere Order. The *Merchant's Tale* prepares both for the magical story of the Wife and her own lusty career with its narrative of May's treetop romance preserved by the intercession of the magical Pluto and Proserpina. Placing the *Squire's Tale* closer to the tale of the Wife of Bath brings to light the significance of her story, generally neglected in the studies of the marriage group in favor of the Wife herself and her experiences. It also serves to emphasize the themes of magical seeing and deception in love, which link together the stories of the Squire, the Merchant, the Wife of Bath, and the Franklin. Another benefit of the arrangement is to force the reader to weigh the various points of view on marriage against one another more carefully: a juxtaposition of the tales of the Clerk and the Franklin makes a total acceptance or rejection of either Walter's authoritarianism or Arveragus's surrender impossible.

These two medieval proposals for reordering and grouping certain of the *Canterbury Tales* are but examples of a great many which the manuscripts preserve. Another, clearly Chaucer's own, is the first fragment itself, whose series of Knight's, Miller's, Reeve's, and Cook's tales is universally recognized as thematically coherent and logically ordered. Efforts to discover similar clusters of tales grouped about a common subject have yielded important readings, as in Bruce Rosenberg's discussion of the tales of group G and Penn Szittya's discussion of structural similarities linking the tales of the Wife of Bath and the Friar.[36] Such an approach to understanding the arrangement of the tales places primary emphasis on content, on what is being discussed; each section of the poem—tale, prologue, enclosed digression, or whatever—is examined for its mutually informing relations with the material around it. This approach, in the light both of medieval editorial procedure and of the clear intention of Chaucer's first fragment, is historically correct.

By contrast, the importance of geography as a clue to the final intended arrangement of the *Canterbury Tales* is questionable for a number of reasons. First, the evidence from geography is limited; references to time and place on the journey occur only rarely in the links and seem to be there more as local color than as direction of the storytellings.[37] Second, the evidence from geography admits a number of contradictory constructions. Efforts to explain the tales as making up a trip to Canterbury cannot resolve the evidence, remaining in the text, that Chaucer was still considering the possibility of giving every pilgrim more than one tale (IX [H] 9-29). Some time conflicts, such as the juxtaposition of the Manciple's brief morning tale followed immediately by the Parson's afternoon tale (X [I] 2-5), remain, even after group B² is relocated in accordance with the Bradshaw Shift. The evidence of geography has permitted other scholars to argue that we have in the tales the remnants of a two-way journey. The principal challenge to this theory in the text is Chaucer's elaborate endpiece of the *Parson's Tale,* clearly identified with the coming to Canterbury. The drawback of arguing from geography, common to both the Bradshaw Shift and to proposals of a two-way journey, is that geography does not answer all the questions of arrangement which remain after the evidence of a geographical reference is fully correlated.[38] The placement of some fragments remains the work of editorial hypothesis, rather than the determination of Chaucer's description of the journey. Third, geography is suspect because early editors take so little notice of it; we realize here that we are reversing the usual direction of this relationship, but we think with good reason. To modern readers, accustomed to think of Chaucer as a genius unappreciated in his own time, the geographical references have become a proof of a narrative plot, structured by the realistic material of the actual road to Canterbury, and almost lost to us because of the blunted sensibilities of Chaucer's first readers. It is argued that Chaucer never would have permitted errors in geography, because he knew the geography so well; yet Chaucer's contemporaries surely were equally well acquainted with the road to Canterbury from London and would have been more disturbed than we are by inaccuracies of this kind, if such inaccuracies were really to be judged important. Both J. S. P. Tatlock and Germaine Dempster argue that early scribal editors willingly sacrificed accurate transmission of the poem for the sake of better sales;[39] scribes frequently departed from their exemplars for the purpose of giving the text a surface appearance of completeness. Several manuscripts manufacture links to connect tales which are not joined, or to introduce tales without prologue material naming and introducing the speaker. Yet, in both alterations of links and manufacture of links, no medieval editor of the poem improved geography to give the poem an appearance of being finished, despite the fact that their readers obviously were closer than modern readers to the geographical facts, and more likely to be sensitive to them if they had been important.[40] For all these reasons we would explain the geographical references in the links as merely realistic details, inserted provisionally to flesh out Chaucer's frame story, and perhaps to be polished in a final revision which never took place. With Manly and Rickert, then, we would call it a probability that "in making allusions to time and place he [Chaucer] may have been guided by the needs of the moment, as Shakespeare was in his allusions to time, and not have considered carefully whether these allusions would fit into his general plan or would harmonize with one another."[41]

In absolute terms, moreover, the sequence of place names between London and Canterbury forms no plausible mnemonic series, either for medieval or for modern sensibilities. The art of memory practiced in the Middle Ages, and derived substantially from the *Rhetorica ad Herennium,* specifies images in places, not times; and universal human experience confirms the fact that it is far easier to remember a number of items in correct order if they are composed in a single visual space than if they are ordered in time. The geographical ordering of the *Canterbury Tales* is not so much based on any temporal experience of the journey, medieval or modern, as it is on the modern scholar's access to reliable maps—that is, to a visual mnemonic for his material. One may make a journey many times, and may know every town along the way, and still not be able to name them *in order*[42]— the senior author remains to this day uncertain whether Cookeville or

Crossville, Tennessee, comes first on the way from Nashville to Asheville, and that after having made the preinterstate round trip once a year for twenty-five years, and with the aid of maps. We therefore conclude that any ordering of the *Canterbury Tales* based on allusions to place names is implausible both on medieval and on absolute grounds, and we therefore do not consult geographical references as evidence for the proper sequence of tales.

The order of tales which we propose is set forth in the following table, which includes also, for contrast, the Ellesmere Order, and, opposite each juxtaposition of fragments which we propose, the name of the manuscript or manuscripts which agree with it.[43] In the rest of this chapter, we will consider the four groups which this order generates, their relation to one another, and their significance, in the light of Ovid's *carmen perpetuum*, as an ordered set of groups. In part 2 of this study, we will make a detailed reading of all the tales, following this new order.

With the tales thus ordered, we can begin to see the full complexity of the unity they achieve. The fundamental movement is one which begins in order, meets challenge by struggle, and finally reinstates order and understands it; this pattern receives full and stately definition in the *Knight's Tale*, to whose parts the four groups serially correspond. Then, echoing Ovid's chronological *carmen perpetuum*, the incipit tales of each of the four groups, taken as a series, define a pagan-to-Christian chronology, from pagan Athens to the early Christian St. Cecilia and the established imperial Christianity of Constance to the high medieval child saint of the *Prioress's Tale*. More important, the four kinds of metamorphoses of the commentators are adapted to the four steps of the action, and to the four groups which reflect and repeat them. In the first great section, fragment A, Chaucer examines social orders resting on a variety of systems of justice from high to low; the transformations in the section are all natural, wrought by men on men. In the section following Chaucer adopts the medieval formula for magical changes, under which "Things appear to be different, but are really the same."[44] Some of the magic is the true marvel of saintly life, some of it is the fraud of alchemist and magician, and some of it is from faerie—in all of the stories Chaucer ties together the problem of true and false sight with the problem of a collapse of order through misunderstanding and misinterpretation. In the third section Chaucer is concerned with moral transformation, and here most strongly he concentrates his attention on the image of marriage as the figure of moral combat,

ORDER OF THE TALES

	Ellesmere Order		New Order	
I (A)	Knight's Tale Miller's Tale Reeve's Tale Cook's Tale	I Natural	Knight's Tale Miller's Tale Reeve's Tale Cook's Tale	(Holkham)
II (B¹)	Man of Law's Tale		Second Nun's Tale Canon's Yeoman's Tale	(Holkham; Corpus Christi 198)
III (D)	Wife of Bath's Tale Friar's Tale Summoner's Tale	II Magical	Squire's Tale Franklin's Tale	(Hatton; Fitzwilliam)
IV (E)	Clerk's Tale Merchant's Tale		Wife of Bath's Tale Friar's Tale Summoner's Tale	(Hatton)
V (F)	Squire's Tale Franklin's Tale		Physician's Tale Pardoner's Tale	(Oxford Trinity)
VI (C)	Physician's Tale Pardoner's Tale			

VII (B²)
Shipman's Tale
Prioress's Tale
Sir Thopas
Melibeus
Monk's Tale
Nun's Priest's Tale

VIII (G)
Second Nun's Tale
Canon's Yeoman's Tale

IX (H)
Manciple's Tale

X (I)
Parson's Tale

III
Moral

IV
Spiritual

Man of Law's Tale   (Laud 600; Paris)

Clerk's Tale
Merchant's Tale   (Holkham)

Manciple's Tale   (Trinity Cambridge)

Shipman's Tale
Prioress's Tale
Sir Thopas
Melibeus
Monk's Tale
Nun's Priest's Tale

Parson's Tale   (Holkham; Hengwrt)

both within a person and between persons. Finally, the last tales in the Canterbury trip reflect, along with Theseus's speech on order, the human effort to regain control of the world through interpreting events; this action is linked clearly with the fourth kind of transformation, the spiritual, with the virtuous descent into hell and, most important, with the admonition to interpret earthly changes in terms of heavenly truths, which is the burden of the whole of the medieval *Metamorphoses.*

Thus, Chaucer does not stumble or ramble for lack of structure, as many critics have argued when stopped short by the question of the whole Canterbury collection. Rather, working from a traditional model, he has adapted the moralistic interpretation of the transformations of Ovid to the problem of the Christian's inability to remain constant before God and his neighbors. To underline the relationship to the model, and undoubtly because he saw that the manner of telling was intimately bound up with Ovid's meaning, he took from the *Metamorphoses* a logic of both large-scale and small-scale design. Most significant of all, Chaucer, like Ovid, built his world of transformations on stories. Like Ovid he constructed a history of civilization built on its literature, on its great stories. We shall return to the significance of such a choice in the Epilogue. Here it is enough to say that by such a choice Chaucer was identifying literature with man's ability to reorganize his universe again successfully, after sin and error had repeatedly thrown it into confusion. In making this choice, Chaucer affirms both the ethical significance of story and the story quality of ethics. He places a higher value on story than can anyone whose categories are merely aesthetic, because he involves them directly in the real ordering of the moral universe. At the same time, because he puts stories at the center of his ethical enterprise, he asserts for reality all the decorous qualities which the stories in fact do have, and for which readers now tend to have only aesthetic appreciations.

In order to show how this structure works, we propose to analyze it in two stages. The rest of this chapter will be devoted to the sections as such, and to the contrapuntal chronology asserted by their four opening stories. Part 2 of this study will, presuming this larger order, focus on the more particular exempla of *consuetudo* and *credulitas* with which Chaucer accumulates his definitions of human nature and social order.

The tales which begin the four sections—that is, the *Knight's Tale,* the *Second Nun's Tale,* the *Man of Law's Tale,* and the *Prioress's Tale*—

cover, as we have said, the chronological range which extends from pagan times to high medieval Christianity. That is, the tales cover the range of history which constitutes the medieval sense of the past. Theseus, the virtuous pagan, achieves in story the same predictive order for which the Middle Ages prized Virgil and the literally pagan *Consolation* of Boethius. Like them, he qualifies as one of John of Salisbury's giants, on whose shoulders the Christians of a later age achieve their vision. As a pagan, he is preliminary, but assimilable; possessed of incomplete truth, he is yet one of the foundations on which later providential history could be built. The *Second Nun's Tale* of St. Cecilia deals with the era of primitive Christianity, and therefore with the saintly paradigm which defines the ideal of individual life. Within the social order governed by the pagan successors of Theseus, she inserts a dialectic of personal holiness before which it is by definition incomplete, and in confrontation with which it falls into sin and eventual defeat. Here, more than anywhere else in the *Canterbury Tales,* we have the intrusive presence of the transcendental ideal; here, and not in the *Parson's Tale,* is the heavenly presence. It is here, we think, in order to confront the social order—that is, it is here, representing its crucial point in salvation history, in order to set in motion an interaction between heavenly definition and earthly particular fact, which the *Tales* as a whole collection will apply to the definition of earthly and provisional orders. Following up this interaction, the *Man of Law's Tale* presents a Christian emperor's daughter, born into a social order now imperially Christian, in confrontation with the pagan borders. Once she fails and once she succeeds; the eventual result, with the help of Providence, is the expansion of the Christian social order. Finally, the *Prioress's Tale* presents the Christian social order in conflict with an internal alien.[45] In all three of these Christian situations, the burden of the definition is carried by an individual—in two cases they are true saints, and in the third, an exemplary, saintly person. Two are women, and the third is a child—all, in a sense, are innocents. All are more acted upon than active; all represent that ideal of Christian patience amid the circumstances of a less-than-perfect world which is the truest posture of any individual.

Cumulatively, they define a progress which defines the social order as well. The order of Theseus is pagan, but noble; subject to attack, but ultimately in a Boethian posture which is immune to absolute disaster. Under the onslaught of personal holiness, this order at first falls into opposition, but finally achieves affirmation, in the cult of the little clergeoun. Here it is important to avoid being misled, on the one hand, by a too modern and too sentimental revulsion at an anti-Semitic pogrom, and too naively historicist a willingness to accept the slaughter in the ghetto as an ideological convention indulged by a society which was not living with real Jews at the time anyway. The truth is something in between, in a society which is Christian, but imperfect; which desires to praise the Virgin, but does not know the meaning of the words; which sustains an alien presence in its midst for the sake of "foule usure and lucre of vileynye," (VII 491 [B² 1681]) but which must then deal with those aliens "with torment and with shameful deeth" (VII 628 [B² 1818]). It is, in short, a society which needs, and gets, the benefit of occasional miracles, such as this childish postmortem singing, which both remind people of the mercies of God and provide a sainted means of obtaining them. Thus, the social ordering which began under the rule of Saturn, whose results were neat but ironic and beyond the calculation of even noble men, ends here in an ordinary, compromised but working society disordered by simple greed and reordered, provisionally, by a pious child and an intrusive miracle. The conclusion which these four incipit tales implies is that society is only a provisional good, but one to be taken seriously; not heaven, but something for the sake of which heaven exerts itself and its powers. This conclusion, as we shall see, is one which the whole series of tales both confirms and richly defines.

1. Nims, *Poetria Nova*, pp. 18 ff.; Faral, *Les arts poétiques*, pp. 200 ff. Commentary treatment is consonant; for example, the material of the *Thebaid* is analysed as follows: "Notandum quod ordo alius naturalis, alius artificialis. Ordo naturalis est rerum gestarum expositio, secundum eundem ordinem quo geste sunt, ut quod primum fit, primo loco narretur, quod statim post, secundo loco, et ita deinceps. Artificialis ordo est quando rerum gestarum fit prepostera expositio, quando quod primum fit, secundo narratur loco, quod secundo, primo exponitur, et hoc ordine hic utitur autor. Nam incipit ubi Edippus precatum suum recognovit de patre interfecto, de matre violata, et sibi ipsi oculos excecavit. Unde ait: Impia iam merita scrutatus lumina dextra. Ibi, inquam, incepit cum multa precessissent que summatim et satis oratorie declarat autor. Vere multa precesserunt. Nam primum rapta fuit Europa a Iove mutato in speciem tauri. Deinde Cadmus exulavit responsum in parnaso accepit, vaccam videns Thebas condidit, in serpentem vertit. Filii sui scilicet athamas et pentheus regnaverunt usque ad Layum. Hunc Edippus eius filius occidit, matrem eius Iocastam nomine in uxorem duxit, ex qua pignora suscepit, quo comperto sibi oculos excecavit, et ab hoc puncto Statius incipit, quod fere ultimo loco gestum erat" (Venice, Biblioteca Marciana MS lat XII. 61 (4097),

fols. lv–2r). "It must be understood that there is one order which is natural and another which is artificial. The natural order is the presentation of events, according to the same order in which they were done, so that what was first, is narrated in the first place, what happened immediately after, in the second place, and so on in order. The artificial order of events is inverted, when what was first is narrated in the second place, what was second is placed first, and the author uses this order here. For the story begins when Oedipus ended his search with father dead, mother violated, and he blinded himself. Thus, he said: 'He probed his sinful eyes with an avenging hand.' There, I say, the author began although many things had gone before which he declares briefly as sufficient for its statement. Truly many things had happened before. For first Europa was carried off by Jove changed into the shape of a bull. Then Cadmus was banished, accepted the command from Parnassus, seeing the cow founded Thebes, and turned into a snake. His sons, that is, Athamas and Pentheus, reigned until Laius. Oedipus, his son, killed him, took his own mother, Iocasta by name, in marriage, from whom he received pledges of love. When he discovered these things, he blinded his own eyes, and from this point Statius begins, which happened almost last." It is most significant that the commentator should feel it necessary to begin the story so far back, with Cadmus; obviously, the material itself is seen as having a canonical shape and content, which any given poet may adapt, but only by deliberate "artificiality."

2. Traugott Lawler, trans., *The Parisiana Poetria of John of Garland* (Yale, 1974), pp. 58–59.

3. Allen, "Commentary as Criticism."

4. The commentator's attitude is clearly betrayed in this gloss on a section of book 1 of the *Thebaid:* "Hoc est capitulum quintum huius primi libri in quo continentur narrationes adrasti et primo facit suam narrationem ad istos, secundo interrogationem sive directionem sermonis. *postquam:* Modo incipit narrare et dividitur hec pars in tot quot sunt ea que narrat sive quot sunt membra huius narracionis." "This is the fifth chapter of this first book in which are contained the narratives of Adrastus; first he tells his narrative, second he [poses] the question or point of the speech. *Postquam;* Now [i.e., at this lemma] he begins to narrate and this part is divided into as many things as there are things he tells—the narrative is divided into as many members as it is." Such language ceases to be circular as soon as one grants that the narration really does have an essence, intrinsically divisible into so many parts. The commentator's job is not hermeneutic, but simply reporting, even though what the medieval commentator in fact does often seems to us exegesis.

5. The difference is that working with medieval patterns, it is almost always unwise to trust to unconscious, archetypal, personalist, or other modern associations of one's own. Formally and structurally, medieval handling of meanings and the associations which meaning made possible was quite similar to the forms and structures now relegated to the unconscious and its "nonscientific" relations; but the specific associations which were in fact made had an explicit conscious statement and were thought at the time to have been made rationally and reasonably, on a true ontological base. We must therefore proceed in terms of associations which they actually made, as well as in terms of their associative logic.

6. Venice, Biblioteca Marciana MS lat. XII. 61 (4097), fol. 2r. "It must be noted that it is laid down sufficiently as in a certain preface, by dividing briefly into three parts, that is, into a proposition, invocation, and narrative, by following elegantly the duties of the beginnings. For a preface makes readers well disposed, docile, and attentive. He proposes where he says, 'Fraternal battlegrounds,' and then he makes them there docile. He invokes where he says, 'Whence you will judge, etc.,' and there he make them attentive. He narrates there, 'Unworthy ones now with a righteous [hand],' and there he make them well disposed. Or he proposes there concerning what thing he is about to say. There, where he invokes, they are attentive as they are well disposed. For then, in that way, the manner of treating is shown, and in the manner of treating the readers are always well disposed. But in the narration they are docile." The reference to *modus tractandi* in this context is most unusual; it probably means that a reader would be expected to be most receptive to a book after he knew its discursive genre—i.e., whether it intended to prove, refute, define, or whatever.

7. Ghisalberti, "Giovanni," p. 19. "After these things let us come briefly to the division of the book. I say therefore that this book is divided after the manner of poetry into three parts, because first it proposes, then it makes an invocation, and third it narrates."

8. Assisi, Biblioteca Communale MS 302, fol. 6r. "It should be known that the author in the manner of the poets makes a prologue in which he proposes also the material he will present. Second, the author also invokes, first in general there, 'Whence you will judge of the wrath of the goddess,' and second particularly there, 'Which of the heroes will you give first, Clio?' In the general invocation he raises two questions or inquiries: the first is whether he ought to begin from the remote ancestors of the Thebans and the city's first founders by setting out its ancient history which preceded the point the author intends to describe, and this question he resolves there: 'a long sequence backwards.' The second question is with whom he ought to begin. There were many who were related to this subject, and he asks whether he should begin with the pious or with the cruel. Resolving this question he begins from the impious, that is, with Oedipus, that is, the house and family of Oedipus."

9. Two studies of Geoffrey's rhetorical works now in progress at the University of Toronto promise to contribute significantly to our understanding of medieval poetic theory. Margaret F. Nims is editing a new, and lengthier, version of the *Documentum de modo et arte dictandi et versificandi*. One version of this work is included in Faral, *Les arts poétiques*. Marjorie Curry Woods's editing of the versions of the earliest known commentary on *Poetria Nova* for her dissertation is "The *In principio huius libri* Type A Commentary on Geoffrey of Vinsauf's *Poetria Nova:* Text and Analysis" (University of Toronto, 1977). She will follow this with a study of the commentary tradition as a whole. Half of the two hundred manuscripts of the *Poetria Nova* have commentaries and marginal notes.

10. Assisi, Biblioteca Communale MS 309, fol. 2r. "By a first division the book, therefore, is divided into two parts, that is, a prologue and a treatise, that begins 'If someone has to found a house,' because in prologues poets are accustomed to invoke and propose, but in the treatise to narrate what they are

setting out. Next the prologue is divided into two parts. And note that I have said 'prologue,' and not into a 'prohennium' and treatise, because as Aristotle says in the third book of the Rhetoric, 'prohennium' is the beginning of a speech just as a prologue is the beginning in poetry and a prelude in a song, from which it is apparent that when the author draws on poetry or on poetic art and we are treating poetry, on account of what has already been said, the part of the discourse should rightly be called a 'prologue,' although it is possible to be called a 'prohennium,' when speaking colloquially, since these things are the same with respect to substance and are not different except by mental distinction." This manuscript is the fullest commentary on the *Poetria Nova* yet identified; it seems to have two *accessus,* not quite duplicates of one another—one at the beginning and the other at the end.

11. Donald R. Howard, "The Canterbury Tales: Memory and Form," *ELH* 38 (1971): 319-28. The work which makes all this possible, of course, is Frances Yates's *The Art of Memory* (Penguin, 1969).

12. Howard, "Memory and Form," pp. 323-25.

13. For further discussion see Beryl Smalley, *The Study of the Bible in the Middle Ages,* p. 246, and the bibliography there listed. Cf. also Lynn Thorndike, "Unde Versus," *Traditio* 11 (1955): 163-92.

14. Among the things which "anima dicitur" in Hugh's *distinctio* on the topic are "vita hominis," "totus homo," and, most useful for our purposes here, "status hominis" (*Opera Omnia* [Venice, 1732], vol. 2, fol. 82rb).

15. A medieval form of the proverb is listed in *Proverbs, Sentences, and Proverbial Phrases,* ed. B. J. Whiting (Cambridge, Mass., 1968), p. 61: "When the clot klyngueth, and the cucko synguth and the brome sprynguth, then his time a youngelyng for to go a wowying." For a discussion of the problem of the literary origins of the General Prologue's springtime setting, see Rosemond Tuve, "Spring in Chaucer and Before Him," *Modern Language Notes* 52 (1937): 9-16.

16. For a summary of the controversy over the attribution of this letter—a controversy which seems to us to exist only because certain critics are so opposed on various a priori grounds to what the letter says that they are forced to deny Dante's authorship—see Robert Hollander, *Allegory in Dante's Commedia* (Princeton, 1966), pp. 40-41.

17. The title of *Dante Studies I, Commedia: Elements of Structure* (Cambridge, Mass., 1965), is indicative of Singleton's principal interest in discovering the manner in which Dante constructed his poem. See, in particular, the final chapter, "The Two Kinds of Allegory," pp. 84-98.

18. Charles Singleton, "The Irreducible Dove," *Comparative Literature* 9 (1957): 129-35. See also the discussion of the complex definition of allegory underlying the action of the *Commedia,* in Hollander, *Allegory,* passim.

19. Hollander, *Allegory,* p. 191.

20. Ibid., p. 123.

21. Ibid., p. 59n.

22. Ibid., pp. 75-76. It is also true that during the period of Dante's own life the traditional insistence that figural meanings be applied only to true

events, and the related insistence that true or pious exempla were more valid than fictional and secular ones, were both beginning to break down, so that by mid fourteenth century all kinds of fantasies and marvels were being admitted into sermons and other religious contexts, eventually breaking down entirely the earlier distinction between the allegory of the poets and the allegory of the theologians. For documentation and discussion on this point, see Allen, *The Friar as Critic.*

23. A similar but more pedestrian example of this syncretism is Peter Comestor's *Historia Scholastica,* which interpolates episodes of pagan mythology into biblical history (see P.L. 198, cols. 1054-1722).

24. Hollander, *Allegory,* p. 74.

25. The reading which follows was presented by Theresa Moritz in an address to the Medieval French section of the Medieval Institute, Kalamazoo, Mich., May 1973, "'Nothing Comes from Nothing': The Structure of Jean de Meun's *Roman de la Rose.*"

26. Rosemund Tuve, in *Allegorical Imagery* (Princeton, 1966), comes closest to this perception of Jean de Meun's ironic evocation of the truth through a miscellany of erroneous attitudes. We are less convinced by the interpretation presented by D. W. Robertson, *A Preface to Chaucer* (Princeton, 1962), pp. 361-65, which is followed closely by that of Charles Dahlberg in his introduction to a translation of the poem, *The Romance of the Rose* (Princeton, 1971), pp. 12-21. An alternative view appears in Wetherbee, *Platonism and Poetry in the Twelfth Century.*

27. Otis, *Ovid as an Epic Poet,* passim.

28. For a fuller discussion of the symbolic dimensions of Chaucer's choice of four parts, see above, chap. 1, esp. n. 79.

29. On the superiority of the text as an argument, see Robinson, *Works,* p. xxxvii; for the view that Hengwrt is in many instances textually superior, see Germaine Dempster, "Manly's Conception of the Early History of the *Canterbury Tales,*" *PMLA* 61 (1946): 394, and Charles A. Owen, Jr., "The Transformation of a Frame Story: The Dynamics of Fiction," in *Chaucer at Albany,* p. 146. On the widespread adoption of the Ellesmere Order in the a group of manuscripts, see John M. Manly and Edith Rickert, *The Text of the Canterbury Tales* (Chicago, 1949), 2:475-95, and Dempster, "Manly's Conception," p. 396; the Ellesmere Order is discussed with reference to a geographical reading in Donaldson, "The Ordering of the *Canterbury Tales,*" pp. 201-4. On the argument from theme, see John Gardner, "The Case Against the Bradshaw Shift; or, The Mystery of the Manuscript in the Trunk," *Papers in Language and Literature* 3, supplement (1967): 80-106.

30. Since no single manuscript contains the order we propose, as a whole, it may well be that these partial correspondences are merely accident. But they do exist, and so we mention them, well aware that their full significance cannot be known until the manuscript evidence has been reconsidered under new assumptions.

31. Both acknowledge, for example, the intelligence and care of the Ellesmere scribe (Dempster, "Manly's Conception," p. 396). At the same time, Dempster customarily finds scribal editors careless and hasty ("A Chapter in the

Manuscript History of the *Canterbury Tales*," *PMLA* 63 [1948]: 482). Tatlock, "The *Canterbury Tales* in 1400," p. 136, defends the authenticity of the Hengwrt arrangement but criticizes the "wit" of the editor who put it together by a logic of grouping similar stories.

32. Dempster, "A Chapter," pp. 472-73; Tatlock, "The *Canterbury Tales* in 1400," p. 111.

33. Manly and Rickert describe and provide charts of these groups in *The Text*, 2:475-95. In addition to the articles already cited, Dempster discusses these various orders, with an eye to their ancestry, in "A Period in the Development of the *Canterbury Tales* Marriage Group and of Blocks B^2 and C," *PMLA* 68 (1953): 1142-59; and "The Problem of Tale Order in the *Canterbury Tales*," *PMLA* 64 (1949): 1123-42.

34. Tatlock, "The *Canterbury Tales* in 1400," pp. 110-12, is generally kinder than Dempster in his characterization of the efforts of early scribal editors to produce good texts; he mentions a number of cases in which blanks are left for tales not at the time available, or in which words that cannot be made out in exemplars are omitted in the copying of new manuscripts.

35. Several manuscripts, including some of the groups c and d, preserve the early tradition of grouping these tales, and providing appropriate links, in a manner different from Chaucer's final plan for the tales, clearly indicated by their pairings through linking material. The problem of this sequence is discussed by Dempster, "Manly's Conception," p. 394.

36. Rosenberg, "The Contrary Tales of the Second Nun and the Canon's Yeoman," pp. 278-91; Szittya, "The Green Yeoman as Loathly Lady,"pp. 386-94; and several other studies of similar type devoted to various fragments: for a partial list, see above, chap. 1, n. 38. To the same end, but with more self-conscious use of medieval critical structures, Glending Olson's "Fragment VIII of the *Canterbury Tales*," presented to the Kalamazoo medieval conference of 1979, shows that the fragment is a unit illustrating what can properly be called a single medieval *distinctio*.

37. Many tales begin without even an identification of the speaker, in the conversational style familiar from the Monk's Prologue; others have only a reference to time, as in the important case of the *Man of Law's Tale*. Still others depend not on any reference to geography, or time, but on some interruption or controversy arising during the journey, as in the Franklin's succession to the Squire, or the logic by which the Friar and the Summoner follow the Wife of Bath.

38. C. Robert Kase, "Observations of the Shifting Position of Groups G and DE in the Manuscripts of the *Canterbury Tales*," *Three Canterbury Studies* (New York, 1932), pp. 3-89; cf. also Charles A. Owen, Jr., "The Plan of the Canterbury Pilgrimage,"*PLMA* 66 (1951): 820-26, who combines the evidence of geography with an argument by thematic appropriateness.

39. Dempster, "A Chapter," pp. 472-73, and elsewhere in her many articles on the subject; Tatlock, "*The Canterbury Tales* in 1400,"p. 129.

40. Sir William McCormick and Janet E. Heseltine, *The Manuscripts of Chaucer's "Canterbury Tales": A Critical Description of Their Contents* (Oxford, 1933), pp. xxv-xxviii, give a list of the spurious links, and their texts are

available by manuscript in the body of the book. None of these spurious links introduces any geographical allusion to pinpoint a story or to give a sense of completing an essential aspect of the original work; the majority of them perform the task of introducing the speaker by name, a conventional rhetorical device for a prologue, and on occasion refer to a possible subject for a story.

41. Manly and Rickert, *The Text*, 2:491.

42. One may of course memorize any arbitrary series of names, as Sunday school children learn the books of the Bible, and as commuters may learn to repeat the conductor's singsong of stations. But such series are learned as unified patterns of sound, not as a set of discrete experiences in time. Had Chaucer let the Host name all the towns along the way in one batch, then subsequent allusion to them might have been significant. But he did not.

43. The table presents, in brief, a comparison between the order we propose and the most familiar arrangement of tales, the Ellesmere Order. The right-hand column mentions some of the principal manuscript justifications for the new connections between the established fragments. See the following discussion, along with notes, for a fuller treatment of each of these significant connections in the proposed order. To summarize the changes we propose: the *Man of Law's Tale* moves down to a position before the *Clerk's Tale*, to open a group of stories on marriage. Groups III, IV, V, and VI are rearranged, with IV moving down along with the *Man of Law's Tale* to form a marriage sequence. Group VIII (G) becomes the new source of a serious theme following the *Cook's Tale*, followed by groups V, III, and VI, in that order. These changes are completed by moving the *Manciple's Tale* into the marriage group, which leaves group B^2 immediately before the *Parson's Tale*.

44. See above, chapter 1.

45. It may have been noted that in our ordering, all the proposed major groups begin a fragment except the last. Here, Chaucer has provided what seems to us an internal clue: in the epilogue of the *Shipman's Tale*, the Host says: "But now passe over, and lat us seke aboute,/Who shal now telle first of al this route/Another tale" (VII 443–45 [B^2 1633–35]). In so doing, with explicit reference to "first of al this route," Chaucer underlines in stronger terms than anywhere else in the links an impression of new beginning. Doubtless there would have been more such hints of large structure had all the fragments received their final editorial joining; here, at least, the underlining of a major division happily reinforces what seems apparent from the stories themselves.

PART TWO

A Reading of the Tales

4

The Natural Group

In this chapter we shall begin to present the tales of Chaucer's Canterbury collection as a normative array of exempla, which accumulate a definition of the good human society. Both their plots and the society they define are founded, maintained, and informed by words—founded on a responsible exchange of vows or promises, maintained by faithful adherence to those promises, and informed by the memory of past moral action, preserved as narrative. The power of words to interpret and direct life is therefore implicitly the focal interest of the *Canterbury Tales,* both in its exploration of the validity of fiction and in its preoccupation with marriage as the representative human situation. Stories bring the past under man's control by presenting it in a form which both preserves and values the experiences of the race, and so makes it possible to learn from them. Promises share with stories their ability to describe and determine the future, because they establish the intentional limits within which action is to be performed and judged. We have seen, in part, what can happen when these stories and promises are misunderstood or misappropriated, because we have confronted the literary misunderstandings of Chaucer's pilgrims. In this part we will deal with further misunderstandings, misappropriations, and misbehaviors, along with much that is actually good and right, as we read the entire series of prologues and tales as an ordered array of exempla. In this array the quality which Chaucer prizes in both stories and promises is the power they hold over the future; bad beginnings, he shows us repeatedly, make bad, or absurdly and ironically good, ends, but good beginnings, whether they come from reading a story or making a promise, are a foundation for good conclusions. His stories enact promises, and their consequences, and so help us both to formulate and to enact our own.

The reading which follows differs visibly from previous analyses, both in its unconventional ordering and in its linear method. The ordering is intended to emphasize the unifying associations which relate tale to tale. The linear procedure, which reads tales and prologues in order at the same level, as parts in series of the same moral discourse, not only has the pragmatic value of permitting richer insights into the meaning of Chaucer's text, but also has the advantage of following both the example of medieval commentary and the recommendation of medieval writing manuals. Necessarily, therefore, our reading differs from previous ones also in its results. Trusting one tale to inform the next leads us to emphasize details previously passed over and to differ from precedent in many details of interpretation. We challenge traditional readings of a number of tales previously taken as Chaucer's straightforward statements on many subjects, including marriage, courtly love, prudential wisdom, and Christian repentance.

On the other hand, a text may mean more than one thing. Medieval commentators regularly react to their sense of the richness of a text by making several different and mutually complementary allegorizations. We do not attempt to exhaust the meaning of every tale, or even of any tale, but rather wish to present those aspects of each tale's meaning made obvious by the fact of that tale's presence in a collection, an array. We therefore intend that our reading should be taken more often as supplement than as contradiction. But however it is taken, it is the only ultimate justification of the method which makes it possible. The reading itself, and its ability to offer new insights and depths of meaning in the tales and in the whole poem, proves itself by its own value. To the extent that it has value, both our medieval method and our selection of the particular details which we discuss are vindicated.

We offer no apology for dealing with what stories have in common, rather than with stories in isolation; we find no medieval justification either for the isolation implied by a story's being taken as a dramatic speech with a Jamesian or Browningesque point of view, or for the isolation required for a story by Aristotelian or new critical notions of aesthetic integrity. In Chaucer's nominalist age, concrete particulars are not universalized by virtue of any close aesthetic attention, but rather relate to and define universals by having been assembled and arrayed for conceptualization. Chaucer therefore uses his largely borrowed plots, and their various styles and genres, in multiple, testing one against the other in the belief that all stories relate to and make possible truthful statements about proper moral conduct. His irony is not the unstable irony of modern fiction, but rather that medieval irony which is one of the kinds of allegory, and one possible expression of clear moral commitment. His irony is pervasive, not because the universe makes no sense, but rather because the predicament of all particulars, in themselves, is ironic. Only in groups can particulars become true. The very variety of Chaucer's tales helps constitute their unity, because this variety arrays them, distinguishes them, in an association which can be taken as a whole.

In the variety of Chaucer's tales, the first group is the one beyond all question he designed himself: the tales of the first fragment. We have already shown how the *Knight's Tale,* in its four parts, defines Chaucer's whole collection. In addition, of course, it also belongs to and begins the first fragment, and thus belongs in the first group, the nature group, as well as being paradigm and introduction to the whole. In this group we have in social and human terms an analysis of *contextio elementorum*[1]—the elements, of course, being those human beings whose condition is a present potentially liable to vice and a future potentially liable to hell. What Chaucer does in this group synthesizes the formulas of the Ovidian and the descent-into-hell tradition; he is concerned with defining the authority—or rather authorities—by which the social *contextio hominum* is to be achieved. The humanity involved is in a state of nature, not grace. The Athenians and Thebans are literally before Christ; the Miller's carpenter, at least, thinks he lives just before the flood; the Reeve's miller defines his life by the lawless state most vividly described later by Thomas Hobbes; the Cook's pimps are riot.

Nevertheless, this group of tales also exemplifies, perhaps more explicitly than anywhere else in Chaucer's work, the operation of justice. We have already seen that Theseus is a just ruler because he wisely rules himself, his family, and his state. The authority he imposes does not control Saturn, of course, but can make orderly and just sense of what Saturn does. The poetic justice of the fact that Palamon and Arcite each gets precisely what he has prayed for is ironic, but nevertheless neat. With Theseus so firmly and responsibly in control of what man can control of society, the work of providence seems mere work of fortune, as it often does to pagan eyes. Beyond the *Knight's Tale* the operation of poetic justice becomes more and more obviously fair and less and less merely ironic. As a group, the tales become a complex and contrapuntal examination of the relation between absolute justice, on the one hand, and the human laws and human authorities through which, or in spite of which, it is achieved. In these terms one may see the four tales as concerned with, respectively, the imposition of law and justice, the unjust intrusion against the law, the imposition of unjust law, and the abolition of law altogether. In each case there is an authority figure who defines the law, or his posture toward it, in a way which makes claims on society: Theseus rules, both Nicholas and his carpenter host expect to intrude into higher places than they own, the dishonest miller affirms theft as the law of his life, and the master of apprentices and the husband of the swyving wife both abdicate their obligation to make law and order. The *Cook's Take* is unfinished; to this point the operation of poetic justice and ordinary human selfishness and self-protection compensates as the law degenerates. It is as if Chaucer is telling us that nature cannot endure too much disorder; if man will not rule properly, then God will dispose fortune into the balance.

Saturn, the god of nature, rules the events of the *Knight's Tale;* it is his decision which disposes of the relative claims of Arcite and Palamon and foresees an eventual reconciliation of the quarreling Mars and Venus. His presence places the tale in an ambiguous a-Christian time, on the one hand a Golden Age of innocence and on the other the fallen age after the Garden and before the saving intervention of Christ. Saturn's complex double aspect, as, on the one hand, the god of human perfection and human justice and, on the other, the god of fortune and of wealth—the most pernicious of fortune's weapons—is expressed clearly in the tale.[2] Chaucer skillfully uses this seemingly contradictory figure to express mankind's complex longing for the ability to perfect himself, without divine intervention. Saturn presides over an age of courtly sentiment and human greatness which seems always at the point of achieving perfection—Theseus has settled his borders and established an age of peace, administered with justice and compassion, from his seat at Athens. He seems to promise, in his thirst for the orderly disposition of love and justice, the very Golden Age which, for the Middle Ages, had been Saturn's realm.[3] On the other hand, in practice, Saturn's justice is rude and peremptory; Arcite will win but will not receive the prize; Palamon will be shamed by defeat and receive a winner's portion only by default. Saturn's identification of his activities with the darkest deeds of human life has led some critics to think that he is exclusively the evil god of bad fortune.[4]

In fact, Chaucer has struck a traditional balance, weighing the problem of man's perfectibility against what is his present lot and what he might have been had he not sinned. Much as Boethius praises Saturn's Golden Age in the midst of his attacks on the tricks of Fortune,[5] so Chaucer presents a two-sided god of nature in Saturn. Saturn rules a society which is in the state of nature, whose homely and earthly virtues are an enticing end in themselves for most readers. There is struggle, but it is in the cause of wedding justice and love, as Jean de Meun had said the Golden Age also achieved. But, on closer examination, this social order is not perfect, because it lacks the divinely given perspective of salvation history. Human justice, without Christ, is the imperfect institution which Jean de Meun found ruling the world and which Chaucer ridicules more and more evidently as the first fragment develops. Theseus takes the first step outside the Garden of Saturn when he appeals to Jupiter as the order-giver and planner of the universe, whose schemes are outside the control or comprehension of man, but still to be trusted. In doing so, he lays the groundwork for the search to understand which will occupy the remainder of the tales, and particularly the final great section devoted to interpretation. It is only a more perfect interpretation of the world which can draw back Saturn's golden mask and reveal behind it the ugly face of Fortune.[6]

The *Knight's Tale* ends with a marriage; Theseus calls the arrangement his "accord" (I [A] 3081). The Knight's final judgment is approving:

> For now is Palamon in alle wele,
> Lyvynge in blisse, in richesse, and in heele,
> And Emelye hym loveth so tendrely,
> And he hire serveth al so gentilly,
> That nevere was ther no word him betwene
> Of jalousie or any oother teene.
>
> (I [A] 3101-6)

But there will be both words of jealousy and other "teene," at least as far as this social institution is concerned. Chaucer gives us a marriage as the fundamental social arrangement of mankind—as the result of the rule of Theseus—not because it is perfect, but because marriage is the example through which Chaucer will examine social order in general.

Therefore, all the rest of the stories of the natural group emphasize a challenge to a householder's authority over his family. Weddings make households, and the conventional phrase "and they lived happily ever after" covers all the more interesting possibilities for trouble and success in human life. Nowhere outside these first tales of the Miller, Reeve, and Cook is the pattern of conflict established in the *Knight's Tale* so thoroughly reproduced.[7] Just as the kingdom of Theseus is disturbed by the presence of Palamon and Arcite, so the households of John and Symkyn are each shaken by the intrusions of two young men whose efforts to undermine the authority of the head of the house include sexual conquests of the family's female member or members. The proper dominance of husband and father in each story following the Knight's is compromised by the cunning of young lovers; in each, the father figure is discomfited. Throughout the group, even in the fragment of the *Cook's Tale*, a man in authority takes into his house potentially disruptive forces, trusting to his own presence and power to keep order.[8] Theseus succeeds; the others, whose bases for authority are progressively lower than his, fail. But whether the authority figure succeeds, fails, or makes disorder his order, the tales as such are about the variety of human attacks on this authority—various efforts to overturn human organizations, thus exemplifying the natural changes which are the subject of the first in the four groups.

The stories of the first fragment concentrate on the ramifications of the situation which opens the *Knight's Tale:* that is, Theseus's conquest of Thebes and his imprisonment of Palamon and Arcite. The *Miller's Tale* opens with a newly wedded couple who provide lodgings for a young clerk. There is an even closer parallel in the *Reeve's Tale*, when Symkyn, after duping the clerks, John and Aleyn, accepts them as house guests for the night. But the wisdom of Theseus in jailing the last disruptive power of Thebes is contrasted with John the carpenter's foolishly harboring the cause of his undoing in the same "narwe cage" in which he guards his Alisoun; the same lack of foresight, compounded by proud self-reliance in Symkyn's case, causes the miller to house the enemies he has bested in his own bedroom. Even the *Cook's Tale* promises a similar situation:

> Anon he sente his bed and his array
> Unto a compeer of his owene sort,
> That lovede dys, and revel, and disport,
> And hadde a wyf that heeld for contenance
> A shoppe, and swyved for hir sustenance.

(I [A] 4418-22)

The stories after the *Knight's Tale* differ in their approach to this beginning: the possibilities they examine descend from the rightful exercise of authority by Theseus through the ignorant hysteria of John to the pride of Symkyn. The reign of Theseus expresses honest, intelligent efforts to control life or, if not to control, at least to understand its providential workings. But the old carpenter with the "wylde and yong" wife helps in the work which undoes him and is unable to punish the man who cuckolds him, this task, ironically, being performed by his wife's other suitor. Still, John's ignorance is pitiable, and his crime, "that he lovede moore than his lyf," earns him some sympathy from us when he is made ridiculous before his neighbors. Symkyn, on the other hand, is a thief, and his initial conquest over the clerks is accomplished by deceit. Not only is he unable to avenge the clerks' swyving, but "Thise clerkes beete hym weel and leye hym lye." The "poetic justice" the Reeve points out with great relish provokes a readier audience response, because there is nothing sympathetic about the proud Symkyn and his wife, the parson's proud daughter.

An exemplum which is intimately related to these problems of marriage and the administration of justice within that institution is the story of Mars and Venus caught in adultery. Within the *Knight's Tale* itself, Mars and Venus may be principally the opposed representatives of two incompatible types of temperament, the irascible and the passionate. Within the Canterbury collection as a whole there are echoes of the adulterous union of the god of war and the goddess of love, a romantic alliance for which the pair was certainly more famous than as the champions of Palamon and Arcite. In the *Knight's Tale* itself, Arcite invokes Mars as lover:

> Whan that thow usedest for beautee
> Of faire, yonge, fresshe Venus free,
> And haddest hire in armes at thy wille—

(I [A] 2385-87)

but recalls the end to this adulterous affair, with the lovers trapped by Vulcan "in his las." Saturn's call for a reconciliation between the warring pair some hundred lines later has an ironic ring, in the light of Arcite's recollection of their adultery; Chaucer might also have intended an allusion to the matter of Thebes, in which the adulterous union produced one of the great plagues of the house of Cadmus, the necklace given to Venus's love-child Harmonia by Vulcan.[9] On at least two other occasions, Chaucer treats the Mars-Venus love affair: first, in the Wife of Bath's horoscope,[10] and second, in the "Complaint of

Mars,"[11] which, in the manner of the *Ovide moralisé*, presents an elaborate astrological treatment of the encounter between a courtly knight and his lady. It is possible that the exemplum is echoed as well in the *Miller's Tale* love triangle of John the craftsman, his young and uncontrollable wife, and her courtly, able suitor.[12]

The attraction of this exemplum for Chaucer is obvious. It came to him treated in many sources and with a variety of meanings. Within the Canterbury collection, the manner in which Chaucer manipulates this story suggests his method in the larger problem of dealing with his many tales of marriage and human relationships. All the possible dimensions of the tale, with due respect, or at least humorous attention, to everyone's point of view, are explored, not for the sake of choosing among them, but rather in the hopes that from all of them some reasonable conclusions may be drawn about principles and practice. The one interpretation which Chaucer chooses to present only implicitly is the standard moralization, which stressed the dire consequences of sin through the figures of the chains of vicious habit preventing the sinner's escape from his fault.[13] Although such a moralization might be implied in the career of such incorrigible pursuers of their private vices as the Pardoner or the Wife of Bath, still it is never stated. Chaucer can rely on his audience to know this allegorization of the chains which bind man habitually to his sins.

Rather, Chaucer stresses perspectives on the story suggested by its affinities to the basic love situation and to the principal interpretations of courtly love poetry and of the fabliau. That is, there is a love triangle, in which an undesirable husband is faced with a lover for his wife. In courtly treatments the worth of the lover is offered as proof that his claims to the woman are superior to her husband's. "Who regneth now in blysse but Venus,/That hath thys worthy knyght in governaunce?" ("The Complaint of Mars," lines 43–44). On the other hand, fabliau traditions tend to stress, first, the wife's crafty ability to dupe her husband and, second, the uncontrollable drive for sexual fulfillment. It is to explain her cupidity that the Wife of Bath mentions her astrological profile:

> Venus me yaf my lust, my likerousnesse,
> And Mars yaf me my sturdy hardynesse;
> Myn ascendent was Taur, and Mars therinne.
>
> (III [D] 611–13)

In much the same way, in the *Miller's Tale*, the passionate nature of Alisoun is explained in a series of animal allusions, which, particularly in the figure of the caged bird, suggest the unnatural constraint of marriage on sexual desire.[14] From both these traditions, which stress the rights of the lovers regardless of the marital claims of the wronged husband, Chaucer creates the exemplum of Mars and Venus, which is suggested by a number of direct allusions and implicit parallels throughout the collection. Within the nature group, the story is an apt figure for a wholly unspiritual treatment of the sordid problem of adultery. Although it is an incident which concerns the gods entirely, it is a story which lends itself readily to treatment as an all-too-human situation.[15] The lovers meet with no special exercise of divine powers and are caught by Vulcan's skill, rather than by divine might. As the result of exposure, Mars and Venus continue their affair openly, with Vulcan powerless to act.

By casting special light on the Mars-Venus exemplum, we reveal within the *Knight's Tale* seeds for the discontent to come. Mars and Venus signal always the ever-present danger that marriage will be undone by discontent, mismanagement, or chance—including the appearance of an ideal lover. When Saturn calls on Mars and Venus to be reconciled, particularly in the context of the story of Thebes, there is a suggestion that we have come full circle, and that the cycle will begin again, a new society to be faced with disruptive forces, within and without. They are a troublesome discordant note sounding against the harmony of wedded bliss forecast by Theseus at the story's close. Finally, the figure of Mars and Venus caught in adultery is taken up by the remaining stories of the first fragment, repeated and elaborated, in a manner which we shall see below characterizes Chaucer's method in linking the tales within each of the groups we have classified under the headings natural, magical, moral, and spiritual. Within the stately harmony of the *Knight's Tale*, even the disruptive clash of Mars and Venus may be restrained; but when we pass outside the reign of Theseus, disorder intrudes more and more insistently in human affairs.

The *Miller's Tale* is an elaborate, outrageous, blasphemous reversal of the proprieties established in the *Knight's Tale*. The young woman being protected by John is not his virgin ward but his own wild, lusty wife. Neither the virgin modesty of Emelye nor the queenly dignity of Hippolyta survives in this willing wife, whose first protestations against Nicholas's wooing are changed to words of love in the space of a few lines:

> This Nicholas gan mercy for to crye,
> And spak so faire, and profred him so faste,
> That she hir love hym graunted atte laste.

> (I [A] 3288–90)

There is nothing of the ethereal goddess in Alisoun, whose discription is filled with allusions to animals.[16] The young men who seek her out are both clerks, both accomplished wooers, whose differences to a certain measure parallel the differences between Palamon, the follower of Venus, and Arcite, the follower of Mars. Absalom trusts to words of wooing and love gifts to gain Alisoun, whereas Nicholas is a schemer intent on winning the game. Their situations, Nicholas in the house and Absalom outside, recall the prison of Palamon and the exile of Arcite, but Nicholas's situation gives him opportunity, rather than preventing him from reaching the object of his lust.[17] John is duped into constructing the elaborate equipment which frees Alisoun for a night with Nicholas; his *constructio* evokes, by the medieval doctrine of concordance, an analogy with the construction by Theseus of the pavilion in which the young men will contend for his ward. The exchange of insults between Nicholas and Absalom is a vulgar exchange in comparison with the stately tournament between Palamon and Arcite, especially because Absalom's actions are dictated by revenge. The pathetic end of Arcite, his complaint of fate and forgiveness of Palamon, offers a significant contrast to Absalom's bitter determination to strike one final blow when it is evident that he may not win the girl for himself.

The tale ends with all the carpenter's pain turned to a public joke. "The folk gan laughen at his fantasye; . . . And turned al his harm unto a jape" (I [A] 3840, 3842). The shame of his situation before his neighbors is that he thought the flood was coming; but for the story's audience, it is his further shame that his wife has deserted him, and that the clerk who won her has been punished for his crime not by her husband but by another suitor. The problem of poetic justice posed by the disposition of Palamon's and Arcite's claims is raised again here. Although the judgment of Saturn determines the ends of each suitor, it is Theseus's authority which stages their conflict and steps forward to offer the human understanding of events. In the *Miller's Tale,* on the other hand, John's authority has no place in the rivalry between Nicholas and Absalom. The settling of their claims with Nicholas's punishment and Absalom's revenge, much like Palamon's defeat and Arcite's victory, ultimately means little to the award of the girl's affections, because Nicholas has already won her, and she is already married to John. Further, Nicholas is not punished for his real crime, adultery, but rather receives the blow intended for Alisoun. Thus, all the merely human intentions are lawless, but their result is, by providential accident, just, and the Miller's list of the punished makes of them the comic butts which their deeds deserve. But we are left without proper authority; the carpenter, made foolish by his lodger, is written off: "The man is wood, my leeve brother" (I [A] 3848). From such a conclusion there can come no interpretation except laughter:

> Whan folk hadde laughen at this nyce cas
> Of Absolon and hende Nicholas,
> Diverse folk diversely they seyde.
>
> (I [A] 3855-57)

It is not so cosmic a laughter as that of Troilus; it is not obviously Boethian, and it involves diversity of individual judgment, but nevertheless it does answer to the great Boethian meditation of Theseus. It affirms, as does he, that the point of a tale is what one does with it, the point of an event is how one reacts to it. The common laughter in which these diverse interpretations find expression is the comic *ars vituperandi,* an implicit recognition of the normative.[18] John the carpenter is a bad husband and a bad man; that Nicholas promises him Noah's vacant realm is Chaucer's ironic indication that he would have been a bad ruler. Nevertheless, there is justice. The ceremony of accidents which gave not only both Thebans their prayers and Emelye a husband but also Theseus the occasion for a noble speech gives here each man his due.

The Reeve, however, has no use for law. His world, more primitive even than the law of revenge, is the world of private revenge, personally inflicted. He takes the law into his own hands and thereby abolishes it. As both the Miller's Prologue and his tale exemplify the theme of unjust intrusion against the law, so the vengeful, quiting Reeve, his hero miller whose only law is that millers must steal, and his students, who accomplish a private revenge, all exemplify the theme of the imposition of unjust law. In this theme the *Reeve's Tale* brings into sharp focus what had been implicit before. The rule of all these tales, in a sense, is quiting—an interruption of the order proposed by the Host and conducted under the rule of the self-confessed drunk, the Miller. His purpose is to offer a "noble tale for the nones, / With which I wol now quite the Knyghtes tale" (I [A] 3126-27). The Cook also threatens a quiting, with Harry Bailly, though he postpones it (I [A] 4356-61). But what the Miller began within the game, as he sought to quite the Knight's story, the Reeve and the Cook continue outside the game, as they attempt to quite real people. Although the Miller slyly argues that the Reeve cannot be insulted by a story of a cuckolded husband without admitting that he is one, still the Reeve, who must announce that he is a carpenter to justify his feeling insulted, is determined to apply the story to himself, and to return insult for insult.[19] The Miller's intention is to answer nobility, a pageant of high seriousness with a burlesque of low comedy. But the *ars vituperandi,* or comedy, is as morally serious as tragedy, the *ars laudandi,* and what quites at one level repeats at another. The Reeve, mistaking game for earnest, intends to insult the Miller by relating the downfall of another miller.

The series of tales descends. From the high management of Theban disorder to the fool undone by prognostications of a supernatural disorder which does not happen, we go to the thief undone by the arrogance he asserts in presuming his right to steal. The *Miller's Tale* is a rich, complex answer to the *Knight's Tale;* the *Reeve's Tale* is a vulgarized looking-glass image of the Theseus, Palamon, and Arcite struggle.[20] The ruler of this tale is a "theef"; his family is a proud wife, a willing daughter, the unawarded daughter of the piece, and a babe whose innocent cradle is used in the clerks' cunning plan to outwit Symkyn. Unlike Theseus, Symkyn does not award his virgin; she is stolen from him, and his wife as well. The shrine of Theseus's lists is obscenely parodied in the "places" of the beds, where prayers and consummations are combined. John and Aleyn are rivals in love, but only in the sense that each wishes equally to have his lust assuaged, in one bed or another. Hilarious coincidence eventually intervenes to expose what has been going on, to unleash chaos for a time, and to bring on the moral summary of punishments.

Aleyn and John are primarily partners in revenge, not lovers. They believe in the law of divine compensation:

> For, John, ther is a lawe that says thus,
> That gif a man in a point be agreved,
> That in another he sal be releved.

(I [A] 4180–82)

But they take the law into their own hands, using love as a mere instrument of a lower and even more lawless purpose. Love, even here, has an integrity of its own. Although it is hardly more than sex and is being consciously manipulated for vengeful and selfish purposes, love resists Aleyn's reduction of pleasure to a neutral return for value lost. Although his purpose is to cheat the miller, Aleyn parts with the miller's daughter fondly, and she has been sufficiently moved to enter willingly into the plan to get the better of her father. Symkyn has trained her and so must receive his reward.

> Right at the entree of the dore byhynde
> Thou shalt a cake of half a busshel fynde
> That was ymaked of thyn owene mele,
> Which that I heelp my sire for to stele.

$$\text{(I [A] 4243-46)}$$

Thus love does justice. Symkyn's cheating costs him not only his honor but the fruit of his deceit, and the clerks' revenge has created a relationship which resists reduction. In the same way, the Reeve's story as a whole exists as something beyond the intended insult of Reeve to Miller. The story is welcomed as a pleasant one; the Cook cannot contain his delight with it. The Cook, moreover, gives it the right moral—the moral which integrates it properly in the series as a whole:

> "Ne bryng nat every man into thyn hous";
> For herberwynge by nyghte is perilous.
> Wel oghte a man avysed for to be
> Whom that he broghte into his pryvetee.

$$\text{(I [A] 4331-34)}$$

It is all, from *Knight's Tale* to *Cook's Tale*, an "argument of herbergage."[21] Whatever is taken in must be dealt with—be it Theban princes or Amazonian princesses, student lodgers, cheated customers, or riotous apprentices. The Reeve's story, as story, is not a mere insult at all but a piece of nature, an exemplum of the *contextio elementorum humanorum*, which succeeds in exemplifying justice even in the lives of unjust men and unreliable authorities. They are practitioners of sin, and they are under threat of damnation, but their descent into hell, however natural, is nevertheless exemplary, and therefore both true and moral.

The *Cook's Tale*, the last of the series, is unfinished. Since the medieval rhetoric of endings was not nearly so elaborated as the technique of beginnings, Chaucer's having simply stopped should cause no trouble. We have neither to speculate about what he might have done nor to justify the *Cook's Tale* as we have it as an organically integrated fragment. Rather, we simply note that the situation which the Cook defines does fit into what has gone before. It repeats the pattern of authority figure, awardable woman, and two males. It confronts the authority figure with a problem of disorder in his household. It even ends, as we have it, with the establishment of another household. Most important, it is a logically appropriate last statement, because it deals with the weakest of authority figures, the least significant of kinds of households, and the least orderly of awarded woman solutions. That the difference between the king's awarding of a ward in marriage and the awarding of a prostitute's favors for an hour is morally so large as to be taken as a difference in kind should not obscure the fact, more important here, that the two acts are structurally in series, and that the one is indeed a degenerate version of the other. Authoritative responsibility for the sexual fate of a woman is one of the most important arrangements which society makes—the exercise of this authority, in a range of its permutations, is an excellent paradigmatic example of authority in general. Chaucer's extremes are socially realistic—some people, and some acts, are high, and some are very low.

The authority figure is the master of apprentices. As a teacher he is a failure; as a master he endures insubordination and embezzlement with increasing discomfort, until finally he simply abdicates his responsibility. Perkyn, his riotous apprentice, is a lover, a skilled servant of fortune with his dice, a sometime prisoner (as were Palamon and Arcite), a frequenter of triumphant parades,[22] and in the end, a suitable member of a ménage à trois. Love is no longer something that a man wins, but rather something because of which "wel was the wenche with hym myghte meete" (I [A] 4374). Family has been reduced to parody, and the duty of awarding the virgin has been transformed into the commerce of selling the whore.

From the first fragment we gain not only the rich and subtle mediations of the interplay between nature and grace, between God's law and poetic justice, provided us by the tales, but also a valuable model for understanding the manner in which the groups of stories within the *Canterbury Tales* will work with one another. We have observed a close thematic unity, which explores the rule of human justice on the earth; Chaucer sets this high ideal in the best light in the *Knight's Tale*, where it brings to mind the medieval longing for the Golden Age, and in the worst light in the *Reeve's Tale* and the unfinished tale of the Cook, where, as will happen so often on the journey, love is replaced by a reverence for money. We have seen that this thematic unity rests firmly on an analogical association of the narrative patterns and characterizations to be found in the tales: Palamon and Arcite are repeated, a little blurred and a little coarse, in Nicholas and Absolom, and in the two young clerks who best the Reeve's corrupt miller; the same with Emelye and Theseus, with motifs of imagery and incident, with the final resolution of the action, all the things we have set forth in this chapter. We have taken note, as well, of the strong sense of descending order in the arrangement of the tales, from an ideal statement of Chaucer's theme—justice in the natural order of human society—to its debasements in the hands of sinful men. These three qualities of a story group, its close thematic unity, the binding of the tales by analogical association, and a descent in ideals and harmony from first tale to last, will all be observed in the other groups of tales discussed in the following chapters—the tales of magic, of morality, and of interpretation.

1. The phrase which for Ovid defined natural changes. Of all the tales, the Knight's is perhaps the most elaborately and elegantly treated by scholars. We are particularly indebted to the following works: Muscatine, *Chaucer and the French Tradition';* Stokoe, "Structure and Intention"; Joseph, "Chaucerian 'Game'"; and Leyerle, "The Heart and the Chain."

2. Raymond Klibansky, Erwin Panofsky, and Fritz Saxl, *Saturn and Melancholy* (London, 1964), trace the various traditions of the god in astrology, art, mythography, and so forth. They find in Chaucer, Gower, and Lydgate examples of the double-sided medieval view of the god, but they suggest that this is due more to a confusing tradition than to an artistic insight into the related aspects of the god's character; in particular, they cite the *Knight's Tale* portrait of Saturn as an example of "the cold, leaden, destructive, planetary god" (p. 193). On Saturn as the god of gold and wealth, see pp. 179 ff.

3. As we have already seen, in discussing the *Romance of the Rose,* the figure of Saturn's Golden Age was associated for the Middle Ages with a time of great innocence and freedom from conflict. But the ambiguous merits of its virtues, which we would suggest are at work in the *Knight's Tale,* are ironically suggested in the *Romance of the Rose,* especially by Reason's criticism of natural justice. See *Romance of the Rose,* ed. Dahlberg, pp. 113–15, lines 5555–692.

4. This is true in Klibansky, *Saturn and Melancholy,* p. 193. It is true, as well, of Alan T. Gaylord's study "The Role of Saturn in the Knight's Tale," *Chaucer Review* 8 (1973): 171–90. Gaylord argues that the tale reflects the dark, planetary aspect of Saturn as the representation of people, like Palamon and Arcite, who have willfully submitted themselves to fortune.

5. In book 2 of the *Consolation,* Lady Philosophy treats the glories of the Golden Age in the context of the evils of the present age, ruled by Fortune. Man's willingness to believe in the goods of wealth and prestige, and his consequent disappointment with turns of Fortune's wheel, are treated in prose 5 and 6; with such slavish devotion to things of no importance, Lady Philosophy contrasts the wisdom of the Golden Age, when men did not disrupt natural harmony by searching for gold or adventure. She suggests, in

fact, that it was the lust for gain which disrupted Paradise: "Heu primus quis fuit ille/auri qui pondera tecti/gemmasque latere valentes/pretiosa pericula fodit?" (book 2 meter 5).

6. As we shall see below, the image of old age, connected both with sexual potency and with experience as the proof of authority, is developed throughout the *Canterbury Tales*. Saturn, too, is a figure of old age, as well as of the old times which men both miss and yet know must pass away. Chaucer states that Saturn's solution to a problem Jupiter could not solve was based on "his olde experience," and offers him as proof that "elde hath greet avantage." But his old man's solution, though it tidies up the problem, betrays a lack of sensibility for the issues at stake in the problem; it is "agayn his kynde" for Saturn to be solving "strif and drede."

7. Although there will be husbands confronted with suitors for their wives, as in the *Franklin's Tale,* and parents challenged for their virgin children, as in the *Physician's Tale,* the pattern of a man in authority contesting with two suitors is nowhere repeated in the *Tales.* Cf. Stokoe, "Structure and Intention," passim.

8. Joseph, "Chaucerian 'Game,'" pp. 84–96, relates the tales of the first group through their use of space. He contrasts the *Knight's Tale,* with its sense of confining limitations, and fabliaux, in the contentment they feel in small spaces. See, also, the treatment of the contrasting image patterns of "links" and "holes" within the first fragment in Leyerle, "The Heart and the Chain," pp. 118–21.

9. Statius tells the story of the cursed necklace in book 2 of the *Thebaid,* lines 269–305. Chaucer alludes to the jewelry, wrought by Vulcan, in the "Complaint of Mars," line 245, as the "broche of Thebes," a charm with the ability to drive man mad with the desire to possess it. Through this necklace Chaucer links the madness of Thebes with love madness, a connection which is implicit in the distress of Thebes's last two sons, Palamon and Arcite, in the *Knight's Tale.*

10. Cf. Walter Clyde Curry, *Chaucer and the Medieval Sciences,* rev. ed. (New York, 1960), pp. 91–118, for the Wife's horoscope. The Wife's discussion of her personality, in astrological terms, applies the heavenly motions of the planets to her most private parts. "I folwed ay myn inclinacioun / By vertu of my constellacioun; / That made me I koude noght withdrawe / My chambre of Venus from a good felawe" (III [D] 615–18). Cf. Chaucer's description of Mars's entrance into the house of Venus in "Complaint of Mars," lines 50–84.

11. Edgar S. Laird, in "Astrology and Irony in Chaucer's 'Complaint of Mars,'" *Chaucer Review* 6 (1972): 229–231, considers both the accuracy of Chaucer's astrological information and the courtly shape the story is given in the poem. Cf. *Ovide moralisé,* vol. 2, book 4, lines 1489–1755, pp. 131–36.

12. Of course, as we readily admit, the general situation of the elderly husband, the young wife, and the suitor is the stuff of a wide variety of medieval love traditions, with echoes and associations extending as much to Mary, Joseph, and Mary's mysterious suitor as to Mars, Venus, and Vulcan. But there are some details of the story which might be attributed to Chaucer's knowledge of the story of Mars and Venus, as it was told by Jean de Meun; these are details whose conjunction cannot be explained by a common source.

Cf. Stith Thompson, "The Miller's Tale," in *Sources and Analogues*, p. 106. Some of these details include the name of Absalom, who occurs as an alternative lover for Venus in the *Romance of the Rose*, ed. Dahlberg, p. 238, lines 13850-74; the smith who aids in the undoing of the lovers—Vulcan was a smith; and Alisoun, like Venus, who is identified with birds, mares, and other animals which must not be restrained in marriage from pursuing their natural drives.

13. Thomas D. Hill, "La Vielle's Digression on Free Love: A Note on the Rhetorical Structure in the *Romance of the Rose*," *Romance Notes* 8 (1966): 112-115, discusses the variety of interpretations given the story. Typical of the tradition is Arnulf of Orleans's comment on the story, as told in the *Metamorphoses* by Ovid, which concentrated on the crippling results of the passionate involvement; Vulcan's chains become, instead, the representation of the lovers' own feelings: "Quae quidem virtus prava consuetudine illiciti fervoris quasi cathena constringitur" (Ghisalberti, "Arnolfo," p. 210). On the other hand, Ovid, in telling the same story in the *Ars Amatoria*, book 2, lines 550-600, emphasizes the lesson that men must not pry too closely into their lovers' activities. Jean de Meun picks up this interpretation in the speech of the Old Woman.

14. We are not suggesting here the richly allegorical sense of natural fruitfulness which Jean de Meun ironically advocates, through his evocation of Alanus de Insulis's *Complaint*. Rather, we are referring to the earthy wisdom of the *Decameron*, which may well be indebted to the tradition of natural fruitfulness growing from Alanus, but which presents a different aspect from Jean. For Boccaccio sexual energy is natural, opposed in its vitality and energy to the restraint and emptiness of the social conventions, of selecting marriage partners, and so on, imposed on its naturally unharnessed power. Without appealing to supernatural defenses for the necessity to allow this power to act in human life, Boccaccio, rather in the manner of Shakesperean comedy, promises that this energy will win out and revivify mankind.

15. See Allen, *Friar as Critic*, p. 101, for a reading of the tale in very human terms from Giovanni del Virgilio.

16. Animal imagery unites the two tales and emphasizes the carnal character of love. Salutati's definition of the "natural" descent as the passage of the spirit into the body is fulfilled in these stories, which reduce the spiritualized love-seeking of Palamon and Arcite to bawdy dalliance. The exegetical overtones of these images, outlined by R. E. Kaske in "The Canticum Canticorum in the *Miller's Tale*," *Studies in Philology* 59 (1962): 480-85, only serve to underscore that love here is carnal, rather than spiritual.

17. Joseph, "Chaucerian 'Game'," p. 89, considers this particular significance of Nicholas's description as "hende."

18. The same kind of comedy is implicit in the tale's exegetical echoes, as Kaske so well shows in "The Canticum Canticorum in the *Miller's Tale*," pp. 479-500. Universally, laughter results from the awareness of incongruity; medieval laughter is more moral than ours, and less often simply an expression of the fact that the one laughing is relieved to distance himself from some threatening or absurd situation, because the medieval sense of the congruous, and so of incongruity, had a larger and more well defined base in reality.

19. As we saw above, the Reeve's error, unlike that of the quiting critics, is to assume that the Miller's story is intended to say something applicable to all carpenters and so necessarily to himself. His error is that he cannot see that the brunt of the story is not John as carpenter but rather John as the authority figure in a marriage.

20. Glending Olson, in "The *Reeve's Tale* as a Fabliau," *Modern Language Quarterly* 35 (1974): 230, distinguishes between Chaucer's fidelity to the fabliau genre in the *Reeve's Tale* and the author's elaborate reworking of fabliau motifs in other tales, particularly the Merchant's. His suggestion that the *Merchant's Tale* is more than a fabliau applies, we think, to the *Miller's Tale* as well. The evocation of Christian symbols, their interweaving in the fabliau, places the *Miller's Tale*, generically as well as thematically, between the high seriousness of the Knight and the low comedy of the Reeve.

21. E. D. Blodgett, in "Chaucerian *Pryvetee* and the Opposition to Time," *Speculum* 51 (1976): 493, characterizes the whole of the first fragment as "the steady play on the notion of 'pryvetee.'" The opposition of moral precept and the secrets that resist it, both in God's perfect knowledge and in man's guilty attempts to conceal his sin, it evoked throughout the tales and is linked clearly to the effort to understand the conflict between "ernest" and "game" (pp. 482–83). The theme of "pryvetee" is discussed profitably elsewhere, as well; Blodgett provides a helpful summary of this scholarship on the first fragment, pp. 473–93.

22. This series of tales began with Theseus's triumphal parade; it is fitting that in the *Cook's Tale* we should return to the same motif, reduced now to a mere amusement, and the occasion of shirking lawful work and responsibility. The ceremonial presence of authority, at first Trajanlike, is now disorder.

23. Perkyn's running off to see "any ridyng was in Chepe" (I [A] 4377) ironically reminds us of the triumphal parade of Theseus, and its evocation of Trajan.

5

The Tales of Magic

After the *Cook's Tale* there is nothing to do but start over. After the givenness of intentional social order has been allowed to degenerate into a commercial ménage à trois, and the duty of awarding a virgin has been transformed, by way of providing for a priest's bastard's daughter, to procuring for prostitutes, Chaucer turns from an array of orders in action to a normative array of disorders as such. These tales, which we consider under the rubric of magic, are the most miscellaneous in Chaucer's collection, and appropriately so, because disorder is infinitely various and miscellaneous. Important here are acts of real magic and the kindred deceptions which result from deceitful or mistaken appearances. In each case there is something, or someone, intrusive and individual, whose particular notion of truth, justice, and order is imposed on a situation. In each case also there is a particular area of human concern, or a particular part or level of reality, upon which disorder intrudes. These three elements—magic, intrusive individual, and the array of situations intruded upon—not only exemplify disorder but also define it. In the General Prologue it was both important and most interesting to ask the question, What general definition of man is implied by illustrating it in terms of arrays of status, learning, and stewardship?; here it is equally instructive to ask the question, What can we learn about human order by seeing what threatens it, and by seeing what areas of human concern are vulnerable to threat?

The importance of individualism as the basis of disorder is well illustrated by Robert Holkot's interpretation of the Phaeton story. After telling how Phaeton took the chariot of the sun and with it brought the world nearly to ruin, he concludes: "Ita contingeret istis fatuis et praesumptuosis qui de divina gubernatione murmurant. Sed si secundum eos fieret gubernatio pro sua affectione sentiunt, et facerent sua fatuitate, ut tota mundi machina solveretur."[1] Such ruin, of course, is one possible result of skepticism, or of a nominalism run to excess. In the chiming slogans of popular rebellion, "When Adam delved and Eve span, who was then the gentleman," Chaucer would have been only too aware of the dangers which come when one tries to "take but degree away." In the tales of magic, Chaucer examines the possibilities and, with one exception, finds them wanting.

It is possible, even here among the magical tales themselves, to find an architectonic and contrapuntal order. In the earlier series, from *Knight's Tale* to *Cook's Tale*, we have a clear and simply linear series, through which authorities degenerate but justice (poetic if not legal) operates almost to the end. In the magic group coherence is, as might be expected, far more complicated. Several principles seem to be operating simultaneously, which together generate an order at the verbal or storial level which at once echoes an order which ought to be operating in the stories but is not, and organizes them into a mutually commenting series, in the typological fashion we have already defined. One such principle is the relationship of parody, by which the basic point of one story is repeated in another, but at another level. Another is the principle of thematic echo—as ordered here, the story series will introduce a theme, such as gentilesse, in one story, and elaborate a treatment of it in the next. These echoes interlock as well, forming a kind of thematic enthymeme. Another is the principle of echoed gloss—very often, here as elsewhere, Chaucer will include a detail which, to the medieval mind, has a conventional association based on some glossing tradition. Then, in the same or the next or a following tale, what was first evoked by allusion to an unstated gloss will receive explicit treatment. Finally, there is the principle of linear series, already established so clearly in the first group of tales.

The series begins with the *Tale of St. Cecilia*. Following the critical principle announced earlier, of taking prologues seriously as prologues, we should pay particular attention to what the Second Nun says by way of introduction, not as a way of understanding her, but as Chaucer's way of making a beginning for a series and of introducing and justifying the large concerns which that series will exemplify and define. In this prologue material there is a good deal of the sententious—a good deal of material that would qualify under the rubric of *accessus* as *definitiva, probativa, refutativa*. The stories which follow, of course, belong to the *modus tractandi* of *exemplorum positiva;* if we are to receive them as exempla, we must first be told what they exemplify. This the prologue does.

At the outset we are advised to avoid the counsel of the *Romance of the Rose:*

> The ministre and the norice unto vices,
> Which that men clepe in Englissh ydelnesse,
> That porter of the gate is of delices,
> To eschue, and by hire contrarie hire oppresse,
> That is to seyn, by leveful bisynesse,
> Wel oghten we to doon al oure entente,
> Lest that the feend thrugh ydelnesse us hente.
>
> For he that with his thousand cordes slye
> Continuelly us waiteth to biclappe,
> Whan he may man in ydelnesse espye,
> He kan so lightly cache hym in his trappe,
> Til that a man be hent right by the lappe,
> He nys nat war the feend hath hym in honde.
> Wel oghte us werche, and ydelnesse withstonde.
>
> And though men dradden nevere for to dye,
> Yet seen men wel by resoun, douteless,
> That ydelnesse is roten slogardye,
> Of which ther nevere comth ne good n'encrees,
> And syn that slouthe hire holdeth in a lees
> Oonly to slepe, and for to ete and drynke,
> And to devouren al that othere swynke,
>
> And for to putte us fro swich ydelnesse,
> That cause is of so greet confusioun,
> I have heer doon my feithful bisynesse...
>
> (VIII [G] 1-24)

That is, to tell the story of Saint Cecilia.

The prologue continues with a lengthy *Invocatio ad Mariam,* the subject of an extensive analysis by Paul Clogan,[2] and a translation of the etymologizing on Saint Cecilia's name from the *Legenda Aurea.* The *Invocatio* talks about faith and works, and makes at least this storytelling a work of business fit for the kingdom. The etymologizing underlines, by elaboration of metaphor, the proper ethical application of the story. Taken as a whole, this prologue tells us three very important things. First, this series of stories will not be concerned fundamentally and sententiously with carnal love—though that, for some of them, is their actual subject. Loving and lusty behavior, rather, is exemplary of something of larger significance, in the way more nearly defined by the original poems of Alanus than by the incorrigibly sex-only orientation of the *Romance of the Rose*.[3] Second, and to the same end, this prologue's emphasis on work, on the human condition, which Mary is supposed to help, and on the metaphoric applications of names, encourages us to take all the stories as exempla of *consuetudo* and *credulitas*, and that to earthly and ethical significances. Third, the prologue is an introduction, by explicit reference, to the *Friar's Tale* ("He nys nat war the feend hath hym in honde") and the *Pardoner's Tale* ("And though men dradden nevere for to dye"), as well as to the *Tale of St. Cecilia*—that is, to the three tales in this nine-tale series which deal with a divine intrusion into human affairs, rather than a human intrusion into some condition of ethical reality. As such, the introduction frames and introduces disorder, as it were, *in bono*, as we shall see. These tales frame the others; together, they are a normative array *in bono* and *in malo*. Pervasive in them all is a sense of what theologians call today "otherness"—one may call it a sense of the presence of God, a folktale atmosphere, a sense of archetype, hauntedness, magic. Under any name this dimension of the tales is appropriate to a treatment of the relation between order and disorder in a world whose ultimate orderliness is achieved either by miracle or after death.

The *Tale of St. Cecilia* is, as first in the series, the special and defining case. The *Friar's Tale* presents the retributive intrusion of the devil into the exploitative world of a wicked summoner; the *Pardoner's Tale* presents the intrusion of death into the order of drunken riot; both come to divinely good ends. But both are still, in human terms, both disorderly and about disorder. Saint Cecilia, on the other hand, is the single limiting case. Only the saint has absolute rights to civil disobedience; only by virtue (literally) of the grace of God does one have the power and the right to oppose one's individual, intrusive, invisibly crowned convictions to the good order of normal society. When the saint confronts the Roman Empire, it is the empire which eventually loses; when the Wife of Bath (and all others like her) wishfully defy the right of time to bring an old age, she must herself lose, and by losing convict and denounce, however nostalgically and with whatever bittersweet and Kittredgean regret, the faerie values and virtues by which one pretends, for a time, to swap loathly old age for youth again.

In this normative array of disorder, then, the *Tale of St. Cecilia* is properly first, to remind us that all human arrangements and all ethical generalizations stand under possible correction from miracle and revelation, and at the same time to point, by contrast, to the futility of all intrusions and all disorders which lack the miracle of divine sanction.[4]

Chaucer underlines this contrast by parody, in the very next tale. Bruce Rosenberg has explained in full and elegant detail the parallelism which at once unites and contrasts these two tales, and so it is unnecessary here to do more than reaffirm the irony and underline the futility of merely human attempts at metamorphosis, by alchemy or magic or any other false power.[5] It is, however, appropriate to mention that this series of human disorders, descending from and introduced by the saint's life, is distinguished from that saint's life, and introduced to the pilgrimage, by the most sweatingly violent intrusion into the world of the pilgrimage to be found anywhere in the links.

When the Canon's Yeoman intrudes upon the company of the pilgrimage, the series of disorders which he initiates seems merely miscellaneous but becomes ostentatiously linear when once we wonder what kind of order, in each case, is being violated. In alchemy, clearly, the fundamental order of elements, of natural substances, is the one which the fraudulent Canon seeks to overturn by changing base metals into gold and silver. In the *Squire's Tale* the slightly less fundamental but still natural barriers between sincerity and treason, between one place and another, between health and ill health, and between species are to be overcome by the magic horse, mirror, sword, and ring. Moreover, the fable of the faithless tercelet has birds aping the status of men and begins a discussion of gentilesse which will extend over several tales. The fundamental distinction made here is that between good behavior or appearance and the intrinsic gentilesse that comes from birth or some other absolute. Values, in the absolute sense, remain ambiguous. The *Franklin's Tale* also involves an intrusion upon an order of nature, in this case, a rocky coastline, but devolves into two more central concerns—the question of sovereignty between husband and wife, and the question of the relative gentilesse of members of three different status classes, knight, squire, and clerk. In the *Franklin's Tale*, moreover, there are quite pointed discussions of magic as false manipulation of appearances, and equally pointed assertions, by Dorigen, that her private notion of the world's good is more correct than God's. The Wife of Bath continues the discussion of sovereignty in marriage but comes to more radical conclusions; both her tale and her prologue, moreover, attempt fundamental misconstructions of the value and power of time—or successive history—the Wife by adopting experience as authority without accepting the old age whose wisdom that experience should produce, the loathly lady by being able herself to renew her youth and beauty. The *Friar's Tale* and the *Summoner's Tale* are both concerned with gifts, and with all the proprieties and agreements and relationships which result when people give gifts to one another. The fact that in both cases the gifts actually given involve elements of disaster should not prevent us from seeing through the ironies to the medieval truth, that *donum* or more properly *beneficium* was a fundamental instrument of social order. The *Physician's Tale* recounts a violation of the responsibility of a judge and governor—the theme of *iudicium,* which involves both the labeling of crime and the corresponding responsibility for the good of dependents, Chaucer underlines in a long initial digression. Finally, the *Pardoner's Tale* returns, inversely, to the beginning. As the saint finds a good end, with a holy virtue which not even the Roman Empire can withstand, so the three rioters find their bad end, representing as they do no order but the morning drunkenness of the tavern.

The progress here, from *Canon's Yeoman's Tale* to *Pardoner's Tale,* is from general to particular. From the general order of nature as a whole, composed of substances and distances and orders of creatures, we move to the smaller question of status, by which human society is ordered, and the still smaller question of time and history, by which changes occur that lead to wisdom. Still narrower in scope is the structure of *beneficium,* which in the Middle Ages never lost the personal involvement of individuals who gave and received and were therefore related. Narrower still is *iudicium,* by which the opinion of a single individual is received as true—and the British tradition of case law, already by Chaucer's time well established, would have underlined this individualism even when it was still possible, scholastically and philosophically, to believe in universal or natural law. At the same time, of course, idealistic notions of office and stewardship, analogous to the doctrine of the king's two bodies, which theoretically protected sovereignty from mere royal caprice, would have seen this individualism as orderly. Beyond this in the *Pardoner's Tale* is riot, chaos, and death.

Nature, status, history, benefice, and judgment are sociological or anthropological factors on the basis of which a coherent understanding of society may be easily formulated; such an understanding, however theoretically and abstractly devised, would turn out to fit the Middle Ages quite well. In order to realize this fact beyond doubt, it is only necessary to see that modern Western society is based on none of them, except perhaps judgment, and that of quite a different and less sacramental kind. We have in fact transmuted lead into gold, and B. F. Skinner at least claims to communicate with pigeons. Our factors, corresponding to these, would probably be technology, rank, process, contract, and expertise—on the basis of these, our society is very different, and very differently ordered, from that of the Middle Ages. Thus, Chaucer's intrusive disorders threaten, and in threatening, define, a medieval set of orders, not a modern one. This is most important. Neither order nor disorder is absolute; both may exist in various modes, depending on their interrelationships, and on the structure of the whole in which they operate. Above a certain level, all perfections must be defined by negation; Chaucer's array of disorders is calculated to define the perfection of his sense of order, and we will miss the greater part of his message if we do not keep firmly and emphatically in mind its difference from our own.

As we have shown, the intrusive disorders with which Theseus had to deal in the *Knight's Tale* traced to the fact that he had taken under his sovereignty an unawarded Amazon virgin and two Theban royal cousins. It is therefore most appropriate that the disorders in this magic group tend to arise most out of two general problems—the problem of awarding some woman (usually a virgin, but once and repeatedly a widow) in marriage, and the problem of male fellowship, usually for the sake of gold. Death, moreover, is much talked about and sometimes experienced in these magic tales. Love, as a source of physical life, struggles with death in the tales of the Second Nun, the Wife of Bath, the Franklin, and the Squire. In the first two, lovers stand under sentence of death, one for a higher and the other for a lower standard of love than their society admitted. In the second two, death is considered a possible relief from the difficulties of love. Lust for gold threatens to kill the souls of the protagonists in the tale of the Canon's Yeoman, the Friar, and the Summoner. The two senses of death, physical and spiritual, unite in the story of the Pardoner, in which avarice leads to violent crime and death.[6] In addition to these obvious links of plot and character, the stories have in common a considerable preoccupation with the imagery of sight and the problem of perception.

The tale of Saint Cecilia begins with a version of Emelye's prayer:

> She nevere cessed, as I writen fynde,
> Of hir preyere, and God to love and drede,
> Bisekynge hym to kepe hir maydenhede.

(VIII [G] 124-26)

The result of this prayer is a rather wife-dominated marriage, based on an initial, private, secret agreement, obviously evoking the marriage worked out between Arveragus and Dorigen.[7] But Cecilia is no Amazon, and these arrangements, miraculous and disordering though they be in earthly terms, have divine sanction. To the unbaptized there is nothing particularly distinguished about Cecilia; for the baptized she wears a halo of heavenly roses and is accompanied by a heavenly guardian. Cecilia is, in a sense, the true alchemist's stone, for she is the material of the earth transmuted into a saint and thus a citizen of the heavenly city. Throughout the tale the emphasis is not on the violences perpetrated against the Christians, but rather on the strength and power of conversion, which has given the Christians themselves, whom Rome perceives as merely disorderly, a vision and foretaste of heaven.

The Canon and his yeoman, on the other hand, would not be able to see the heavenly crown. The prologue to their tale introduces two themes or narrative motifs—intrusion into an existing world, and the betrayal of fraternal relationships. The intrusion motif is fundamental for this group of tales; some variation of the motif of fraternal relationship occurs in a great many tales throughout the collection, and all relate to that initial fraternal relationship, itself betrayed, defined by the interaction of Palamon and Arcite. The intrusion parodies the miraculous one which preceded it; the Canon's Yeoman's betrayal of his master both evokes the fraternal dissension between Palamon and Arcite and introduces the confidence game which will be the object of the tale itself. These two tales, the saint's life and the tale of alchemical fraud, make an elegantly balanced pair. Rosenberg's explanation of this relationship we have already noted; here we should mention his emphasis on sight: "Insight leads Cecile to love God; mere physical sight causes the Canon and the priest to love the things of this world, and thus they turn away from God."[8] Rosenberg goes on to identify the bonds of imagery which draw together, through common words and descriptions, these two stories of heavenly and earthly transformations. As a pair, these two stories serve as guideposts to the two types of stories which will follow. In one, God creates a kingdom of safety and glory for his virgin brides, preparing for them crowns of glory which mark them out among the faithful—there follow other brides and other safeties, more and more ironic and disastrous until, for Virginia, her bodily beauty is merely bad luck. In the other, the devil brands his dupes with a special kind of blindness which makes them see gold where there is none—there follow other dupes who see a good business partner where there is none and a chance for a pot of gold where there is none.

In the *Squire's Tale* we have a kingdom with a perfect king: "So excellent a lord in alle thyng./Hym lakked noght that longeth to a kyng" (V [F] 15-16). For him the usual disorders which beset society are to be solved by magic tools—the horse, the ring, the mirror, and the sword. He has an unawarded virgin, a daughter, who is to be won (eventually) much as was Emelye. As it stands, the tale is introductory, expository, almost eventless.[9] The only complete action is the enclosed tale of the faithless tercelet, which the ring permits Canacee to hear, and perhaps be warned by.

In this tale we might pause at two significant allusions—the incident of the knight's riding armed into the banqueting hall, including a reference to Gawain, and the description of the faithless tercelet as like a snake and a tomb. The first permits one to suppose that Chaucer knew the *Gawain and the Green Knight;* the second, given Chaucer's language, seems clearly to relate to Christ's denunciation of the scribes and Pharisees in Matthew 23: as "whited sepulchres" and "generation of vipers." It is, we believe, generally recognized that Chaucer often derived his best ironies from implicit allusion and gloss.[10] From these we should learn two very important things about disorder.

First, the intrusive, magical knight in *Gawain and the Green Knight* brings disorder, not order, as do his conventional analogues in the romance tradition. *Gawain and the Green Knight* has been variously interpreted;[11] but all critics would certainly agree that the poem deals with an apparently disorderly intruder into an ordered world, who brings one member of that world to see that the full truth about whatever is true is more complicated and less stable than he had thought. The Squire's intrusive magic knight, clearly, teaches rather the opposite lesson. To the court of the already perfect king he brings a magical icing on the kingly cake—after this, nothing should ever go wrong. The ironies are obvious—and once seen in terms of secular order and disorder, the gifts of the intrusive knight are a parallel and parody of the gifts of God personified in Saint Cecilia and her Christian fellowship.

It is therefore most appropriate that the Squire's developed interpretation of these gifts should be a "lewed" one, full of disagreement and comic pretentiousness, and references to contradictory legendary analogues. Chaucer is implicitly telling us what our opinion is worth if we wish to be impressed with these marvels. There is no need to analyze such obvious comedy in detail. For the sake of illustration, however, one might note that the word *horsly* with which the commons commend the magic horse, a word that Chaucer possibly coined,[12] is itself a parody of the human interest in definition. Such words as *manly, kingly,* and *queenly* are common parlance and indicate by their existence a pervasive human interest in the essence of something admired. But normally and straightly, such words tend to be made on the names of things noble, superior, and human—in contrast to which this "horsly" seems as incongruous as Eliza Doolittle's father in his wedding clothes.

The relation of the faithless tercelet to the hypocritical scribes and Pharisees of the Gospel is clear in Chaucer's introduction of him:

> Right as a serpent hit hym under floures
> Til he may seen his tyme for to byte,
> Right so this god of loves ypocryte
> Dooth so his cerymonyes and obeisaunces,
> And kepeth in semblaunt alle his observaunces
> That sownen into gentillesse of love.
> As in a toumbe is al the faire above,
> And under is the corps, swich as ye woot,
> Swich was this ypocrite, both coold and hoot.
>
> (V [F] 512-20)[13]

According to Hugh of St. Cher, the exegete who most frequently seems to fit Chaucer,[14] the Gospel denunciation may be applied to "prelati et magistri nostri temporis exterioris nitidi, interius fetidi."[15] For our purposes this connection between the faithless tercelet and the scribes and Pharisees, and through them to "praelati et magistri," expands the significance of this bird-fable love story to politics in general and permits us to relate this hypocrisy and irresponsibility to the frauds and crimes of the alchemist and the unjust Apius at least, and probably to the appearance-making magician of the *Franklin's Tale* as well. The allusion, that is, permits one to generalize from a tale about love to a general insight about true and false responsibility in human relationships at large—that is, to see the faithless tercelet as representing a specific case of general disorder.

This love affair of birds also looks forward to the *Franklin's Tale:* the courtly love posturing through which both relationships are established; the falcon's agreement to obey, "kepynge the boundes of my worshipe evere" (V [F] 571), balancing Arveragus's agreement to obey "save that the name of soveraynetee" (V [F] 751); the departure of both males for the sake of honor—all these resemblances link the two stories. If the *Squire's Tale* is first of all an ironic undercutting of the magic that overcomes natural and inevitable difficulties, it is in its enclosed exemplum about gentilesse, and the rhetorics and hypocrisies and relationships within which gentilesse is defined, achieved, and betrayed. Gentilesse, of course, is the ground and definition of medieval status, the basis of social and even moral distinction.

It is therefore fitting that prologue material should have to do with gentilesse. The Squire's prologue is inconsequential; the Franklin's seems to be largely concerned with the relation between rhetoric and gentilesse, and with the desirability of learning "gentillesse aright."[16] As the *Squire's Tale* has already made clear, the fit description of any ideal (in this case Canacee) requires

> ... a rethor excellent
> That koude his colours longynge for that art,
> If he sholde hire discryven every part.
>
> (V [F] 38-40)

Though the Squire does not think himself such a rhetor, the Franklin admires him as at least well on the way toward it and wishes that his own son were the equal of the Squire. That he is not, the Franklin blames on gambling (a link with the chaos of both the *Cook's Tale* and the of *Pardoner's Tale*) and on lack of good example. This, since the Franklin is a self-confessed "burel man," and since the Squire has presumably the example of his knightly father, is an admission of the Franklin's own deficiencies as an exemplary father. The prologue material, then, which links the *Squire's Tale* and the *Franklin's Tale*, relates status or gentilesse to rhetoric, to example, and to family. In doing so, the prologue announces the terms of the debate implicit in the stories, since the relative merits of birth and breeding, or family and example, are explicitly discussed and the necessity of rhetoric is equally explicit in Chaucer's skill as a storyteller.

The importance of rhetoric, both as a verbal technique and as the name for a complex focus of human ethical concern, cannot be too strongly emphasized. Aristotle's *Rhetoric*, after all, is in practice a manual for the expert manipulation of status differences as this manipulation enhances persuasive communication. Its medieval circulation in ethical and political contexts rather than in contexts involving the verbal arts makes clear the very practical value which medieval people placed on such activities.[17] Rhetoric, perceived medievally, was the prescribed behavior by means of which one constituted one's self a certain kind of social person. Rhetorical behavior determined kind, because it expressed status; it necessarily determined one's social being, because it governed all intelligibly decorous communication.

It is in these terms that we must see the *Franklin's Tale*—not as the deciding tale in Kittredge's marriage group,[18] but as a tale in which disorderly agreements about sovereignty and disorderly aspirations to possession and power come to no bad end largely because people try, in further disorderly fashion, to be more genteel than they really are. The fact that, in merely human terms, Dorigen and Arveragus have a happier marriage than does the Wife of Bath, or the Merchant's January and May, or Walter and Griselda, is significant only when thrown into relief by a modern determination to see it in the context of a marriage group. In isolation the courtliness of their relationship is ironic, even a little silly, and the contest in gentilesse is compromised by overtones of social climbing. In the context of a group of tales in which things are not as they seem—that is, in Ovidian terms, tales of magic—the fundamental disorderliness of their attitudes and arrangements becomes more visible. The happy ending is, in its own way, as much an ironic accident as is the poetic justice of the *Miller's Tale* or the double twist of the *Knight's Tale,* whereby each of the rivals gets what he prayed for, but no more. What the accident overrules is, in fact, the most explicit preference for human desire over what God has done in all the *Canterbury Tales.* The Summoner and the alchemical Canon are uglier, and the Pardoner's rioters are more blasphemous, but Chaucer's language here in the *Franklin's Tale* is the most clearly theological:

> Eterne God, that thurgh thy purveiaunce
> Ledest the world by certein governaunce,
> In ydel, as men seyn, ye no thyng make.
> But, Lord, thise grisly feendly rokkes blake,
> That semen rather a foul confusion
> Of werk than any fair creacion
> Of swich a parfit wys God and a stable,
> Why han ye wroght this werk unresonable?
> . . . .
> I woot wel clerkes wol seyn as hem leste,
> By argumentz, that al is for the beste,
> . . . .

> ... this [is] my conclusion.
> To clerkes lete I al disputison.
> But wolde God that alle thise rokkes blake
> Were sonken into helle for his sake!
>
> (V [F] 865–72, 885–86, 889–92)

And when Dorigen explains to Averagus her predicament, her language explicitly prefers her own judgment above the will of God: "This is to muche, and it were Goddes wille" (V [F] 1471).[19]

What this theologizing wants, really, is what the intrusive knight brings to Cambyuskan—that is, the magical power to overcome all naturally imposed obstacles to private desire and private good. To Dorigen nature has no purpose except to make her emotionally comfortable, and her fundamental and disorderly silliness is betrayed by the fact that she expresses her need and love for her husband and his safety by an impulsive promise to betray the very relationship with him which made her worry in the first place.[20] The happy ending of this relationship, which evokes that of the *Knight's Tale,* is as privately idyllic as can be desired:

> Arveragus and Dorigen his wyf
> In sovereyn blisse leden forth hir lyf.
> Nevere eft ne was there angre hem bitwene.
> He cherisseth hir as though she were a queene,
> And she was to hym trewe for everemoore.
>
> (V [F] 1551–55)

She is, however, not a queen, and "sovereyn blisse" is, in fact, reserved to heaven. The desire for an intrusive miracle, which will overcome natural evil, and the desire to pass responsibility, in a pinch, to someone else, which are the chief characteristics of Dorigen's sense of the order of things, are really appropriate to, and workable for, the saint. And in fact, as Donald Howard has shown, there are substantial parallels between this tale and the story of Saint Cecilia.

> The marriage of Cecile and Valerian begins with a vow of chastity ... just as the marriage in the *Franklin's Tale* has begun with a vow of courtesy and mutual concession. The husband, with a lack of resistance probable only in hagiography, agrees to baptism and a life of chastity and he joins Cecile in the destiny of purity and martyrdom which the angel announces for them. The marriage here, unlike any previously mentioned, is the vehicle for Christian works.... There is a kind of mutuality in their relationship, a lack of any noticeable element of "maistrye." This, of course, is strikingly like the relationship in the *Franklin's Tale,* and it points to a crucial contrast. The vow in the *Franklin's Tale* is one of mutual concession; its purpose is the establishment of earthly concord. But the vow of the *Second*

Nun's Tale is a mutual subjugation of both their wills to the will of God, and its end is an eternal reward.[21]

The parallels redound ironically to reprove the *Franklin's Tale*'s values, particularly since we should admit that the vows here are not really for the establishment of earthly concord but rather attempt the creation of a special case of concord, disorderly in its very essence because of the contradictory commitments it involves.

The other significant feature of the *Franklin's Tale* is the gentilesse contest, in which a squire attempts to demonstrate that he is as good as a knight, and a clerk that he is as good as a squire. Their mutual emulation is a parodic echo of the recognition in the Franklin's prologue that gentilesse depends upon good example; the fact that in each case, from knight to squire to clerk, the exercise of gentilesse consists of undoing rather than fulfilling the obligation of a plighted "truth" further underlines the essential disorderliness of this contest, whose only accidental result is an all-around happy ending—apart, we must presume, from Aurelius's continued amorous frustration. There is, in fact, no personal desire expressed in the whole of the tale—neither Arveragus's desire to adore his wife, nor her desire to rule him, nor her desire to change nature, nor Aurelius's desire for Dorigen and therefore for the help of magic, nor the magician's desire for real pay in exchange for illusory goods, nor anyone's desire for equivalent gentilesse, which would not, if allowed free rein, upset the *totam machinam mundi*. And we should not allow the "poetic injustice" of the tale to blind us to what it proposed, however harmlessly, in the end.[22]

The Franklin, as he ends his tale, invites his audience to judgment: "Which was the mooste fre, as thynketh yow?" (V [F] 1622). With this invitation he begins a discussion of judgment which will climax with the disorderly Apius, who judges wrongly of a beautiful virgin. The same invitation is implicit in the *Wife of Bath's Tale,* covertly addressed to the audience.[23] In the tales that follow, judgment, and wrong judgment at that, becomes more and more obviously the explicit concern within the tales, and the audience is invited, not to judge, but to observe judgment being made. That is, the act which the audience is overtly invited to perform becomes by gradual and implicating degrees the subject of the fiction itself; the posture of the audience is gradually absorbed into the series of tales in order to be evaluated by the events in those tales. Rhetorically, the audience faces a picture which turns out, eventually, to have the faces of the audience on the bodies in the story, after the manner of carnival photographers' props.

The last disorder before final calamity is bad judgment pure, in the case of Apius. Before that, however, we have other disorders, which arise as bad judgment is applied to specific situations—status, history, and *beneficium*, as we have said. The tale of the Wife of Bath, fifth in the series of tales of magic, is a story neglected too often in favor of the Wife's own very colorful life history. However, this tale of Arthur's court and the sinful knight who must go on a pilgrimage to discover woman's greatest desire is an important commentary on most of the major themes of disorder we have noticed. It deals with the problem of the unawarded virgin with brutal directness. It asserts, even more radically than do the interceding ladies in the *Knight's Tale*, the desire of courtly ladies to assume control over justice—the Arthurian queen and her attendants are the ones who decide the case and send the rapist to find "what thyng is it that wommen moost desiren" (III [D] 905). It admits, more radically than either Valerian or Arveragus, the sovereignty of woman in marriage. It continues, in explicit theoretical terms, the debate over gentilesse. It treats, in most miraculous terms, the theme of magical appearance and transformation.[24] It ends with the predictable (and in practice unattainable) perfection: "And thus they lyve unto hir lyves ende / In parfit joye" (III [D] 1257–58).

It has been said many times and in many ways that the Wife of Bath's tale is a projection, into fiction, of what she desires most—the power to be young again, and to have in thrall a husband "meeke, yonge, and fressh abedde" (III [D] 1259). Failing this, she desires her audience to think of her, aged and somewhat coarse though she is, as still charming, attractive, lively, good company, and fun in bed. In this at least she has succeeded with a numerous company, of which Kittredge and Curry are only the most famous of many.[25] But in the end she will come, like Hamlet's ladies, to Yorick's end: "Now get you to my lady's chamber and tell her, let her paint an inch thick, to this favor she must come—make her laugh at that" (act 5, sc. 1, lines 212–16). And in pretending that this is not, or should not be, true, the Wife of Bath associates herself with the Pardoner's three drunken rioters, who wish to kill Death and only find him after the doom of all mortals. What the Wife wants is true only in fairy tale, and so she tells one, from a time when the realm of England was "fulfild of fayerye" (III [D] 859) instead of friars. In so doing, she wishes violated for her sake the fundamental order of time or history, which makes experience into authority by transmuting it into remembrance and wisdom. She wishes the west-to-east motion of the planets to rule the firmament; she refuses the paradox of life through death to which Donne gave classic statement in "Good Friday, Riding Westward"; she refuses to see what has always been true, though we have been best reminded of it only in modern times by Tolkien, that the Gospel is the consummate and defining fairy tale, and that its catastrophe is the only happy ending which is finally possible. Thus the Wife desires what only Saint Cecilia knows properly how to get, but refuses the saint's way of getting it, and such are the charms of her vitality and sex that we are, for a moment, distracted into believing her. Her tale, by a happy and, we hope, not accidental result of linkages and fragments, is the middle tale in this magic group, and tempts us to ignore both the first tale and the last—to avoid the necessity of sainthood by denying, for a time, the death of which the Pardoner warns, instead of accepting, as we must, both.[26]

But though the Wife's tale is a projection of what she most desires, we must not be misled by the dramatic principle into too exclusive a focus on her motivations, desires, and biography. Following the example of Shakespeare criticism, Chaucer scholars need to transcend Bradley-type concerns. Considered in medieval categories, the Wife of Bath's material consists of a vastly overblown prologue and a rather short *tractatus in narratione;* in terms of the fivefold formal cause, that is, *definitiva, divisiva, probativa, refutiva,* and *exemplorum positiva,* what we probably have, after the sententious exordium, is a section *refutiva,* the exemplum of autobiography, the exemplum of the rapist and the loathly lady, and the enclosed defining sermon on gentilesse—rather a mixed bag taken altogether as a discourse instead of as a dramatic monologue. But if one takes the Wife's beginning as Chaucer's, that all this has to do with "wo that is in mariage," then an outline emerges. The first woe of marriage is that it is the end of virginity, second that it is the destroyer of peace, third that it is almost the pain of death, and fourth that it is not conducive to nobility. It is almost a crime against human high spirits to work so homiletic an outline on what the Wife of Bath has to say, yet the ironies point this way, the habits of medieval literary criticism point this way, and the discursive context points this way. We have already seen how disorderly the first three of these themes are, relating as they do to Saint Cecilia, to the question of marital sovereignty, and to the desire to avoid old age and death. The fourth, that is, the question of and contest over gentilesse, reaches its proper conclusion here only as we see it fitted into the proper outline and labeled with the proper heading.

Gentilesse, according to conventional opinion, was to be equated with virtue,[27] not with lineage, or wealth, or any other worldly asset which might well be, and often was, possessed by scoundrels. This is true enough, both historically and morally. Yet as modern readers trying to get our history right, we must remind ourselves that this opinion was held in spite of the fact that distinctions of gentility in Chaucer's real world were very largely determined by inheritance. Organized threats to the security of this system of inheritance were put down with considerable violence, and with every appearance, on the part of the "gentle" classes, of sincere righteous indignation.[28] In the light of his situation, thus, Chaucer puts his most elaborate defense of an ethical meritocracy in exactly the right place—in the context of marriages which so far as we know neither have nor desire children, and in the mouth of a magical creature from faerie who can renew her youth.

In balance, we have the Franklin's admiration for the gentilesse of another man's son, and his concern for the deficiencies of his own—we have an emphatic connection between gentilesse and rhetoric, and a contest to see who can be the most genteel, by emulative and competitive generosity. All this is probably to be taken as the real, by contrast to the loathly lady's ideal. As an ideal, only saints are both permissible and assimilable, because their proper environment is heaven, and they impose on the world only a sweet example of moral suasion. Otherwise, idealism impinges on society as a principle of disorder, however well intentioned. It is a mark of Chaucer's genius that he puts even gentilesse here, in a tale of magic and in the context of all those private and disordering desires which intrusive individuals wish to impose on the world. He is too honest to settle only for denouncing easy and obvious evils; he deals as well with those so near good as to daunt all but the most precise of moralists. As Pratt has shown, this section grew on Chaucer[29]—the *Shipman's Tale,* the autobiography, and the tale of the loathly lady were by turns assigned as the Wife of Bath's tale; how much poorer and less profound would have been our moral profit had the Wife merely concluded, "score it upon my taille." Instead, we have the bittersweet and universal desire to get without paying the full price what the psalmist described:

> Bless the Lord, O my soul: and let all that is within me
> bless his holy name.
> Bless the Lord, O my soul, and never forget all he hath

> done for thee. . . .
> Who redeemeth thy life from destruction: who crowneth thee
> with mercy and compassion.
> Who satisfieth thy desire with good things: thy youth shall be
> renewed like the eagle's.
>
> (Ps. 102: 1–

From this point on, in the magic group, the temptations are smalle
There is no human being over forty who ever lived, medieval c
modern, who has not assented to the desire of the Wife of Bath, an
only the wisest of them have fully known what price had to be paid t
do so. The Friar and the Summoner, whose tales deal with disorde
ings of *beneficium,* and the Physician, whose tale deals with disorder c
judgment, more warn than tempt; the Pardoner, in himself and in hi
tale, drives men from sin with horror.

The *Friar's Tale* and the *Summoner's Tale* have been an embarrass
ment to fragment 3 ever since Kittredge settled lamely for the notio
of "interlude."[30] Clearly Chaucer was setting something up; it is th
Friar and the Summoner who are allowed to interrupt the Wife an
who provide the transition from her autobiography to her finall
assigned tale. And we properly expect friars after faeries, because th
Wife herself tells us to expect them.[31] Yet these tales have nothing t
do with gentilesse, nor with marriage; the fornication which alway
hovers like a leitmotif in the backgrounds of the Chaucerian regula
clergy is not really what the tales are about. Tales like this are the te
of any critical method which seeks unity, because the analysis mu
proceed tale by tale, following the divisions which are the *form
tractatus,* but it must arrange its material for analysis fragment b
fragment, accepting such relationships as have clearly been estab
lished. In our reading the *Friar's Tale* and the *Summoner's Tale* ar
here because the Wife of Bath's is clearly, on the literal level, abou
magic. It is reassuring to find that, once the fragment as a whole i
placed in the magic group, it is possible to say such coherent an
informative things about these two odd tales, as well as about the tal
of the Wife of Bath.

The tales of the magic group have to do with deceitful appearances
with trickery, with what seems to change and is really the same, wit
intrusive disorder which attacks, and in attacking defines, some aspec
of order and good. We have already said that these two tales of th
Friar and the Summoner have to do with *beneficium,* particularly in it
disorderly manifestations, and with the place of *beneficium* in the se
ries of orders, descending from general to particular, on the basis o

which society is constituted. It remains here to show in more detail just how the stories treat the theme and how the material of the stories, understood discursively, brings to bear upon the theme the theological overtones which justified its importance in medieval society.

Beneficium is a social virtue now so thoroughly out of fashion that it can hardly be understood, much less justified. Modern economic and social ethics define themselves so largely in terms of contract and quid pro quo that the rhetoric of patronage is dismissed as degrading, and gifts of any substance tend automatically to be seen as bribery. Nevertheless, the notion of *donum* or *beneficium* is at the very heart of the ordering process of medieval society and therefore should be expected to appear, in its place, in any serious treatment of social order.

The basis of the notion of *beneficium* was a God defined as gracious, whose creation and whose sacraments alike were received by men as gifts from God, and whose example of liberality was the proper model of healthy social behavior. One of the conventional duties of human sovereigns, therefore, was to be magnificent, and that magnificence includes the giving of gifts. The continual gentrification of commercial wealth, especially in the later Middle Ages, expresses the desire to rise from a world of quid pro quo (for which there was little theological and sacramental significance) to the world of fiefs in the gift of magnate or king. There may in fact have been a good deal of commercial enterprise involved in the transition, but the rhetoric was of *beneficium*. Even salaries paid to retainers, and especially those portions paid in kind, as new clothes for festive occasions, indulge the rhetoric of gifts. Though tithes may have been hard to collect, the early successes of the friars, the need for such laws as the statute of mortmain, and the popularity of cathedral building all testify to the fact that gift-giving was an important social structure, regardless of how mixed its motivation may have been. In theoretical terms, Aegidius Romanus even bases his attack on communism and his defense of private property and unequal distribution of wealth on his desire to encourage the virtue of liberality.[32]

The relation of the tales of both Friar and Summoner with gifts and gift-giving is obvious. Summoners live by bribery, and friars by gifts. The *Friar's Tale*'s point has to do with a gift sincerely given—as it happens, to a devil. The point of the *Summoner's Tale* is another gift—Thomas's fart. The final episode in the set contains a squire, in a feudal setting, earning a gift of "gowne-clooth" (III [D] 2252). These gifts, all but the last, are parodies of true *beneficium*. As do all other disorders in this magic group of tales, they intrude upon order, in this case the order of *beneficium,* which is restored in the action of the lord and his squire. But this intrusion is more than literal. It is also parodic and this dimension of parody, which is underlined and reinforced by the parodic dimensions of the discussion of devilish bodies, the location of friars in hell, glossing, "ars-metrike" (III [D] 2222), and the "transubstantial" fart, answers to the fact that *beneficium,* more obviously than any of the other orders we have considered in this group, has a transcendental dimension. Creation, once made, operates in a way which can be taken as simply natural, and status, being intimately connected with pride, tends to be exercised in a more secular manner the more one is conscious of it at all. Both, of course, have ultimate validation from God—but his presence is not in practice necessarily insistent. On the other hand, the most important *beneficium* in medieval culture, the Incarnation and its continuance in the Mass, is truly divine.[33] Of the double nature of the sacramental, of "being divine in the world," the genre of parody is structurally, as well as meaningfully, appropriate.

We begin therefore with a prologue which takes the doctrine of the Wife of Bath seriously, rejects authorities (as she had in her turn, even though she is herself one), and defends game. More serious matters are to be left to preaching and clerical pronouncement—and this in introduction of what will in fact be a good deal of explicit discussion of theological matters and an excessive straining after authority through the strategem of gloss. The topos of quiting is mentioned again and rejected. In the company there shall be no debate. What all this says, of course, is that "yes" will be "no" and "no" will be "yes." The game will be to play games with serious matters, as an activity fitting this "compaignye" or society which the rule of the Host has constituted.

If we divide what follows discursively, a diptych pattern emerges involving five elements. First, there is a definition—of ecclesiastical justice and of the place of summoners in it; then, in parallel, a definition of friars. Second, a society is constituted as a result—the summoner swears brotherhood with the fiend, and the friar claims his privileged relation with Thomas and his wife. Then there is an elaborate discussion of doctrine—on the nature of hellish bodies and their function in the world; and of glossing, intercessory prayer, and the sin of wrath. Fourth, there is a two-part exemplum, which poses a problem—the two curses in the *Friar's Tale,* and the fart and its discussion at the Lord's dinner in the Summoner's. Finally, the problems are solved. We find out from the Summoner that friars live in hell in the devil's anus; we find out from the lord's squire how to divide a fart. Both these solutions, moreover, are made distinctive and separate by rubrication. Procedurally and formally, the whole thing could not be more obviously something usually left "to prechyng and to scole eek of clergye" (III [D] 1277). And the fivefold *forma tractandi* which medieval critics were accustomed to find in their stories and poems is also obviously governing: *definitiva, divisiva, probativa, refutiva, exemplorum positiva.*

What is missing, of course, is the central panel, *in bono*—the divine definition which makes good society possible, the doctrine by which that society lives and believes, the actions which that society's history and its accumulation of exempla preserve, and the heavenly solution which causes all exempla to make sense. Irony is a form of allegory here. And the overtones which might be noted in these tales—why the devil wears green,[34] that devilish appearance and substance resemble those of angels, that the hell of the devil's anus parodies the bosom of Mary of mercies,[35] that this gift of wind blasphemously parodies the coming of the Holy Ghost upon the Apostles, with the "sound from heaven, as of a violent wind blowing"[36]—all evoke elements of truth and value appropriate to this literally absent but ironically present central panel. That these ironic stories are literally about gift-giving, then, properly implies that the central fact of the true story is God's gracious gift of salvation and his commandment that analogous graces be the chief exercise through which earthly hierarchies express themselves.

Incongruities further underline the point. The friar's willingness to take seriously the problem of the division of the fart is Chaucer's way of labeling him a materialist—a person unable to deal with the spiritual (or at least insubstantial) problem, and therefore disqualified from appreciating, or participating in, a social institution which properly is always more than material.[37] More important still is the old woman's curse against the Summoner. In orthodox terms she cannot damn her enemy without his consent; the Summoner effectively damns himself by refusing the opportunity to repent.[38] Even the fully serious and validated cursing of excommunication is of no effect, if it does not really correspond to the actual state of grace of the one being cursed.[39] But cursing and blessing are still a valid and necessary part of religion, because mutuality is the essence of it. This widow's cursing corresponds, thematically, to *beneficium*—and no less clearly because *in malo. Beneficium* is always accomplished by the agency of another; it always generates a mutuality between two or more people.

The allegorical strategy through which much of the meaning of the Friar's and Summoner's tales is generated continues in the rest of the tales of this magic group. The full meaning of the *Physician's Tale,* and of the judgment which is its theme, is only defined by considerations of the medieval glosses which it evokes and the framing exempla of the tale—the references to Pygmalion and to Jephthah's daughter. Even more, the *Pardoner's Tale* is allegorical, not just in details, but as a whole in the full typological sense defined by biblical exegesis. The reason for this larger allegorical presence in the latter tales of the magic group is, we think, that in these tales the theme of order being treated has become quite particular. In the series as a whole, from nature and status to judgment, we are going from general to particular, from universal to singular. Since, philosophically, singulars cannot be the basis of certain knowledge, the allegorical strategy functions as validation, or, as it were, universalization, of something which needs to be both particular and true.

The *Physician's Tale* is a true story, a "historial thyng notable; / The sentence of it sooth is, out of doute" (VI [C] 156–57). The relationship between the true letter and the possibility of further meaning, of true sentence, is a commonplace of exegesis and strengthens Chaucer's assertion of the value of the tale's sentence. But here, as so often in Chaucer, the allegorical overtones which allusions and the investigation of commentaries make possible are not the end for which the tale is meant, but rather reinforcements and amplifications of the literal force of the tale itself, and validations of it.

Most obviously, the tale is an exemplum of the unjust judge. As such it addresses a human problem serious at all times, but for Chaucer not quite the same problem as it might be now. In his society the judicial and the executive functions were not so thoroughly distinguished as they have since been, and the judge and his functions had sacral, or at least theological, overtones, of which secularization has since deprived us. In a society with more case law than statute law, with a great many matters theroretically decided on the basis of customs, and with relatively inefficient public administration, the individual judge and his personal activity were of great practical importance. Pierre Bersuire's definition is helpfully comprehensive:

> Nota, quod iudicare idem est quod discernere. Unde de homine sapiente et discreto in aliqua arte dicitur quod ipse est homo boni iudicii. Iudicium enim nihil aliud est quam discretio inter qualitates et conditiones rerum.... Quia nomen ergo iudicii importat status iurisdictionem negociorum cognitionem, et negociorum diffinitionem, bene patet, quod

officium iudicandi debet committi viris autenticis et honestis, viris pruden-
tibus et discretis, viris etiam Deum timentibus et perfectis. Iudex enim in
populo est sicut oculus in corpore, a quo dependet regimen corporis uni-
versi. Nam sicut oculus habet de coloribus iudicare, foveas, et pericula
precavere et praeiudicare, et cunctis membris aliis de debito regimine
praevidere, sic vere iudex debet de coloribus idest de personarum con-
ditionibus discernere, reipublicae pericula cognoscere, et omnia membra
corporis, idest omnes personas suae iurisdictionis debite gubernare.[40]

A few details might be singled out for comment. First, judgment is
grounded in perception; the judge is a person of discernment. His
discernment has much to do with the crucial element of *conditio,* with
which Chaucer was concerned in his General Prologue and which we
have already related to the *consuetudines* and *credulitates* which the
Averroistic *Poetics* of Aristotle uses to define the content of poetry. He
is clearly a ruler as well as an interpreter of statutes. On his personal
goodness the health of the body politic greatly depends.

After Dante the classic biblical citation for justice and judgment is
Wisd. 1:1, "Diligite iustitiam, qui iudicatis terram." Hugh of St. Cher's
comments on this verse define judges as spiritual men who in judging
the earth deal with "terrenos, terrena nimis diligentes." He associates
the activity of judgment with the command in Genesis, given to Adam
and Eve, to subdue the earth. Finally, he allegorizes: "Diligite iustitiam, qui iudicatis terram, idest, qui carnem vestro subditis iudicio,
ut obediat spiritui, discrete, et cum amore hoc facite, et quod iustum
est, iumento reddite, scilicet, onus, virgam, et pabulum, Eccl. 33.d.
Unde Apostolus Rom. 12.a. Rationable obsequium vestrum, nemo
enim unquam carnem suam odio habuit, sed fovet, et nutrit eam,
Eph. 5.f."[41]

All this corresponds to Apius where he is typical and reproves him
where he is wicked. He is a governor, as well as a judge, with a great
deal of discretionary authority. The responsibility which he professes
to owe to "right," that is, to natural law, to what is true rather than
merely correct, is thoroughly medieval.

> . . . "Of this, in his absence,
> I may nat yeve diffynytyf sentence.
> Lat do hym calle, and I wol gladly heere;
> Thou shalt have al right, and no wrong heere."
>
> (VI [C] 171–74)

In his lust, in his subornation of the witness, in his inability to rule
himself and his own body, in his desire to alter the "condition" of the
maid Virginia, knowing that he could never persuade her "for to

make hire with hir body synne" (VI [C] 137), he violates definition. In his desire to misappropriate his high and spiritual office as a means to accomplish, if not legalize, an act of rape, he is a bad judge by medieval standards, not only because he is attempting to do an injustice to Virginia and Virginius, but also because he has distorted himself, has turned upside down the proper relation between his own flesh and his proper spiritual wisdom, and so acts in a way which denies, rather than affirms, the metaphoric possibilities of his existence as judge which allegorically validate and confirm judgment fully accomplished.[42]

It is these dimensions which the framing exempla, of Pygmalion and Jephthah's daughter and of the evocation of the *Romance of the Rose*, emphasize and define. In the first place, though we must admit Virginia's beauty, we must also admit from the *Romance of the Rose*, and ultimately from the poem of Alanus, that the chief complaint against man was that he was too physical and not sufficiently fecund in the spirituality of good works. In addition, the evocation of the *Romance of the Rose* gives special importance to the allusion to Pygmalion, whose love of his beautiful statue, in the main tradition of commentary, meant either that his wife was frigid or that he was masturbating with the statue.[43] In neither case, nor in the very promising treatment of the *Romance of the Rose* itself, does Pygmalion's accomplishment deserve ideal commendation.

Bersuire's gloss, in fact, finds for the Pygmalion story a meaning very closely analogous to that of Apius:

> Per istum factorem imaginum intelligo predicatores qui animam sciunt sculpere, et pingere correctionibus et virtutibus, per istam puellam eburneam intelligo quamlibet sanctimonialem, que eburnea dicitur pro eo quod casta frigida ponderosa et honesta esse dicitur. Sed saepe contingit quod aliquis bonus pigmaleon, idest aliquis bonus religiosus proponit perpetuo nec mulierem nec carnales amplexus appetere et talis convertit se ad imagines eburneas faciendas, idest ad benignas sanctimoniales et matronas in castitate et sanctitate informandas, et in moribus spiritualibus sculpendas, et accidit quod quandoque unam inter ceteras sibi eligit quam sororem vel filiam dicit et eam bono ac casto animo et amore associat et tangit. Sed pro certo tandem accidit quod venus dea luxurie idest carnis concupiscentia se interponit et ipsam imaginem mortuam convertit in vivam, et ipsam castam mulierem facit carnis stimulos sentire et eam mutat de bona in fatuam. Ipse enim pigmaleon predicator hoc a venere expetit, et istam mutationem appetit. Sic igitur cum more solito ad colloquia redeunt simul se mutatos invenit, ita quod illa que fuerat eburnea, fit carnea et ille qui mulieres horrebat, incipit carnis spurciciam appetere. Isti igitur carnales sic se mutuo accipiunt, et quandoque filios generant. Non est igitur tutum religioso cum mulieribus nimiam familiaritatem contrahere vel econverso.[44]

Just as Apius was "caught with beautee of this mayde" Virginia, so the *predicator* of Bersuire's interpretation "incipit carnis spurcicia appetere." But Bersuire's gloss makes explicit what in the *Physician's Tale* is only implicit, and that is the positive duty of right judgment. The preacher exhorts the women in his charge to chastity and holiness; the judge must love justice as he judges earthly things and people. As described, Virginia, this most wondrous of nature's works, exists as an occasion for right judgment as well as a temptation to wrong judgment, and Chaucer's digression dealing with the obligation of parents and chaperones to rule their charges wisely and well is evidence that he considered her so. Apius is guilty of a sin of omission as well as commission.

So, also, in a way, is Virginius. The loss of chastity is a serious matter, but the loss of physical chastity by rape, without consent, is neither sin nor justification for suicide,[45] and Virginius's remedy is extreme. In this attempt to preserve the flesh from taint by destroying it, he has overmagnified the importance of the flesh.[46] Thus he has failed to appreciate its relatively lesser, but still true, value. Just as in the *Manciple's Tale,* the spiritual good achieved at the expense of the flesh, upon reflection, proves a hollow prize. Virginia's evocation of Jephthah's daughter is therefore precisely to the point.[47]

Glosses on the story of Jephthah's daughter are generally disapproving, and generally because human sacrifice is not considered the thing to do. But all angles are considered: Nicholas of Lyra says, for instance, "Licet autem illud votum processerit ex devotione, tamen factum fuit indiscrete: quia de domo sua primo poterat egredi obviam ei canis: qui non est animal immolaticium."[48] Hugh of St. Cher cites Augustine's suspicion of ulterior motive, "Item dicit Augustinus quod votum suum retulit ad uxorem, quam habebat odio, cogitans eam sibi occurrere primo, et ita patet, quod mala intentione vovit, ergo malum fuit eius votum."[49]

For the allegorizations of the story,[50] Pierre Bersuire's commentary provides a convenient summary. After various applications of the fact that Jephthah was a concubine's child, rejected by his family, he comes to those applications which include the daughter:

> Exponamus allegorice de Christo, dicamus itaque quod iste Iephthe significat Christum, qui revera quasi ex concubina nascitur, pro eo quod ex Deo patre et virgine matre, quae erat alterius thori et fori generatus videtur.... Iste igitur quamvis repudiatus a Iudaeis, tamen contra Amon, idest diabolum, princeps et dux filiorum Israel, idest fidelium constituitur, et pro victoria obtinenda propriam filiam, idest humanitatem Deo patri immolavit, et ipsa pro salute humani generis et pro victoria mortem

patitur, et Amon et populus suus, idest diabolus et vitia superantur, et filii Israel, idest fideles populi liberantur.... Vel dic quod Iephthe est homo, cuius filia est propria caro, quam scilicet Deo debet vovere, et per poenitentiam Deo immolandam promittere, ut contra Amon, idest contra diabolum et peccata possit obtinere victoriam. Quando igitur contingit quod homo victoriam contra vitia vel contra tribulationes habuit, vel quod a Deo donum spirituale reportavit, et videt filiam, idest, propriam carnem cum tympanis et organis, idest cum delitiis et delectationibus occurrere, et sibi in via morum obviare: statim pro certo debet dicere et clamare: Filia mea decepisti me, et ipsa decepta es. Decepisti me, dico, vitia suggerendo, sed tu ipsa decepta es, per peccatum et poenitentiam promendo. Istam igitur statim debet Deo per poenitentiam immolare, et sibi fletum proprie virginitatis, idest, compunctionem et virtutum sterilitatem iniungere, et tandem virginitate seu sterilitate deplorata, debet eam per charitatem comburere, et per laborum fatigationem et poenitentiam Deo sacrificare vel offerre.[51]

Just as the judge may by analogy be likened to the eyes, which guide the body, discern colors, and discriminate dangers, so the social relationships between father and daughter may be analogous to the relation of spirit to flesh, whereby the individual keeps his values straight and his heart right.[52] Ideally, however, the level must be good, though God can make good significance of evil events. An earthly beauty defined in terms of the kind of beauty Pygmalion made is, when fully understood, the kind to which Apius's lust is appropriate; a flesh defined by the terms of Jephthah's vow deserves the judgment of Virginius and the fate of Virginia.

We may turn profitably from the story itself to the judgment Chaucer's pilgrims make upon its meaning. The Host's interpretation is a version of Virginius's attitude—a rejection of the flesh:

> Allas, to deere boughte she beautee!
> Wherfore I seye al day that men may see
> That yiftes of Fortune and of Nature
> Been cause of deeth to many a creature.
> Hire beautee was hire deth, I dar wel sayn.
>
> (VI [C] 293-97)

Nature's achievement, from this limited perspective, is not only vain but positively harmful. Better we were all born ugly, and chastity would be easier to achieve.

No one of these many judgments on Virginia's beauty, whether coming from within the tale or in its surrounding link material, provides us with the whole truth, but from these erroneous judgments we may gain a sense of the understanding they ironically evoke. Nature's achievement is good, but not supreme; Apius, the judge, exists to place on the facts of this world, including people, value labels—good, bad, wicked, criminal, liable, innocent. Virginius exists to foster his child, and Virginia to be properly loved. And all of this should, when retold and remembered, be of some moral use. From beginning to end it is a matter of discernment, and discernment is the essence of *iudicium*. The allegorical overtones, which relate personal to social and social to personal, and make possible good insight even from bad events, tell us what the ideal harmonies are. *Iudicium* is at once so important and so difficult because it is a particular act which makes universal claims. When a human being renders sentence, an individual's perception of particulars is the basis for affirming, defining, and then applying the universal. It is the duty of a judge to be right—and at once his privilege and his awesome responsibility to create right in terms of what he decides, even when sometimes what he decides is less than perfect. This duty to be right gains complexity, in Chaucer's time, from a context in which particulars cannot, by definition, be right as objects of true knowledge, and in which universals and the possibility of knowing them are far more palpable than for us. It is the allegorical overtones, contributed primarily by the allusions which surround this simple true story of Roman injustice, which celebrate the resonances by which alone particulars may guarantee universals and which impose on the judges of Chaucer's audience the obligation to discern all of the many truths they perform in their particular attention to a cause.

The *Pardoner's Tale* is more allegorical still. Some years ago Judson Allen argued that it was one of those late medieval poems demanding a fully exegetical spiritual sense reading.[53] We still think so, but would go further, first, by relating the *Pardoner's Tale* to the structurally defined schema of the four levels and, second, by showing how both the literal and the allegorical features of the tale are thrown into sharper and clearer relief by their having been seen as a part of the group of tales to which we have assigned it. We do not intend to offer any new interpretation of the tale, or of any of its parts, characters, or details. Scholarship on the *Pardoner's Tale* has been unusually rich, and the allegorical overtones defining the old man, the tree, the Pardoner's complex sterility, and his homiletic effectiveness all have been fully and, we think, correctly explained.[54]

All four allegorical levels are present, both in the biblical sense and in the structural sense we developed earlier. The actual tale is the same for both, of course. Doctrinal overtones are unusually strong, as

Robert P. Miller has shown;[55] in merely secular terms, the tale has about it an abstract or hieratic quality which constantly forces the reader to the sense that these characters are typical and not merely individual. In addition, the readers cannot avoid some personal involvement. People who behave like these rioters will die—all men must die, we know, but the sudden end of the rioters is an insistent reminder that the death which is our common fate, and which cannot be avoided or postponed, can be hastened. Finally, there is about the tale still another dimension, which the tradition would have labeled anagogy or eschatology, and which we label prosopopoeia. Others might attempt to get at the same quality by referring to "folktale" atmosphere. What we mean has been most brilliantly explained, in secular terms, by Donald Howard, in an analogy with the work of Jean Genet.[56] The perversions which Genet's characters enact, Howard said, like the perversion which the Pardoner is and recounts, reveal to the audience, as it were like the sudden opening of a pit, the potential for evil in every one of us. A part of the effect is the powerfulness of the revelation, a part is the shock of recognition, and a part is the almost heart-stopping relief provided by the possibility of aesthetic distance. What all this awareness adds up to, we believe, can in medieval terms be labeled prosopopoeia—at least for nominalist sensibilities. It is the awareness of the presence, not just of evil people, or even evil kinds of people (or good, had it been a different story)—but rather of evilness itself, palpable and real. One of the greatest powers literature has, in all times, is this power to bring people into the presence of universals. It is a power not always present, nor even always intended, and sometimes not achieved when intended. One of the great burdens of Hardy's fiction, for instance, is that our misfortune is to live in a world without universals, yet the child in *Jude*, like the Pardoner's Old Man, comes very near to being totally transparent to that dark underside of the world outside Plato's cave. The difference between medieval and later literatures at this point is not a difference of power, but rather a difference of clarity—there were more abstractions, with names, and one could recognize the powers when they appeared and give them names. Hence prosopopoeia—a very different kind of mental state from the rationalist trick of poetry it later became.

As is universally recognized, both the Pardoner and his tale are about death. Here, as in the tale of Saint Cecilia, we are in the presence of paradox. The sainted martyr, whom the world that kills her perceives as mere disorder, is the intrusive, authentic, particular individual who has the right to be disorder in any world which so perceives her. Rome must fall, that there might be a new Rome, and ultimately a new Jerusalem. In the context of the tales of the magic group, which begins with the *Tale of St. Cecilia*, it is possible to see just what this death in the *Pardoner's Tale* is about, just how it relates to the comprehensive treatment of order and disorder in society. Death is the intrusive order, which intrudes upon all the mere arrangements of this world, defines them as disorders, and reduces them to peace (or hell). Taken in isolation, the Pardoner's exemplum of the three rioters who meet death is moral enough. We have a sense of earthy riot and deserved punishment. But if we define the *Pardoner's Tale* as, in a sense, that part of saint's life visible to merely mortal eyes, then the redeeming ironies become much larger.

The death of Death is an event whose expectation and achievement are central to the faith of Christendom. Saint Cecilia and her co-religionists were, from the point of view of orthodox pagan Rome, no less foolish than the Pardoner's rioters in their insistence that they would conquer death. The difference, of course, is that we view Saint Cecilia, whether we are personally Christian or not, from the point of view of an insider who shares, within the "fiction," her faith. We know more than the Romans do and can appreciate the ironic value of their postures and their claims to be right. In the same way, but even more naively and automatically, we know more than the Pardoner's rioters do (because the expectation of death is more universal in human experience than in Christian faith) and can appreciate the ironic values of their postures and their claims to be able to murder Death. But—and this is the difference the grouping makes—the ironies are enlarged when we see that ultimately the rioters equal the Roman empire, that all merely human arrangements are disorder before their common end, and common peace, which is death. The rioters proposed, in the drunkenness of a morning, to kill death. Rome proposed for one thousand years to be the Eternal City. The end of the rioters, though haunted by archetypes, is expected and unsurprising; the end of Rome was a cosmic shock, even to such a man of faith as Jerome. All mortal things are, by ultimate standards, disorderly, even Rome. The cry of the crusader aginst the Albigensians, "Kill them all; God will recognize his own," is at one level an unhuman horror, but at another the only proper posture of true faith. The end of the rioters is a mortal horror, and a seeming disorder at all levels. But the allegorical resonance, which was becoming increasingly audible in all these last tales and inescapable in the last, redeems that disorder even while it is dying, reminding us that facts do connect, while they last, to the truth which neither changes nor dies, whose symbol is the crowns of lilies and roses that only faith can see. Of the great ordering structures into which facts may fit themselves, and from which they derive their meaning—sainthood, nature, status, history, *beneficium, iudicium,* and death—the last and most difficult is death. But in context we are given a double vision of death—as just punishment within the world of the rioters and the Pardoner, and as the last and anagogical peace from the point of view defined by having seen order in dialectic with disorder throughout the series. And we are reminded once again of that quality of Chaucer's faith in life which is the central measure of his greatness—that ironic, gentle handling of fallible facts which accepts their failures even while it sees the truth they bring in resonant focus.

1. Robert Holkot, *In librum Sapientiae* (Basel, 1586), lectio 9, p. 33. "Thus it would happen to those foolish and presumptuous ones who complain about the divine authority. But if the administration were conducted according to what they feel would be in their interest, and they would act according to their foolishness, the whole machine of the universe would be destroyed."

2. Paul Clogan, "The Figural Style and Meaning of the Second Nun's Prologue and Tale," *Medievalia and Humanistica,* n.s. 3 (1972), pp. 213–40.

3. The ironic contrast between the sterility of fecund concupiscence and the fecundity of childless chastity is often invoked, with its roots growing perhaps from the complex redefining of love relationships going on in all the intellectual movements of the Middle Ages. Cf. Abelard's comforting remarks to Heloise on her spiritual children, who must replace the children of her body, which she regrets being unable to bear (letter 4, p. 90, in "The Personal Letters between Abelard and Heloise," *Mediaeval Studies* 16 [1953]: 47–94).

4. This is the lesson of the prologue combat as well. Unholy interruptions and confusion are rewarded by rude insults and verbal abuse. Only the Knight, at the conclusion of the tales of the Pardoner and the Monk, speaks in the cause of peace.

5. Rosenberg, "The Contrary Tales," pp. 278–91.

6. The problem of old age, exemplified by men in their efforts to recapture youth by marrying young and wild wives, is raised in the first fragment. In the *Miller's Tale,* a family unit is formed of a foolish old man and a young, straying wife—a pattern which will be repeated in the story collection and then in the Reeve's Prologue, with its ironic evocation of the humility topos, as the Reeve excuses himself from indulging in ribaldry because of his advanced age (I [A] 3867–98).

7. Cecilia's love is praised by Edmund Reiss, in "Chaucer's *fyn lovynge* and the Late Medieval Sense of fin amor," pp. 181-92, in *Medieval Studies in Honor of Lillian Herlands Horstein*, ed. Jess B. Bessiger, Jr., and Robert R. Raymo (New York, 1976); by Clogan, "The Figural Style and Meaning of the Second Nun's Prologue and Tale," pp. 237-40; and by Howard, *The Idea of the Canterbury Tales*, pp. 290-92.

8. Rosenberg, "The Contrary Tales," p. 290.

9. On the Squire's problems in managing his rhetorical flourishes, see D. A. Pearsall, "The Squire as Story-teller," *University of Toronto Quarterly* 34 (1964): 82-92.

10. A very brief theoretical definition of this technique, relating it to the ironic mode of allegory, may be found in Allen and Gallacher, "Alisoun through the Looking Glass." The same presumption is the basis of Allen's "The Old Way and the Parson's Way" and "The Ironic Fruyt: Chauntecleer as Figura," *Studies in Philology* 66 (1969): 25-35. The most elaborate study of this kind, and the one leading to the most properly subtle conclusions about the effect of the Chaucerian story, is Kaske, "The Canticum Canticorum in the *Miller's Tale*."

11. We are most convinced by J. A. Burrow, *A Reading of Sir Gawain and the Green Knight* (New York, 1966), and Larry D. Benson, *Art and Tradition in Sir Gawain and the Green Knight* (New Brunswick, N.J., 1965).

12. "Therwith so horsly, and so quyk of ye" (V [F] 194). The *OED* lists this line of Chaucer's as the only medieval occurrence.

13. Cf. Matt. 23:27, 33: "Vae vobis scribae et pharisaei hypocritae quia similes estis sepulchris dealbatis, quae a foris parent hominibus speciosa, intus vero plena sunt ossibus mortuorum, et omni spurcitia! . . . Serpentes genimina viperarum, quomodo fugietis a iudicio gehennae?" "Woe to you, Scribes and Pharisees, hypocrites! because you are like white sepulchres, which outwardly appear to men beautiful, but within are full of dead men's bones and of all uncleanness. . . . Serpents, brood of vipers, how are you to escape the judgment of hell?" This allusion may suggest a connection between the blandishing tongues of the tercelet and of Chaucer's clergymen, the friar and the summoner, who will soon appear in tales devoted to their wicked speech. Penn R. Szittya, in "The Friar as False Apostle: Antifraternal Exegesis and the *Summoner's Tale*," *Studies in Philology* 71 (1974): 41, finds this same quotation from Matt. 23 serving as a link between Chaucer's Friar and the Pharisees. In these tales of magic. Chaucer suggests that smooth-tongued rascals, particularly the clergy, succeed in making things appear to be what they are not, with dire consequences for their dupes.

14. Allen, in "The Ironic Fruyt," argues for Chaucer's debt to Hugh for twelve of thirteen details allegorizing the relation between preachers and roosters; in "The Old Way and the Parson's Way" he points out an irony which many commentaries permit but only Hugh requires. Two swallows, of course, do not make a summer, but the fact that Chaucer's debts to exegesis in these cases involves not just atmosphere and general drift of doctrine but precise dependence on *ipsissima verba* seems at least quite strong evidence.

15. Hugh of St. Cher, *Opera Omnia*, vol. 6, fol. 73v: "prelates and masters

of our time [who are] externally clean, internally corrupt." Hugh's comment on the generation of vipers permits the same generalization: "Serpentes astuti sunt, sed in malo tantum. Semper aspiciunt quomodo mordeant, et cum momorderint, quomodo se occultent, sic hypocritae cum aliquem laeserint, ita simpliciter ambulant, ac si nulli nocuerint. . . . Item serpentes varii sunt, et hypocritae variores, quia nunquam os consonat cordi. Ideo enim dicuntur hypocritae, quia aliud habent in ore, aliud in corde, ut dicit Hieronimus. Huic serpenti dicitur Genes. 52. c [*sic*]. Pectore et ventre repes, quia hypocritae omnia faciunt propter ventrem, et inanem gloriam, quod est super pectus repere. . . . Sed et eidem dicitur: Terram comedes omnibus diebus vitae tuae, quia hypocritae nihil aliud, quam terrena concupiscunt. Item serpentes venenum portant in lingua, sic omnes hypocritae detractores sunt" (fol. 74r). "Snakes are cunning, but only for evil. They always take care how they bite, and when they bite, how they hide themselves; in the same way, hypocrites when they injure someone, walk about simply, as if they had done harm to no one. . . . Next serpents are various, and hypocrites more so, because they never make their speech accord with their heart. For that reason they are called hypocrites, because they have one thing in their mouth, and another in their heart, as Jerome says. Genes. 52. c is addressed to this serpent: You will crawl on your chest and belly, because hypocrites do everything to satisfy their bellies, and for the sake of vainglory, which is to crawl on the chest. . . . But to him it is also said: You will eat dirt all the days of your life, because hypocrites do nothing else except lust after the earthly. Next serpents carry poison on their tongue, in the same way all hypocrites are detractors."

16. For a discussion of the relationship between the two tales, see Joyce E. Peterson, "The Finished Fragment: A Reassessment of the Squire's Tale," *Chaucer Review* 5 (1970): 62–74. Charles F. Duncan, in "'A Straw for Your Gentillesse': The Gentle Franklin's Interruption of the Squire," *Chaucer Review* 5 (1970): 161–64, discusses the vexed question of whether Chaucer intended the Franklin to interrupt a bad story or, rather, used the interruption to make the Franklin look ridiculous. He also surveys the scholarship on the subject. As Peterson shows, the question of proper speech, and proper speech as a demonstration of virtue, as well as of virtuosity, is at stake in the two tales.

17. J. J. Murphy is much impressed with this feature of the *Rhetoric's fortuna;* see his *Rhetoric in the Middle Ages* (Berkeley, 1974), pp. 92–101. Aristotle's *Poetics,* in the Averroistic version put into Latin circulation by Hermann the German, also tended more often to circulate with ethical than with grammatical or logical texts. It is therefore improper to distinguish too sharply the Ciceronian tradition of colors and ornaments from the Aristotelian tradition of persuasive postures. Similarly, it is necessary to see Chaucer's frequent praise of rhetoric, especially intrusive in this prologue material of the Franklin's, as insisting on sound ethical existence as well as on goodness at storytelling, and that without being much interested in distinguishing the two. The modern convention which takes Chaucer's relations to rhetoric as either stylistically immature or as ironic is beside the point. To the modern sensibility, rhetoric is by definition artificial in a pejorative sense; to the medieval one, rhetoric is artificial in a way which helps existence achieve truth. Chaucer's irony is directed, not at rhetoric per se, but at failed rhetoric. For amplifica-

tion of this point, see the review of Murphy's *Rhetoric in the Middle Ages* in *Speculum* 52 (April 1977): 411–14.

18. Gertrude M. White, in "The *Franklin's Tale:* Chaucer and the Critics," *PMLA* 89 (1974): 454–62, provides a survey of criticism; she emphasizes the recent critical emphasis on the character of Arveragus. Kaske's article "Chaucer's Marriage Group" is both the most cogent and the most enjoyable analysis in print of this aspect of Chaucer criticism; in it Arveragus emerges very subtly as a ruler more in control de facto than de jure. But the whole question takes on a very different complexion if one presumes, as we do, that Chaucer's stories are not about particulars but rather use them, exemplum fashion, as normative arrays leading to definition.

19. A. C. Baugh, in *Chaucer's Major Poetry* (Englewood Cliffs, N.J., 1963), p. 482, translates the line "if God allow me to say so" and thus misses the easiest construction of the subjunctive. The line might better be read: "This is too much [even] if it were the will of God."

20. Kenneth Kee, in "Illusion and Reality in Chaucer's *Franklin's Tale*," *English Studies in Canada* 1 (1975): 1–12, speaks of the tale as a discussion of magic. He argues, however, that Chaucer's ultimate purpose in depicting Dorigen's trust of magic is a refutation of Boethian philosophy, rather than an ironic criticism of Dorigen's philosophical misunderstandings.

21. Donald R. Howard, "The Conclusion of the Marriage Group: Chaucer and the Human Condition," *Modern Philology* 57 (1960): 228–29.

22. Rhetorically, the strategies of this tale and the *Miller's Tale* are precisely the same. In each case the ending is so arranged as to make the audience able safely to entertain the story. The ending of the *Miller's Tale* permits us to enjoy the romping disorders which lead up to it, knowing that the harm they do will be punished; the ending of the *Franklin's Tale* permits us to enjoy the sentimental disorders which lead up to it, knowing that no great harm will come from them. In both cases comic distance encourages precisely the empathy necessary to entertain (in the logical sense) the propositions made in the tale and, at the same time, precisely the objectivity necessary to judge them. In the same way, pornography ceases to be sordid as soon as it stimulates laughter—that is, the social and distanced judgment which keeps the ethical universe in order.

23. For a full analysis of the significance of the exemplum of Midas in the *Wife of Bath's Tale*, which establishes the central importance of the implicit theme of judgment and which shows how the Wife is attempting to manipulate the tale rhetorically so as to make herself the *object* of a favorable judgment, see Allen and Gallacher, "Alisoun through the Looking Glass."

24. In the analogues the choice is between fair by day and foul by night, or vice versa. Chaucer's version of the choice, between faithful plainness and possibly faithless beauty, underlines the false dilemma between flesh and spirit, or carnality and the religious ideal, which the Wife of Bath has been posing in order to defend her sex-oriented value system. The ironic juxtaposition of her desire for youth and her confidence in her own experience links her with the Old Woman of the *Romance of the Rose*, and thence to the *Ars Amatoria*, as a woman whose behind-the-scenes knowledge of mores has not freed her from love's illusions. Cf. Margaret Schlauch, "The Marital Dilemma

in the Wife of Bath's Tale," *PMLA* 61 (1946), pp. 416-30. William Matthews, "The Wife of Bath and All Her Sect," *Viator* 5 (1974): 413-44, correctly identifies the issue of the tale as related to the medieval interest in old age, but ends by concluding, with most critics, that the Wife is "unique." Old age, in its struggle to maintain itself in authority and to retain its participation in the joys of life, was a theme of the first fragment, as well. Here, in light of the *Pardoner's Tale*, we may say that just as virginity is paired with true riches and virtue in this second group of tales, so old age is linked with avarice and with sexual cupidity.

25. Owen, in "The Transformation of a Frame Story," p. 134, identifies the Wife as one of the three key characters of the poem: "it was the Wife of Bath who was to transform the collection into drama." Curry, *Medieval Sciences*, finds the Wife "so vividly feminine and human," and quotes Kittredge, from *Chaucer and His Poetry*, who called the Wife "one of the most amazing characters . . . the brain of man has ever conceived" (p. 91).

26. We are happy to thank R. A. Shoaf for an archetypal insight which adds a last and neatly climactic twist to this whole argument. Writing, in a letter, of the separations from the world which human self-consciousness causes, and of the encounter with the loathly lady, he says: "The old hag is the world and the young knight is you or I and all our self-conscious ideals. But the young knight must accept the old hag, and then, only then, does beauty happen, the beauty of the world." This of course both modernizes and universalizes Chaucer's message, and places the miracle in the phenomenological world of the acceptance of a transcendence which mortal men can know but never absolutely be, rather than in the faerie transformation of the hag herself. But this placement gives us immediate possession of the miracle.

27. Cf. the *Parson's Tale:* "Now been ther generale signes of gentillesse, as eschewynge of vice and ribaudye and servage of synne, in word, in werk, and contenaunce;/and usynge vertu, curteisye, and clennesse, and to be liberal, that is to seyn, large by mesure; for thilke that passeth mesure is folie and synne" (X [I] 464-65). See, also, Dante's *Convivio*, 4. xx, and G. M. Vogt, "Gleanings for the History of a Sentiment: Generositas Virtus, non Sanguis," *Journal of English and Germanic Philology* 24 (1925): 102-23.

28. The principal spokesman for this righteous indignation must be John Gower, who in both the *Vox Clamantis* and the *Mirour de l'omme* attacks the "common multitude for the lawless destruction in England." Cf. *The Works of John Gower*, ed. G. C. Macaulay (Oxford, 1899), 1: 1-334; (1902) 4: 3-314. In *Vox*, p. 20, Gower contrasts the "serviles rustici" with the "ingenuos et nobiles regni," blaming the "serviles" for the trouble. For other documents of the Peasants' Revolt, particularly reflecting the dangerous character of the lower-class outbreak, see, *The Peasants' Revolt of 1381*, ed. R. B. Dobson (London, 1970), pp. 98, 359-61; and R. H. Robbins, *Historical Poems of the XIVth and XVth Centuries* (New York, 1959), "The taxes hath tened us all" (pp. 55-57), and "Yit is God a curteis lord" (pp. 57-59).

29. Robert A. Pratt, "The Order of the Canterbury Tales," pp. 1141-67, an article whose proposals on the evolution of the poem still hold wide influence.

30. "Chaucer's Discussion of Marriage," in *Chaucer Criticism*, ed. Schoeck and Taylor, p. 138.

31. With the same rhetoric, we are led to expect the Pardoner as well, and as it turns out, his is the last tale of the magic group.

32. "Possessiones et res civium debere[nt] esse proprias, et communes, proprias quidem quantum ad dominium, communes vero propter virtutem liberalitatis. . . . nam quilibet dominans bonis propriis adhibebit debitam diligentiam circa illa. Expedit autem talia esse communia secundum liberalitatem; quia cives inter se debent liberales esse, communicando sibi invicem propria bona" (*De Regimine Principum* [Rome, 1607; rpt. Aalen, Germany, 1967], p. 430). "The possessions and goods of the citizens ought to be private, and common, private indeed in the sense of ownership, but common for the sake of the virtue of liberality. . . . For any owner will devote to his own goods the care owed them. But it is proper that such things should be common for the sake of liberality; because the citizens ought to be liberal, by giving their own goods to each other reciprocally." "Tertia via ad ostendendum legem Phaleae non esse decentem de aequatione possessionum, sumitur ex parte virtutum quas decet habere cives: decet enim ipsos esse liberales et temperatos: non ergo bene dictum est quod ad bonum regimen civitatis sufficit cives habere possessiones aequatas, nisi aliquid determinetur de quantitate possessionum illarum; possent enim cives adeo modicas possessiones habere, quod oporteret eos ita parce vivere quod opera liberalitatis de facili exercere non valerent. Rursus habendo possessiones aequatas possent ita abundare in eis, et adeo deliciose vivere, quod non contingeret ipsos temperatos esse" (p. 442). "The third way for showing the law of Phalea not to be proper, in the equality of possessions, is based on the virtues which it is proper that citizens have: for it is appropriate that they should be liberal and temperate: therefore it is not well said that it is enough for the good management of a city that the citizens have equal possessions, unless something may be determined concerning the quantity of their possessions, but then citizens might have modest possessions so that it might be necessary for them to live simply, and they would not be able to exercise the works of liberality easily. On the other hand, by having equal possessions they might be able to have them in such an abundance and they would live so luxuriously, that it would not be necessary for them to be temperate."

33. The friar's problem resembles the difficulty of the disciples in Matt. 14:17; they must divide the five loaves and two fishes to distribute to the multitude. The spiritual associations suggested would link the tale with the Pardoner's, whose description of the robbers' last meal has been discussed recently in terms of a parody of the Last Supper and the Mass. See Rodney Delasanta, "Sacrament and Sacrifice in the *Pardoner's Tale*," *Annuale Mediaevale* 14 (1973): 43–52.

34. D. W. Robertson, Jr., "Why the Devil Wears Green," *Modern Language Notes* 69 (1954): 470–72.

35. John V. Fleming, "The Summoner's Prologue: An Iconographic Readjustment," *Chaucer Review* 2 (1967): 95–107.

36. Cf. Alan Levitan, "The Parody of Pentecost in Chaucer's Summoner's Tale," *University of Toronto Quarterly* 40 (1970–71): 236–46, and Bernard Levy, "Biblical Parody in the Summoner's Tale," *Tennessee Studies in Literature* 11 (1966): 45–60.

37. Mary Carruthers, "Letter and Gloss in the Friar's and Summoner's Tales," *Journal of Narrative Technique* 2 (1972): 208–14, establishes a helpful tie between the two tales through their common emphasis on glossing. She shows that both the tellers and the characters in their tales suffer from an inability to perceive the allegorical dimensions of language and experience.

38. It is, after all, the Summoner who has struck a bargain with the devil to work as his business partner and who refuses to draw back, even when he learns that his companion is a devil (III [D] 1395–1405, 1447–60).

39. "Not all excommunications imposed in the middle ages . . . were necessarily valid; . . . perhaps the person had not been guilty of mortal sin" (F. Donald Logan, *Excommunication in the Secular Arm in Medieval England* [Toronto, 1968], p. 15). "injusta autem excommunicatio caritatem alicui auferre non potest, cum sit de maximis bonis, quae non possent alicui invito auferri" (Thomas Aquinas, *In 4 de Sententiarum, Opera Omnia*, vol. 10 [London, 1873], Dist. 18, Qu. 2, 2. sol. 1, p. 534). "Unjust excommunication cannot take charity away from someone, since it is among the greatest goods, which cannot be taken away from a person unwilling."

40. Pierre Bersuire, *Dictionarii seu repertorii moralis . . . pars secunda* (Venice, 1589), p. 352, s.v. "Iudicare." Bersuire gives a detailed analysis of the real and ideal behavior of judges, including a number of exempla. "Note that to judge is the same thing as to make distinctions. Wherefore concerning the wise and discreet man in any field it is said that he is a man of good judgment. For judgment is nothing else than discretion among the qualities and conditions of things. . . . Therefore, since the name of judge indicates authority of status, understanding of affairs, and determination of affairs, it is very apparent that the duty of judging ought to be committed to upright and honest men, prudent and discreet men, also God-fearing and perfect men. For the judge in society is as the eye in the body, on which the health of the entire body depends. For just as the eye must judge concerning colors, to forewarn and forejudge pits and dangers, and to foresee for all the other members together, concerning the proper guidance, thus truly the judge ought to distinguish concerning colors, that is, concerning the conditions of people, to know the dangers to the republic, and to govern all members of the body, that is, all the persons of his jurisdiction, rightly."

41. *Opera Omnia*, vol. 3, fol. 139r. "Love justice, you who judge the earth, that is, who submit flesh to your judgment, that it should obey the spirit; do this discreetly and with love. Give the ass what is just, that is, a burden, the rod, and fodder, Eccl. 33.d. Whence the Apostle, Rom. 12.a. Your reasonable service, for no one ever hated his own flesh, but cherishes and nourishes it, Eph. 5.f."

42. Peter G. Beidler, "The Pairing of the Franklin's Tale and the Physician's Tale," *Chaucer Review* 3 (1969): 275–79.

43. Both Arnulf and Giovanni del Virgilio offer the explanation that Pygmalion had conceived a love for a statue of his own making. "Re vera Pigmalion mirabilis artifex eburneam fecit statuam cuius amorem concipiens ea cepit abuti ad modum vere mulieris" (in Ghisalberti, "Arnolfo," p. 223): "What happened was that Pygmalion, a marvelous craftsman, made an ivory statue, fell in love with it, and began to abuse it as if it were a true woman." Cf.

Ghisalberti, "Giovanni," p. 91, where Giovanni adds an alternative explanation: "... ideo aliter potest dici quod Pigmalion habebat quamdam uxorem pulcherrimam ut ebur. Sed erat immobilis id est sine blanditiis, et nesciebat operari sicut alie in coitu et ideo dicebatur esse statua"; "... otherwise it can be said that Pygmalion had a certain wife as beautiful as ivory. But she was frigid, that is, without seductiveness, and did not know how to behave as others do in sex and therefore she was said to be a statue."

44. Pierre Bersuire, *Ovidius Moralizatus: Reductorium moral Liber XC, cap. ii-xv,* Werkmateriaal (2) (Utrecht, 1962), p. 152. "Through this maker of images I understand preachers who know how to sculpt the soul, and to adorn it with corrections and virtues. Through this ivory girl I understand some holy woman, who is said to be ivory, through which she is called chaste, cold, dignified and honest. But often it happens that some good Pygmalion, that is, some good religious man, promises always to seek neither woman nor carnal embraces, and such a man devotes himself to making ivory images, that is, to teaching holy women and matrons in chastity and sanctity and for molding them in spiritual practices. And it happens that he may choose one from among them for himself, whom he calls sister or daughter, and he is with her and touches her with a good and chaste spirit and with love. But certainly it happens that Venus the goddess of lechery, that is, the lust of the flesh, intrudes and converts the dead image into life, and makes the chaste woman feel the stirrings of the flesh and changes her from a good person into a fool. For, Pygmalion himself, the preacher, seeks this from Venus, and desires this change. Thus, when as they were accustomed, they return to their conversions immediately, he finds both of them changed, with the result that she who was ivory has become fleshly and he who feared women, begins to desire the pollutions of the flesh. Therefore, these carnal beings receive each other mutually and generate children. So, it is not safe for a religious man to contract too great a familiarity with women or vice versa."

45. Augustine, in discussing the life of the Roman matron Lucretia, contrasts her suicide with the lives of Christian women who had endured the same evil as she had when she was forced to submit to rape. Augustine judges her suicide to be murder: "Non hoc fecerunt feminae Christianae, quae passae simila vivunt tamen nec in se ultrae sunt crimen alienum, ne aliorum sceleribus adderent sua, si, quoniam hostes in eis concupiscendo stupra commiserant, illae in se ipsis homicidia erubescendo committerent" (*P.L.* 41, col. 34, bk. 1, chap. 19, *De Civitate Dei Libri, Corpus Christianorum Series Latina,* 47:21 "Christian women who suffered rape did not do such a thing; they lived and did not revenge upon themselves the crime of another, lest they add their own sin to that of others by murdering themselves for shame because lusting enemies committed rape upon them."

46. Ibid. Augustine suggests that Lucretia, although she knew herself that she was innocent, attached too much signficance to a bodily defilement and so took her life.

47. Richard Hoffman, in "Jephthah's Daughter and Chaucer's Virginia," *Chaucer Review* 2 (1967–68): 20–31, makes the point that Jephthah's daughter died wasting her virginity, whereas Virginia died to save hers. But the real point of the story is not chastity but judgment; it is the two judgments of the

flesh—that is, of a beautiful young woman as a potential sex object and, alternatively, as a piece of property not to be soiled—which are exemplarily wrong, and postures about virginity per se are not centrally relevant.

48. *Biblia Sacra, cum glosa ordinaria . . . et postilla Nicolai Lyrani*, vol. 2 (Lyons, 1520), fol. 46v. "Though the vow may well have proceeded out of devotion, nevertheless it was made indiscreetly, because there might have come first out of the house to meet him a dog, which is not an animal suitable for sacrifice."

49. *Opera Omnia*, vol. 1, fol. 206v. "Augustine said that the vow referred to his wife, whom he hated, thinking she would meet him first, and so it is clear that he vowed with bad intention, therefore his vow was bad."

50. Allegorizations, *in bono*, do not, however, justify the literal act. The *Glosa's* lengthy discussion is very clear at this point: "Vel per scientes ergo, vel per nescientes significationem futurorum spiritus domini propheticis temporibus operatus est, nec ideo peccata eorum non fuerunt peccata, quia deus qui et malis bene utitur usus est eis ad significanda que voluit. Si ergo peccatum non fuit cuiuslibet necis humane: vel etiam paricidale sacrificium vel vovere vel reddere: quia magnum aliquid et spirituale significavit: frustra deus talia prohibuit: et se odisse dicit: quia et illa que fieri iussit ad significationem spiritualium rerum referuntur, sed humana deo sacrificia non placuerunt: quando non pro iusticia quisque recte vivit vel peccare non vult, interimitur: sed homo ab homine tanquam electa hostia more pecoris immolatur. Si autem dicet aliquis: quia pecorum victime iam usitate ad significationem licet relate minus faciebat intentos ad sacramentum magnum christi et ecclesie requirendum: propterea deus re insigni et inopinata volens animos hominum excitare: eo magis quod sibi talia sacrificia offerri vetuerat: curavit sibi aliquid offerendum, in quo ipsa admiratio magnam gigneret questionem: et questio exigeret studium ad perscrutandum mysterium: pie vero scrutans mens hominis altitudinem prophetie velut hamo piscem christum de profundo scripturarum levaret. Huic rationi non obsistimus. Sed alia questio est de animo voventis, alia de providentia dei" *Biblia Sacra*, fol. 47r). "Therefore, the spirit of the lord worked in prophetic times, either through those knowing, or those not knowing, the significance of future things; their sins were not sins, because God, who uses evil things for good, used them to signify the things he wished. If therefore the sin was not of some murder of a person: either the father's sacrifice, the vow or the return, because it signified something great and spiritual, then in vain God prohibited such things. Yet he says he hates them: those things which he ordered to be done refer to the sense of spiritual things, but human sacrifices did not please the Lord. It is unjust when someone who has lived rightly and does not wish to sin, is killed, but a man is sacrificed by another as a chosen victim in the manner of a beast. If someone says: since it is permitted in this account to use the accustomed animal as sacrifice, it made us less intent on requiring the great sacrifice of Christ and the church. For that reason, God, wishing to excite the spirits of men, with an unexpected and notable event, especially because he had prohibited such sacrifices to be offered to him, arranged that something be offered to him, in which this wonder might raise a great question, and the question might require study to penetrate the mystery. But the mind of man, piously searching the heights of the Prophets, might as he raised a fish with a hook raise Christ from the depths of the Scriptures. We are not opposed to

this argument. But the soul of the man promising is one question, and the providence of God another."

51. *Reductorium morale super totam Bibliam* (Cologne, 1631), p. 88. "We may expound this allegorically concerning Christ. So, we may say this Jephthah signifies Christ, who truly is born as from a concubine, since he seemed to come from God as father and a virgin as mother, who was of another place and bed.... Although he was repudiated by the Judeans, nevertheless, he is made prince and leader of the sons of Israel, that is, of the faithful, against Amon, that is, the devil. For the sake of obtaining victory he sacrificed his own daughter, that is, his humanity to God the Father, and she suffers death for the sake of the health of the human race and for victory, and Amon and his people, that is, the devil and vices, are overcome, and the children of Israel, that is, the faithful people, are liberated.... Or say that Jephthah is a man, whose daughter is his own flesh, which he ought to offer to God, and to promise to be immolated for the sake of penance to God, so that against Amon, that is, against the devil and sins, he is able to obtain victory. So, when it happens that a man had victory over vices or tribulations, or brought back from God a spiritual gift, and he sees his daughter, that is, his own flesh, to come toward him on the road of practice with drums and pipes, that is, to come with pleasures and tempting things, he ought to say and cry out immediately: My daughter, you have deceived me, and you have been deceived yourself. You have deceived me, I say, by offering vices, but you have been deceived yourself by bringing forth sin and repentance. He should sacrifice her to the Lord immediately as a penance, and bringing forth tears for his own virginity, that is, for the shame and the sterility of his virtues, nevertheless, his virginity or sterility having been deplored, he ought to burn her for charity, and to offer or sacrifice to God for the sake of penance and through the fatigue of labor."

52. Throughout this group of tales, the emphasis on right judgment has been coupled with images related to sight: Cecilia's crown seen only by the believer, the Wife's loathly lady with her options of fair by day or night, the magic mirror in the *Squire's Tale,* Dorigen's hated rocks, and so on. There is a corresponding image from the senses that appears in the third and fourth groups of tales, particularly in the tales of interpretation: images of the tongue and speech. See below, chaps. 6 and 7.

53. Allen, *The Friar as Critic,* pp. 135–36.

54. The best of these studies is Robert P. Miller, "Chaucer's Pardoner, the Spiritual Eunuch, and the Pardoner's Tale," *Speculum* 30 (1955): 180–99.

55. Ibid.; cf. Delasanta, "Sacrament and Sacrifice in the *Pardoner's Tale,*" pp. 43–52; and Robert E. Nichols, Jr., "The Pardoner's Ale and Cake," *PMLA* 82 (1967): 498–504. E. R. Amoils, "Fruitfulness and Sterility in the Physician's and Pardoner's Tales," *English Studies in Africa* 17 (1974): 17–37, links the tales of fragment VI as a diptych of physical death redeemed by spiritual values and spiritual death reinforced by murder; in this he provides us with a pattern of ending the magic group which recalls and reinforces, although on a lower scale of perfection, the grouping of tales with which we began, the Second Nun's and Canon's Yeoman's.

56. Donald Howard, "The Pardoner: Actor and Martyr," read to the meet-

ing of the Medieval Academy, 11 May 1974, Kalamazoo, Michigan. Those privileged to hear Howard's paper performed will never forget how powerfully the moral effect of the *Pardoner's Tale* was reenacted. Our report is based on memory, and so may well be an extrapolation of Howard's doctrine. We are confident that it is at least fair to its moral effect. Cf. Howard, *The Idea of the Canterbury Tales*, pp. 339-70.

6

The Moral Group

Chaucer's third group of tales the Ovidian *distinctio* labels moral. In the *distinctio* of descent into hell, the moral descent is simply the descent into vice. In this category, combining both traditions, we have all those human arrangements of order capable of being labeled good or bad. It corresponds to, and is defined by, the third section of the *Knight's Tale*, which is full of catalogues of typical human actions—most of them calamitous. But it is also the most formal of the parts of the *Knight's Tale*, and it is this paradoxical combination of general formality and particular calamity which defines medieval ethics. In this section Theseus builds his grand stadium, and the three principals offer themselves at the shrines of Venus, Mars, and Diana.

It would seem, at first glance, that our four-part order is faulty here. Section three of the *Knight's Tale* is superficially more magical than any of the others, with its atmosphere of pagan shrines—and, to modern eyes at least, the easiest and most obvious division of the tale into natural, magical, moral, and spiritual would seem to take parts one and two as natural, part three as magical, the actual tournament of part four as moral, and the Boethian speech and its circumstances as spiritual. But properly understood, it is the disguises of part two, and not the prayers of part three, which best fit the medieval category of magic. And part three, properly understood, is the best definition of the moral.

In part three of the *Knight's Tale*, human intentionality reaches its highest level of control of its world. This intentionality may be virtuous, or it may be vicious. What the powers invoked in this part actually do, or patronize, is for the most part quite bad. But the framing postures are wholly good.[1] Here Theseus does the best that he can do to build a world, a perfect circular microcosm, in which the events that accumulate as human history can be defined and controlled. Combat here can be moral—combat, like beasts in the forest, was not immoral so much as amoral. The prayers which occur within this microcosm, shrine by shrine, are an array of particular intentionalities each of which attempts to plan the world in ideal fashion. Nothing really happens in the section, but everything is planned. Such action as there is occurs in catalog and betrays the vice and evil of which humanity is capable, even (or perhaps especially) within the ethical frame. This section is, in sum, the most ceremonial, the most iconographic, the most hieratic, the most pageantlike in the whole of the *Knight's Tale*.

All this is the ideal to which medieval morality aspires. For modern critics, accustomed to the rhetoric if not the practice of situational ethics, the medieval ideal requires a considerable adjustment of sensibility. It is not simply that medieval standards of ethics were normative rather than situational—they were, but they were more. Huizinga well describes the heightening of decorum, of form, which was involved.[2] This heightening, this formality, more than anything else, is the quality which both justifies and explains the medieval association between literature and ethics. Actions are more than mere acts—they are acts which can be associated with, possessed by, their particular daemon—Mars, Venus, Diana, or Saturn. Human beings enter into these patterns of action by means of prayer—that is, by means of the words of intentionality—in a setting which, as a shrine, physically confirms the association between act and definition.

The tales which constitute the moral group are the *Man of Law's Tale,* the *Clerk's Tale,* the *Merchant's Tale,* the *Manciple's Tale,* and the *Shipman's Tale*. Each of them is the story of an attempt at ordering—at constructing a microcosm within which the world can be defined and history can be controlled. Each of them involves human intentionality; in most, this intentionality is expressed formally in the words of some vow. In none of them is the action, either intended or accomplished or both, wholly admirable, but all of them record the achievement of some kind of stasis—an acceptable orderly arrangement of human affairs, which one must trust to structure the future bearably, if not virtuously or wholly comfortably. Further, they are, like the tales in the previous groups considered, arranged in descending order, both in terms of the sociopolitical status of the principal characters and in terms of the quality of moral achievement which is defined. Finally, all these tales, for reasons which touch at the essence of Chaucer's art, have to do with marriage.

The traditional marriage group—*Clerk's Tale, Wife of Bath's Tale, Franklin's Tale, Merchant's Tale,* with the *Friar's Tale-Summoner's Tale* interlude (and with the *Squire's Tale* awkwardly hanging about)— seems to us not helpfully labeled, because looking at the tales this way tells us not about marriage but about marriages, and ignores the fact that if one is simply considering tales about marriages, there are a large number of others to be included. The schema of husband-wife-attacker, in fact, can be applied to most of Chaucer's tales, and after only minor transformations to all of them except the final sermon. We shall eventually try to show just why it is that tales involving some actual reference to marriage were so central a part of Chaucer's strategy of social definition in the *Canterbury Tales* as a whole.

Here, however, we wish to use an array of tales of marriages as a normative array of something else—that is, of intentional structures designed to achieve, or exist as, order. Some marriages are structures to which, or within which, things happen. Others are structures created for the sake of making something else happen. In the first category, marriages are simply parts of life and history—things are always happening. The second category, however, is quite different; the intentional event is an event defined, caused, and determined by its final cause, and secondarily by its formal cause. Material cause is relatively unimportant, and efficient causality may even be defied. The feature of this moral group of tales, which is also our marriage group, which gives it coherence is intentionality, or final cause. Each tale involves an arrangement (a marriage, or in one case the canceling of a marriage) brought into being for the sake of generating greater order, stability, and satisfaction than had existed before. The plot of each tale is the gradual definition and accomplishment of this arrangement; each story ends with the arrangement in existence.

The order of the tales is from high to low, greatest to least, most to least admirable. Here as in the other groups Chaucer has put his best exemplum first and then gradually trails off. In the *Man of Law's Tale* the marriage of Constance is intended to extend the boundaries of empire and of Christendom. It fails, but Providence arranges that a second marriage will accomplish the intentions originally frustrated. In the *Clerk's Tale* a sovereign marquis is persuaded to marry for the sake of perpetuating his line and his rule, and does so. In the *Merchant's Tale* a knight persuades himself to marry in order to legitimize his access to sex, and succeeds in legitimizing the sexual morality for which his life really stood. In the *Manciple's Tale* a married bachelor kills his wife in punishment for adultery, and succeeds only in proving that ignorance was bliss. In the *Shipman's Tale* a merchant treats his marriage as an extension of his business, and succeeds in making it so.

The tales are of marriages, but the normative array is of orders, for whose definition Chaucer found marriages exactly suitable. The first order is of empire, the second of sovereign realm, the third of family, the fourth of person, and the fifth of property—once again a descending series, from general to particular, from the universal of imperial society to the particular of an accident of a single person. The difference between this array and the first one—*Knight's Tale* to *Cook's Tale*— is that in the first group the focus of attention was narrowly on authorities, and the kinds of law and order those authorities generate. Here the focus is on what surrounds, generates, and results from authorities—on the one hand, the intentionalities because of which people enter into social orders (representatively, the social order of marriage), and on the other hand, the resonances and analogies for total order which those intended and created orders generate. Thus, in the *Knight's Tale,* Theseus, already married and king of Athens, with his order already established and defined, must deal with an intrusive test personified by Palamon, Arcite, and Emelye. In the *Man of Law's Tale,* on the other hand, a marriage is intended which will, it is hoped, create a new order. The plot of the story is the history of the adventures and trials of this intention, rather than of the order which it will eventually accomplish.

In a second way these tales are also in descending order—that is, in terms of the activity of God (or the pagan gods). It would seem that in this group Chaucer is playing games, both seriously and comically, with the notion of the divine presence. In the *Man of Law's Tale* the providentially assisting Christian God is fully and powerfully present. In the *Clerk's Tale* we have a man functioning as God, with his godlike activity clearly underlined by allusions to Job. In the *Merchant's Tale* there are pagan gods, with real powers, working in a kind of parody of Providence to give the tale its outcome. In the *Manciple's Tale* we have a pagan god without powers, acting merely as a bachelor. In the *Shipman's Tale* there is no god at all. The rhetoric of the tales, in turn, both underlines and complicates the point. As Chauncey Wood has so well shown, there is a great difference between the simple, committed faith of Constance and the Man of Law's disaster-preoccupied and loudly expressed desire that God act as a kind of omnipotent bodyguard.[3] In fact, the Man of Law so overdoes his prayers as almost to transform these adventures of sweet Constance into the perils of Pauline. Thus, the providential guiding of history is comically undercut even while its successful and wholly proper course is narrated. On the other hand, Walter's sadism is protected, by careful allusion both to the fallibility of the human condition and the testing of Job, from ever being comic, in spite of the fact that his pretentious exercise of his right to test his wife is very little more justifiable than the Miller's carpenter's promised sovereignty over the drowned world as a second Noah. The gods in the *Merchant's Tale* are radically humanized into a standard argumentative married couple, and the game they play on January and May evokes the irresponsible and at times sadistic presence of the gods in the *Metamorphoses*. But the richly allusive texture of the tale,[4] with irony and allegory undercutting the letter and each other, constitutes a level of seriousness which prevents our settling for either the Merchant's misanthropy or January's pathos as the point of the tale. Apollo, in the *Manciple's Tale*, is even more humanized; when we see him sunk in remorse for rash and foolish action, an ironic dimension is imposed on the wisdom he represents. And in the merely commercial world of the *Shipman's Tale*, it is gold, not God, which can protect from the evil chances of Fortune. The *Shipman's Tale*, in fact, is a precise inverse of the *Man of Law's Tale* in this matter of Fortune and Providence—the merchant, with gold, must look out for himself:

> And therfore have I greet necessitee
> Upon this queynte[5] world t'avyse me;
> For everemoore we moote stonde in drede
> Of hap and fortune in oure chapmanhede.
>
> (VII 235-38 [B² 1425-28])

The character, extent, and manner of involvement with some kind of divine will which these tales exhibit is, of course, an indicator of moral value. The fact that, beyond the first tale especially, the divine presence has something wrong with it fits with the fact that the array of moral values and orders being presented is a human one merely—even though the outcome of the *Man of Law's Tale* is a happy part of *Heilsgeschichte*, it is clear that the narrator goes beyond the bounds of faith and pure religion in demanding it so selfishly for his heroine.

In all this Chaucer's ultimate point, delivered as always in a complex, ironic way, is that divine sanction and protection are always desirable but not always available. When they are available they may be compromised by wrong attitudes. When they seem available they may in fact be merely something human, projected on the transcendent. They may be mere natural chaos, or something out of the psychomachia of temperaments and humors (which allegory perceived under the names of pagan gods),[6] wrongly perceived for the moment as orderly and providential. Man always likes to believe that what he does bears some relation to the will of God; the games Chaucer plays with what is really going on as the context of that desire show how much of delusion there may be in faith. We cannot know, of course, one way or the other—faith is always prudent, but it is equally prudent to keep always a little irony in reserve.

These stories, however, are not about faith. Faith, and the divine powers which faith evokes, are present in the tales, as is the irony which protects faith from the full consequences of being mistaken, but both faith and irony are accidents rather than essence here. What the tales are about is order—order intended and order accomplished. In the best sense, these tales are worldly. They are, therefore, appropriately much concerned with two important aspects of worldly life and worldly order—vows, or promises, and property. Both these themes are made more emphatic still by their prominent introduction in the prologue material which serves to introduce the whole group.

A vow, or promise, is a form of words which describes the future and commits the speaker to perform actions which will make that particular description of the future come true. In the medieval experience there were three kinds of act which, by their very commonness, would particularly define the act of vowing or promising. These were the vow of holy orders, the pledge made to one's feudal overlord, and the vow of marriage. Of these, the most common, and the most accessible to experience at all levels of society, was marriage. For this reason, if no other, marriage would have been the most suitable vehicle for Chaucer's analysis of the human order that results from intentional creation of structure.[7]

It is most important to notice that the act of vowing has a connection with the act of storytelling. A vow is a story in the future tense whose claims on reality complement and balance those made by an ordinary story, or exemplum, which exists in the past tense as a moral and prudential influence on the present and the future. The present, the sphere of moral action and existence, is thus surrounded by words, which enclose, define, evaluate, and guide it, and, as it exists through time, are also narrative. These stories, as they grow out of vows, thus enact the verbal quality appropriate to the real moral world, as well as the fictive ones of Chaucer's Canterbury collection, and celebrate the fact that real human orders arise out of the power of words to make commitments which pattern and order the real world. In all these stories the primary vow is the wedding vow, which intends and describes the order being created, whose history the past tense story will preserve as an example for other vows and other stories. Thus the foresight of the right vow and the memory of the right story surround the intelligence of the present and make possible that prudence whose parts are these acts of past, present, and future. But this primary vow exists in the presence of other vows—to do murder, to obey one's sovereign husband, to interfere with January and May, to keep secrets—which compromise and comment, as we shall see, on the primary vow of marriage which generates the context of order.

The theme of property ends with sexual bookkeeping and the invitation to "score it upon my taille" (VII 416 [B² 1606]). It begins, in most complex fashion, with Chaucer's prologue—the "wordes of the Hoost to the compaignye" and the "prologue" properly so called. This, as was the Second Nun's Prologue, should be taken as an introduction to the whole group. In the Second Nun's Prologue, we were warned against the *Romance of the Rose,* and especially against Idleness, and exhorted to that good work which consists of making and understanding words. Idleness, there, seemed to imply the loss of full significance or full dimension, as in the *Romance of the Rose* Idleness tempts one to diminish love to its merely sexual literalness. In the introductory material to the *Man of Law's Tale,* we are once again warned against idleness, but now in the context of the speedy passage of time. One must "bewaillen tyme moore than gold in cofre" (II [B¹] 26) because, unlike property, it can never be recovered once it is past. Implicitly, what we are being warned against is the idleness that refrains from any action at all (rather than against acting, but acting idly)—that is, we are being warned against wasting history, or not making any. The fit destiny of man and woman is to fill time with acted exempla, worthy "to drawen to memorie"—idleness is a waste of that property in time more valuable than gold.

There follows a seemingly miscellaneous, dramatic passage in which the Man of Law honors his promise, complains that Chaucer has told all the good stories, disclaims literary ability, and indulges an apostrophe denouncing poverty. But all this ceases to be miscellaneous as soon as we see it in relation to the whole of the group, and to the example and precedent of the third part of the *Knight's Tale*. All of it, from beginning to end, is about property, and subtly expands the time-gold *translatio* with which we began.

In the first place, the Man of Law has made a promise—to obey the Host by telling a story. Such a vow, he admits, is a debt. A story, then, is property, to be paid over in satisfaction of the debt. But Chaucer owns—that is, has told—all the good stories. There follows a list, remarkably similar when one thinks about it, to the catalogues in the third part of the *Knight's Tale*. By an analogy not at all unfair to the storyteller, Chaucer is the patron, or daemon, or divinity of his stories, and they are his property.[8] In contrast, the Man of Law is very poor, with only his prose "hawebake." It is a bad state to be in, and so the Man of Law complains of it, but translates his condition out of the literary and back into economic terms: "O hateful harm, condicion of poverte!" (II [B¹] 99). Far better it is to be a rich merchant, a man whose figurative dice always roll winning numbers. Such people seek to become landed. Finally, they know the "estaat of regnes" and are "fadres of tidynges / And tales, bothe of pees and of debaat." From financial property we return to tales, to literary property. It is from such people, rich in money and in lore, that the Man of Law gets his tale.

Three of these tales, in fact, are merchant's tales—the Man of Law's at second hand, the tale of January and May at first hand, and the *Shipman's Tale* in actual subject matter. This dialectic, whereby the content of the frame is eventually absorbed into, and becomes a part of, the level of story, matches the dialectic of judgment operating from the *Wife of Bath's Tale* to the *Physician's Tale* by which an audience reaction in the Wife's tale is absorbed and becomes the subject matter of the *Physician's Tale*. But all of them are about "tidynges . . . of pees and of debaat." More important still, they all have to do, explicitly or by analogy, with the "estaat of regnes"—with that "commune profyt" which is true commonwealth and which is precisely defined (since literature is ethics) by the seesawing *translatio* of story into property and property into story.

The tale of Constance itself is the third in the framing series of incipit tales which are the *carmen perpetuum* of this medieval *Metamorphoses*. With Christianity established as the religion of the empire, the sacred and the secular are at least normatively and theoretically in harmony, and the conflict will properly be with the borders. Constance herself is largely sweet and passive—more so than in

Chaucer's source—we think because ideally in Christian society eventualities are more given than striven for and achieved. "Take no thought for the morrow" is an exhortation more to serenity than to mere passivity; still, whatever achievements of holiness and even sainthood there are tend to come upon people who were doing something else, and often something else wholly ordinary and daily. Even the large transitions of history are often more visible to hindsight than to observation; the Renaissance is the only age that ever called itself anything other than "moderna tempora"; and expansions of Christendom such as the one of which Constance was the instrument tend always to happen in a way which should encourage us to view with irony even the best laid plans of men.

This is not to say that Constance's adventures lack significance in themselves. Most important, there are two of everything—two marriages, two different pagan realms (and at opposite edges of the empire), two mothers-in-law,[9] two sexual assaulters, two sea voyages, two framing episodes with her father. This doubleness forces us to realize, at the very outset, that the difference between success and failure in human arrangements does not depend as much on the shape and character of what is done or planned as on the quality and character of the divine intention involved. Constance's imperial father had in mind, when he married his daughter off to the sultan, exactly the result which Providence eventually accomplished. But the emperor is not God, and his plans do not necessarily work out, at least not the first time. At the same time, this doubleness reminds us that there is an analogical energy at work in the world between divine and human levels, and that what eventually receives divine approval and providential help must be, in shape and character, appropriate to that divine preoccupation. At the highest and most general level of meaning, therefore, this doubleness reminds us, first, that allegory is not identity, and second, that an event must in a sense await its interpretation. The emperor cannot be God, cannot literally assert for himself divine prerogatives and divine actions, but he is nevertheless obligated to act in analogy with God, in some way he will never, at the time, understand.[10]

A second feature of the *Man of Law's Tale* most important for its meaning is that the Man of Law is not "good at parties" but is good at pathos.[11] In the *Knight's Tale*, as has been shown, the use of the rhetorical strategy of *occupatio* contributes greatly to the richness and elaborateness of the ceremonial, tapestrylike quality of the tale.[12] The more the Knight protests that there is not time to tell, the more rich description he heaps up. The Man of Law, on the other hand, uses *occupatio* to avoid descriptions of ceremony:

> Me list nat of the chaf, ne of the stree,
> Maken so long a tale as of the corn.
> What sholde I tellen of the roialtee
> At mariage, or which cours goth biforn;
> Who bloweth in a trumpe or in an horn?
> The fruyt of every tale is for to seye:
> They ete, and drynke, and daunce, and synge, and pleye.
>
> (II [B¹] 701-7)

Or again:

> The day goth faste, I wol no lenger lette.
> This glade folk to dyner they hem sette;
> In joye and blisse at mete I lete hem dwelle
> A thousand foold wel moore than I kan telle.
>
> (II [B¹] 1117-20)

At the same time, the tale is full of effective rendering of pathos; Chaucer never achieved a greater or more telling comparison than one he gives to the Man of Law in description of Constance:

> Have ye nat seyn somtyme a pale face,
> Among a prees, of hym that hath be lad
> Toward his deeth, wher as hym gat no grace,
> And swich a colour in his face hath had,
> Men myghte knowe his face that was bistad,
> Amonges alle the faces in that route?
> So stant Custance, and looketh hire aboute.
>
> (II [B¹] 645-51)

In poetic effects as well as in vivid characters, there is in Chaucer's work God's plenty. But it is not enough to notice that these effects are indeed masterfully achieved—one must go further and notice where they are put, and to what effect. The dramatic principle, which is pleased to assign these effects to the Man of Law and to account for them by projecting from his imagined character their efficient cause, makes it possible to say interesting things about a hypothetical medieval lawyer but prevents us from asking and answering more interesting questions about Chaucer's art. It is true, after all, that he wrote everybody's speeches, and if it is true, as we believe, that morally and doctrinally the Canterbury pilgrims are the result of their tales, and not the other way around, then one accounts for the nature and distribution of Chaucer's "beauties" in terms of the larger coherence of tale with tale.

The tapestrylike quality of the *Knight's Tale,* which has been well enough noted as a merely aesthetic virtue and as evidence of "medievalism," is in fact precisely the right quality for a tale of definition as we have defined it. The whole enterprise of the *Knight's Tale* is, as it were, to persuade the inevitable emergent disorders of this world to accept the shrine-bounded stadium of Theseus as the fit circumstance of their resolution and to persuade the hearers and readers of the tale that a successful progress from existence to understanding—from an order intruded upon by Palamon and Arcite to an ending made acceptable by having read Boethius—is to be achieved only by the ceremonialization of facts, or (in Chaucer's terms) the assimilation of earnest into game. Therefore, at the level of answerable style, the rude facts of this Theban rivalry must be contained within the ceremony of a verbal *occupatio* whose dense and hurried pressure achieves their verbal ceremonialization.

The tale of Constance, on the other hand, exists at the level of a fact searching for, and still not confident of, its definition. Constance's father intends that the bounds of Christendom shall be enlarged, but he is not God and cannot make Providence his puppet. Rather, Providence, definition, the perfection of what will be is hidden and must be aspired to by people who can in fact see only the chaos and not the shrine-bound stadium. The *Knight's Tale* contains the reconciliation of fact and definition; the *Man of Law's Tale* contains facts in search of definitive affirmation. Therefore necessarily their visible aspect must be pathetic; likewise, ceremony must therefore necessarily be hidden, unreachable, unachievable. Chaucer's orchestration of effects is thus program music—we can know why he is good at this, here, and that, there, only after we have learned what the program is. Then everything is clear.

In terms of the precedent of the *Knight's Tale,* then, the *Man of Law's Tale* reproduces in larger and more foreground detail what the catalogues of human conditions associated with Mars, Venus, Diana, and Saturn listed. When Saturn says

> Myn is the drenchyng in the see so wan;
> Myn is the prison in the derke cote;
> Myn is the stranglyng and hangyng by the throte,
> . . . .
> And myne be the maladyes colde,

> The derke tresons, and the castes olde;
> My lookyng is the fader of pestilence.
>
> (I [A] 2456-58, 2467-69)

his words are followed by the providential promise, echoing the promise of Apocalypse that "God shall wipe away all tears from their eyes" (Apoc. 21:4):

> Now weep namoore, I shal doon diligence
> That Palamon, that is thyn owene knyght,
> Shal have his lady, as thou hast him hight.
> . . . .
> Weep now namoore, I wol thy lust fulfille.
>
> (I [A] 2470-72, 2478)

In the context of the *Knight's Tale,* the calamities of life are contained within their daemonic supervision; in the *Man of Law's Tale* they are forced for a time to stand alone, unsupported even by daemon, let alone the Christian God of Providence, and are therefore necessarily pathetic.

All this is literally appropriate to Christendom, where life must be by faith and not by sight. There are, in the church, ceremonies and securities, but they are tentative, provisional, and ad interim. The revelation of the *opus restaurationis,* which is and will be the career of the church, is ultimately eschatological, and the shrine-girt stadium in which everything will be clear is only in heaven. "We see now through a mirror in an obscure manner, but then face to face" (1 Cor. 13:12). To be good at pathos and incapable of celebration is, sub specie aeternitatis, to be precisely qualified to describe the visible part of the present life of the church, of Christendom, in history. It is a provisional order, capable of using the full resources of merely mortal intentionality but at the same time incomplete, because we do not now see face to face. Since in the *Man of Law's Tale* we have as subject the extension of Christendom, we appropriately see it only literally, but with the *Knight's Tale* resonating in the analogical background to reassure us that all this pathos will not be in vain and to predict the happy ending.

The *Clerk's Tale* is about an earthly kingdom. As it stands it deals with an implausibly monstrous man and an implausibly obedient wife, the marquis and marquise of Saluzzo. At the level of psychological realism, Talbot Donaldson makes more sense of the tale than any other critic we know when he says that constancy, not patience, is Griselda's virtue—"of her own volition she has made constancy to him supreme.... While Walter remains the visible symbol of the vow Griselda made him, it seems less Walter than the vow itself"—her own vow, to which Griselda remains unflinchingly constant.[13] It is this quality of strength in Griselda—a strength so indomitable in its very meekness as to be an awesome self-assertion—which fascinates students who universally find her acceptance of the happy ending implausible. But in this they, and Donaldson, are wrong. He says of Griselda that it "is not human to go on loving a monster."[14] But of course it is, and has been ever since the first husband came home drunk and beat his wife.

The *Clerk's Tale,* as all critics know, is a naturalized version of a generic folktale motif, Beauty and the Beast, which generates an array of plots extending from the Cupid and Psyche myth to the story of the princess who marries a frog in order to break the enchantment and make her frog a prince again. In all versions, whether the ending is happy or not, a woman is asked to accomplish the ordeal of loving and obeying a repulsive, sadistic, unintelligible, supernatural, sometimes invisible, or otherwise impossible consort. Eventually, if faithfulness is perfect (or almost perfect), it is rewarded by having the monstrous consort transformed into an ideal lover or husband. It is impossible to know how much Chaucer knew of the folktale roots of his story.[15] But it is even more impossible to believe that he could have been ignorant of the profound truth of human nature which it expresses. The marriage vow, for better or for worse, and even more because it evokes the faithful saving love of Christ, presumes a radically and stubbornly persistent redemptive power. Wives, and husbands too, who truly marry commit themselves to a faithfulness strong enough to redeem and transform a monster and are perhaps most radically glorified in this world when that is the ordeal they are given.

We need to remember, though, that there is not one vow, but three. Walter vows to God a devotion which Chaucer makes a precise equivalent of Griselda's to Walter;[16] and Walter imposes on his people, before he chooses a wife, the same vow again. These vows reflect the triple duty of the sovereign, as defined by Aegidius Romanus, to rule wisely himself, his family, and his realm.[17] Self-rule, of course, is the very opposite of autonomous self-assertion; rather, it is a cultivation of virtue which is the earthly expression of one's subservience and service to God. The story begins, therefore, with the levels announced and sorted out. In trusting God, Walter implicitly puts himself in the place of Constance—a member of the visible world, dependent upon the invisible workings of the providence of God to provide a meaningful outcome in the *opus restaurationis.* It is his place to be, as marquis, merely human, while God, who has divine use for human actions, provides the allegory.

In the *Man of Law's Tale,* the action of the plot really does expand Christendom; the doubleness consists first in the two parallel actions, one of which fails and one of which succeeds, and then in the pathetic predicament of people who must necessarily see this *opus restaurationis* as a processs in time rather than as an ordered and eschatalogical whole. In the normal career of the human sovereign, however, the doubleness usually consists of the fact that earthly events have a heavenly allegory—the king's practical and daily acts of rule may be devotionally and allegorically compared to the activity of God in Christ, for both the spiritual correction of the king and the spiritual edification of him and of his people. The lesson of the *Man of Law's Tale* is that this doubleness must be accepted.[18]

But Walter does not accept this advice. He is compulsively anxious to play God—as it were, to force the divine level into identity with the human level, rather than to accept it as the analogy that it is and must be. Instead of being the sovereign who is a figure of God, he wishes literally to perform the acts of God—though in terms of the comparison with the Job story, what he actually performs are the acts of the devil. Instead of expanding Christendom by the faithful performance of earthly life, he wishes to expand the scope of earthly sovereignty to include, literally, heaven.[19]

In thus wishing and thus doing, Walter is unfaithful to the pattern of the three vows with which his story began and unfaithful to the ideal of justice which, as sovereign, he was obligated to serve. William Peraldus's definition is instructive:

> Quia virtute iustitiae reddimus unicuique quod debemus, dividetur iustitia secundum ea quae debemus, et quibus debemus.
>
> Notandum ergo quod quaedam debemus omnibus, ut dilectionem, veritatem et fidem: quaedam vero non omnibus et inter ea aliquid debemus superiori, aliquid inferiori, aliquid pari. Item aliquid speciale debemus nobis specialiter coniunctis, ut parentibus, et patriae benevolis, quod debitum solvit pietas, prout Macrobius et Tullius de ea loquuntur. Item debemus aliquid his qui beneficia conferunt: scilicet gratiam, de qua loquitur Tullius. Et aliquid his qui mala inferunt: scilicet vindicationem, de qua idem loquitur. Et aliquid etiam his qui mala ferunt vel sustinent, scilicet misericordiam.[20]

Peraldus goes on to define, as a part of the office of "latria," which we owe to God and only to God, a kind of committed obedience. "Tertium est vitam nostram Deo committere. Qui enim agnoscit per fidem se habere vitam suam a Deo, vult illam ei offerre, et oratione, et obsequiis impetrat eam a Deo dirigi. Tob. 4. Omni tempore benedic Dominum, et pete ab eo ut vias tuas dirigat, et omnia consilia tua in ipso permaneant."[21] It is not at all clear that Griselda's vow of obedience, or that of the people, is overdone, though in the absolute sense, of course, it is ultimately appropriate only to God. However, Walter is clearly in the wrong by not performing his debt of "dilectio, veritas, et fides"—he is harsh rather than cherishing, deceitful rather than true, and faithful only in the sense of technical chastity.

Throughout Peraldus's discussion of justice, which is of course one of the supreme obligations of the sovereign, there runs most strongly the notion of what is due—the actions and relations which are demanded by the very nature and definition of the entities (usually people) involved. We are dealing with definitions and types, not cases: normative procedure at its most normative. The pressure of the medieval conviction that stories are about *consuetudines* and *credulitates*, rather than things obvious to sense, is very strong here. Equally strong, in the story, is the magnificent and indeed iconic perfection of Griselda's constancy—real women are not like that, though in the divine economy of God in which people are tested and tried as if by fire, women and men are expected to be like that, and do indeed sometimes measure up. Therefore, because of the heavy pressure of abstraction, of the perfection of the typical, of the *consuetudo* which is definition, Walter's compulsive playing of God is an imitation made all the more outrageous, all the more absolute and absolutely pretentious, by the perfection of the response to it.

The outrage, as we have said, is that Walter's actions intend literally, rather than analogically and allegorically, to be godlike actions. In this dimension, what the story is about is the abuse of allegory by virtue of the refusal of doubleness—by virtue of an absolute and outrageous demand for unity, singleness, and unequivocal existence. It is an abuse which the doubleness of the *Man of Law's Tale* warns against; it is an abuse which the tales following will compound in various ways, as we shall see; and it is an abuse which gains special meaning because it is committed in the context of marriage, as well as in the context of sovereignty.

We have repeatedly claimed that allegory is, in the later Middle Ages, a principle of structure rather than, or more significantly than, a linguistic strategy of reference. It is in the *Clerk's Tale,* more than anywhere else in Chaucer, that this medieval structural principle is most blatantly and obviously violated.[22] This is true, we think, because it is in the merely human moral order represented by this combination of a sovereign in his realm and a husband in his marriage that there is the greatest human temptation to feel self-sufficient and complete, to refuse or ignore the analogies, and at the same time the greatest opportunity for devotion or insight to develop an awareness of the analogies. The love of Christ for the church should be present to the marriage bed; the sovereign love of God for his Creation should be present to the functions of the king. That they so often are is cause of the human sense that these earthy human functions are both supremely important and superbly meaningful. But when one wishes to have the importance and the meaning, without the humility to keep in mind their ultimate basis, one has the all too easy and natural sin of which Walter's playing God is type and emblem, so radically that one must know, not only that it is perverse, but also what is the norm of doubleness which it violates. The *Clerk's Tale,* then, represents the moral order of the merely human, evil or lacking only when it fails to remember that it is derivative and not absolute, and even then capable of being the context of great individual moral achievement.

Walter is a monster, irredeemably. Yet the tale is not monstrous— or at least it is tantalizingly close to being acceptable. Therein lies its fascination. Just as the *Man of Law's Tale* takes a feature of the third part of the *Knight's Tale,* the pathos of the human condition catalogues, and makes that pathos the theme and essence of the whole tale, so the *Clerk's Tale* takes a part of the *Man of Law's Tale.* When Constance bears Alla's child, the messenger and the constable condemn it (with its mother) to possible death, and with every appearance and conviction of having acted on Alla's instructions. Given Griselda's absolute and absolutely kept promise not to complain or even question, it would take only the smallest of adjustments of the plot of the *Clerk's Tale* to transform Walter's monstrous test into an innocent act of some sort, which his wife unquestioningly misconstrued as a murder. The motif "father rejects innocent child," which in the *Man of Law's Tale* really is an occasion of Job-like endurance of testing, becomes in the *Clerk's Tale* the horror it is only because we have Walter's motivations explained to us. The *Clerk's Tale* permits the horrid mistake of the *Man of Law's Tale* to come true, precisely in order to rid the story of the need for the operation of Providence, to reduce the moral order involved to the merely human by the smallest possible change, so as to preserve for that merely human moral order as much of the absolute character appropriate to definitional paradigms as possible.

The result can perhaps be best defined, briefly, by calling it an exactly medieval equivalent of surrealism. It has the same haunting, troubling quality of overdefinition, of more meaningfulness than meaning, which must accrue to a story which claims to be the act of God while it admits that it is not God.

What are we to make of it? Essentially, that we cannot accept any moral order which insists on unifying all levels of allegory into its literal self. Moral questions depend for their answers not only on the nature of the act involved but also, and perhaps even more importantly, on the nature of the structures, and the structures of structures, which surround and condition and interpret (or fail to interpret) that act. This is the statement that the *Clerk's Tale* makes, partly because it is the tale it is, and partly because we have seen it as a tale that comes immediately after the *Man of Law's Tale*, the third member of a descending enthymeme of tales whose initial proposition is part three of the *Knight's Tale*.

But this tale, uniquely in Chaucer's collection, has an Envoi, which has been on medieval authority labeled as Chaucer's. Dramatically it belongs to the Clerk, but this fact is irrelevant. We are not reading on dramatic principles. In fact, it belongs to Chaucer, and the medieval scribal label properly recognizes the fact that here the author, Chaucer himself, has added something, and speaks from behind his puppet show in his own voice. In the tale Chaucer has not been allusive. Beyond some obvious "ox stall" underlinings of Griselda's identification with Christ, and some quotations from Job which repeat the tale's point and its overt ostensible moralization, the verbal texture of the *Clerk's Tale* is spare, lean, literal, and direct. Such a style is absolutely appropriate, because the point of the tale is to claim (perversely, as it happens, but the style is still answerable) that life can be thus spare, simple, unified, and absolute. But with the Envoi the Chaucerian wit becomes more ostentatiously complex. In the Envoi Chaucer reverts to his favorite ironic technique, a richly allusive statement contradicted or complicated by external commentary.

The tale begins with Petrarch dead, and "nayled in his cheste" (IV [E] 29); the Envoi begins with Griselda dead, along with her patience. In both cases there is a related quality—Petrarch's rhetoric, which illumines (as does Lanyan's philosophy and law), and Griselda's patience. Presumably abstractions can die as well as people—the reality of the *consuetudo* is no more. Therefore, since the old world is dead, we must welcome the new. Follow Echo; answer back. The medieval glosses on Echo repeat and complicate the theme and advice of the

Clerk's Tale marvelously and, when taken with the text, predict and advise the following tales.

Literally, Echo is one who answers back, and therefore by example advises wives to be like the Wife of Bath rather than Griselda. One of Bersuire's glosses says the same thing: "Vel dic quod tales echo sunt quedam litigiose et brigose mulieres vel etiam quidam servitores queruli qui ultimum verbum semper volunt habere: et ad omnia que dicuntur a maritis atque dominis respondere. Etsi ab eis reprehenduntur semper murmurant. Contra illud leviti. xix. Non eris criminator aut susurro in populis."[23] Chaucer's reference to the camel is also appropriate, because he is a strong beast and swift, and able to carry heavy burdens—at the same time a camel will refuse a load that is too heavy or a trip that is too long.[24] The tiger is notable chiefly in the bestiaries for being swift and for being deceivable by a hunter with a mirror.[25]

Other glosses, however, rather contradict the real implications of what Chaucer says. In addition to representing "litigiose et brigose mulieres," Echo may also mean a good reputation: "Per Echo hominis bonam famam, que arrogantem amaret et benedicendo extolleret nisi ipse se cunctis preferendo bonam famam contempneret. Quia igitur contempta fuit, latuit nichil boni dicendo de eo."[26] Or Echo may mean flatterers: "Dic quod echo significat adulatores qui et montes, idest prelatos: silvas idest religiosos: flumina idest seculares et delicatos frequentant et circa ipsos resonant et clamant. Si enim contingat aliquid ab aliquo dici statim solent ad verba ipsius respondere: et verbum eius tanquam benedictum replicare."[27] The camel is allegorically an exemplum of patient endurance of penance: "Sic pro certo veri patientes debent esse agiles, per obedientiae velocitatem, onera poenitentiae et praelia adversitatis sustinere, per patientiam, et firmitatem. Unde ad Gal. 6. Unusquisque onus suum portabit. Et ideo quando magister Cameli, idest, prelatus vel sacerdos, vel etiam quando Deus indicit, iniungit et immittit aliquod opus poenitentiae, laboris vel adversitatis, statim nos debemus incurvari per humilitatem, obedientiam et subiectionem, et genua flectere, per gratiarum actionem."[28] Thus, to follow the example of Echo, and to be like the camel, means to answer back and be stubborn. But these examples also advise us to be like Griselda, careful for the *bona fama* of our Walters, even to the point of flattery. In the camel we are allegorically exhorted to the precise patient endurance of testing which the Envoi says is no longer possible or necessary. Thus Chaucer contradicts himself, if we are learned enough to know the glosses and see the irony. If we see the irony, then we can accept Petrarch's allegorization, and Griselda's death does not mean the death of patience as well. If we know only that Echo is "litigiosa et brigosa," then we are led to Leviticus 19:16: "Non eris criminator aut susurro in populis," a verse which predicts the actual recommendation of the *Manciple's Tale.* If we accept the merely literal recommendation of the Envoi, always to answer back, we will have the gift of ready answer that Persephone gives to May in the *Merchant's Tale.* If we are like Echo, who "evere answereth at the countretaille," then we are prepared to deal with tallies, and with the wife's answer in the *Shipman's Tale:* "Score it upon my taille." Taking all levels together, Griselda's example is both denied and affirmed, and all the following tales are predicted. In a world defined by a man who acts as if he were God, real truth tends to be obscure.

The *Merchant's Tale* accepts Chaucer's advice: always have an answer. It picks up and makes absolute a detail from the *Clerk's Tale,* just as the *Clerk's Tale* had done from the *Man of Law's Tale* and the *Man of Law's Tale* from the *Knight's Tale.* Walter's proposed January–May marriage to his own daughter, which is of course pure pretense, becomes in the *Merchant's Tale* the serious basis of the narrative. And the complex irony of Chaucer's Envoi, with its literal statements contradicted by the glosses which come with allusions and comparisons, is the basic strategy of the whole of the *Merchant's Tale.*

We have said that the *Man of Law's Tale* represents the moral order of imperial Christendom, which properly exists, *ad interim huius mundi,* in a state of pathos out of which providence eventually works good ends. The *Clerk's Tale* represents the moral order of any earthly realm, which sees itself as absolute and so misappropriates to itself divine functions, but which nevertheless can be the context of superb moral achievement. The *Merchant's Tale* represents the moral order of any merely human marriage.

Properly, marriage is not a good in isolation. In the full dispensation of Providence, marriage exists for the sake of engendering children, for the sake of avoidance of sin, and for the sake of figuring the divine truths and relationships which centuries of biblical authority and human devotion had related to it. Necessarily, therefore, January's narrowly sexual reasons for marriage are wrong primarily (discounting his advanced age) because they are incomplete. Avoidance of sin is but one-third, and the least third at that, of the full meaning. To affirm the part as, and instead of, the whole is to make one's self liable to the ironies generated by the whole's inevitable presence; like the *Romance of the Rose,* the *Merchant's Tale* is allegorically haunted by what is missing.[29]

The tale is haunted as well by the true version of what is literally there. Reduced to outline, the *Merchant's Tale* is about an old man who accepts his wife as innocent after he has seen visual evidence of what seems to be her sexual relation with a man in a tree. The most famous old cuckold in the medieval tradition is Joseph; the most famous apparently guilty but acceptably innocent young maiden is Mary.[30] The man in the tree is Satan, if we can accept the testimony of the *Biblia Pauperum.*[31] On the other hand, Christ was also in a tree,[32] and since Mary is pregnant, and May only in danger of being so, the substitution of child for lover is plausible. Nicholas of Lyra comments extensively on Joseph's predicament; one bit is an especially telling parallel with May's pagan goddess–given ability to talk her way out of difficulty: "Sed queritur hic quare maria non dixit ei divinum secretum. Est dicendum quod talia non sunt revelanda: nisi quantum se extendit voluntas divina. et ideo beata virgo tacuit: tenens firmiter quod sicut istud secretum fuerat revelatum sancte eliçabet: ut habetur Luce primo: sic revelaretur aliis competenti tempore ex beneplacito divine voluntatis. Similiter queritur quare ioseph non petivit ab ea? Dicendum quod pro nihilo petisset: quia ipsi marie pro se dicenti non credidisset: et iterum ex divina dispensatione hoc factum est, ut per revelationem angeli ipse ioseph sic certificaretur quod de cetero nullo modo dubitare posset."[33] A husband (or an espoused husband) has a right to be doubtful, in such a case as this; the irony is intensified as, in the *Merchant's Tale,* May herself is made the medium of the divine certification. In thus being able to answer back, she takes the advice of Chaucer's Envoi and at the same time accomplishes, by morally blinding her husband as his real sight is restored, precisely the same detachment from allegorical validity which the tale's assertion of sex-for-its-own-sake marriage has already generated.

Morally, "Per ioseph cogitantem dimittere mariam: qui certificatus de mysterio per angelum accepit eam ut dominam: significatur homo dubitans in fide vel moribus qui per predicatorem vel confessorem bonum in fide solidatur: et subiicit se ei in illis que fidei sunt orthodoxe."[34] January has a great deal of good advice given him, before he marries, *in moribus bonis,* but he will not take it. His marriage is an example of the literal contradiction of what Joseph's marriage morally means.

This neat ironic layering of gloss upon event is, as we have said, the strategy of the tale. So much has been obvious for a long time, especially from Emerson Brown's work. Our point, in adding to this rich texture a gloss or two from Nicholas of Lyra, is not simply to note that the ironies are there, but rather to claim that their presence is a comment upon allegoricalness of a certain sort, and at the place in this descending enthymeme of merely moral orders where that comment has most point.

The merely human marriage is what the Wife of Bath defends— "Whos lyf and al hire secte," says Chaucer's Clerk, may "God mayntene" (IV [E] 1171). It is intrinsic to the nature of marriage, and especially good marriage, to be preoccupying. The Wife of Bath wants husbands who are good in bed. Sovereigns wish to expand their sovereignty, even at the expense of God; lovers, even married ones, wish simply to be left alone.[35] But to be thus left alone is ultimately to have nothing but the predicament of the flesh—this is why the Wife regrets her pith; this is why the sweating Lover of the *Romance of the Rose* has aged so much in his staff-assisted pilgrimage; this is why January's slack skin and badly shaven whiskers are so repulsive; this is why Chaucer forces on his audience in the *Merchant's Tale* the half-fascinated, half-sick repulsive point of view of the voyeur; this is why the gods who rule in this new Eden of the second fall are pagan gods, and from hell at that. The flesh is necessary, and good. The predicament of the flesh, however, is by definition, and because of the Incarnation, self-imposed, unnecessary, escapable. The hovering allegories of the *Merchant's Tale,* which its literal sense constantly contradicts and rejects, are a persistent reminder to the predicament of the flesh that it is unnecessary, and that the whole truth of January's marriage, or of any marriage, as an ideally intended moral order of use in this temporary world, is larger than January knows. Because January refuses to know, the allegories hover ironically; because what he refuses is in fact true, they must be present.

The *Manciple's Tale* and the *Shipman's Tale* elaborate this predicament of the flesh. If marriage is merely carnal, then adultery is its normal complication—the eternal triangle is profoundly grounded in human nature. Two reactions to adultery are possible—outraged condemnation and acceptance. The *Manciple's Tale* has for its matter January's wrath, the *Shipman's Tale* the blindness which May's ready answer imposes on him. Neither order is very good, but we are in a descending series, and lower than the *Merchant's Tale* is at best far from ideal.

The *Manciple's Tale* is really two tales and three discursive essays. The first part is a narrative of the Manciple's prudent reconciliation with the hung-over and drunken Cook, to prevent the Manciple's embezzlements from being found out. The second part is an essay dealing with the relationship between a creature and its nature or definition. The third part is another essay, which deals with the relationship between a thing and its right name.[36] The fourth part is the tale of Apollo and his crow. Finally, there is an essay on the tongue, warning us against too much talk. Four of these five have to do with the kind of order an individual generates, or tries to generate, around himself to make himself comfortable in the world. The Manciple obviously has an interest in the continued benign intoxication of a potential witness against him. The examples of the caged bird, the cat, and the she-wolf would seem to argue that lower impulses, being natural, must find indulgence.[37] Apollo, who is comfortably married, destroys his wife and his situation in defense of principle, and concludes bitterly that he was wrong. The essay on the custody of the tongue then generalizes, advising against any talk which might cause mischief.

In order to see what is the true sum of this miscellany, we must reconcile the tale of Apollo to its context. In the descending enthymeme of tales of marriage, this is a tale which values definitions so far above facts as to be willing to destroy the facts for the sake of definition. This may seem a strange way of describing what he does, but it is deliberately done in order to find a place for what might be called philosophical idealism, or, in modern terms, utopianism, in this descending series of human moralities by which the world is provisionally ordered. Robertson's willingness to give up the Wife of Bath for the abstract name of a grotesque is the critical equivalent of this idealism,[38] and the too easy acceptance of the Parson's condemnation of all that has gone before him is, we suppose, the devotional. Both are ultimately destructive, both of life and of definition. To say, as Apollo does by implication, that it is better to have a dead wife than an unfaithful one is to destroy the marriage along with the wife and be left with nothing. His solution was manifestly unsatisfactory and was instantly repented of. As a god, Apollo is a failure—and precisely the kind of failure to define, by his existence, the influence of idealism upon human morality.[39] He is supposed to be the god of wisdom, but he is in fact a mere bachelor, without powers or *numen*,[40] whose providential working in the world begins in jealous rage and ends in disaster. We are far removed from the providential God who guarded Constance, and even from the lesser gods who gave to January and May (and Damian) what they needed to make a bad situation livable.

It is gratifying to have idealism so far down. We have seen that one of the ruling strategies of this moral group of tales is the evocation, in an array of ways, of some kind of allegorical resonance, overtone, assertion, or relationship. In the *Man of Law's Tale* the allegorical or providential dimension was hidden behind pathos, but eventually, by the power of God, was made part of the literal. Walter acted as if godlikeness could be made literally his merely by behaving like God. January, May, and Damian are pleased to pretend that there is nothing but the flesh, accepting its carnality, and are reproved by the ironies which their unintentionally resonating actions evoke. Apollo, still lower, would pretend that mere flesh can be perfect, and gets nothing. And the merchant and his wife, in the *Shipman's Tale*, mistake the metaphor of the marriage debt for something literal, equate sex and gold, and get the kind of love which results from that equation.

Apollo's foolishness is surrounded by a context which interprets and corrects it. Chaucer's discussion of the propriety of the word *lemman*, and his suggestion that the name of thief is equally applicable to Alexander as to a petty outlaw, speak directly to the problem of the relation between words and things—the relation which Apollo so foolishly and destructively tried to make perfectly pure. The problem Chaucer specifically addresses here is the problem of the correct name, in two opposite senses. First, can a word be used which carries with it a moral evaluation as well as a definite meaning—can one "talk dirty" about dirty things? Second, can a word be expanded beyond its normal usage to expose a truth usually ignored—can we call an emperor a thief when his legitimizing force is nothing but a very large army? The questions seem obvious to the point of triviality, but they are not. First of all, the word *lemman* is not, in fact, a dirty word, since it can be used in perfectly straightforward fashion in religious contexts.[41] Second, the Alexander story, which was enormously popular,[42] tended normally to be told as a story recounted to Alexander himself, to make the point that Alexander would reward a culprit with a brave and ready answer. Chaucer's point would seem to be that one can handle things by using words, but not without admitting that the way between "is slider." The claims which a nominalist would make for words would be high claims, but not at all absolute ones.

The same kind of comment is appropriate to the essay on the nature of birds, cats, and she-wolves. The very fact that the examples echo the *Romance of the Rose* should put us on our guard. Even though the nature of birds is to eat worms, and of cats to chase mice, such low lusts are not absolute, because birds and cats are not absolute. One must ask of Nature, whose gift these natures are, not only what they are but also what they mean, since no single thing can be taken in isolation. Such a question, of course, is ultimately beyond Nature's competence.

Therefore we begin with a Manciple who uses wine to make himself friends of the Mammon of unrighteousness, lest true but inconvenient words about his own history be spoken. And we end with the exhortation to tell nothing, lest we tell too much. Such a philosophy of language is a poor one, but it is the best response that life can make of the ironies of the *Manciple's Tale*. There Apollo, unwise in action though the god of wisdom, has a concept of marriage which leads him to kill his wife. Since concepts are empty words unless they attach to the world, and since the murder which Apollo's notion justifies destroys his marriedness along with his wife, his conceptual use of language empties his language of reference and nullifies his ideal. Silence is indeed better than this.[43]

The action of the *Shipman's Tale* begins with a double vow: on the part of Don John, "That nevere in my lyf, for lief ne looth,/Ne shal I of no conseil yow biwrey" (VII 132–33 [B² 1322–23]), to which the merchant's wife responds: "Ne shal I nevere, for to goon to helle,/Biwreye a word of thyng that ye me telle" (VII 137–38 [B² 1327–28]). Both vows assent to the final advice of the *Manciple's Tale*. Secrets will not be told; cuckolded husbands will never be given a chance to kill in haste and repent at leisure. From this promising beginning the tale goes on to make absolute the result of the *Merchant's Tale*—a stable arrangement for probable further adulteries, with the wife in command and fully aware of the commercial value of her principal assets.

Priest John is a member of the merchant's household—a familiar, an honorary cousin, who gives good tips to the servants and causes no comment when he visits in the merchant's house while the merchant is away. He is, in fact, such a familiar that the merchant is embarrassed to have given him the impression of wanting to have his money back. And the merchant's wife shares with him the secrets of her "privitee"—that her husband is not good in bed. The whole arrangement, in fact, is liberated enough to be modern instead of medieval. The only household in the whole of the *Canterbury Tales* to compare with it is that of the *Cook's Tale,* where sex was actually sold, rather than simply used in payment of debt. This is a world in which there are no gods, no powers except gold (and its sexual equivalent). As a moral order it is the most pragmatic, the most merely human in the eries. Beyond this point one cannot go and still be orderly, or maintain even the pretense of morality.

The irony of the tale involves one metaphor and two puns, whose use defines the verbal potential of this kind of order. The metaphor is that of the *debitum,* or marriage debt; the two puns are of "cosynage" and of "taillynge." The metaphor of the marriage debt is a sufficiently arid-seeming justification for sex, but in rational terms it fits very well. Like marriage, a debt is created by a vow or a promise, it involves something physical or material, and it creates a relationship between two people in which the major concern of the debtor is for the satisfaction of the creditor. The only adjustment which marriage makes is that the status of debtor tends to be maximized, for both parties, and the status of creditor is ignored, or at least not encouraged. Once past the commercial overtones of the word, one must admit that a metaphor which encourages each member of a marriage to be primarily concerned for the satisfaction of the other is a good and noble thing, not to be condemned out of hand because celibate moralists may have made it joyless and repulsive.[44]

But the connection with money does linger; this metaphor, like all metaphors, is subject to abuse. What the characters in the *Shipman's Tale* do is take the metaphor literally. Sex can be bought, as Priest John buys it; once bought and sold, it can, and indeed must, be a currency capable of satisfying debt:

> Ye han more slakkere dettours than am I!
> For I wol paye yow wel and redily
> Fro day to day, and if so be I faille,
> I am youre wyf; score it upon my taille,
> ....
> By God, I wil nat paye yow but abedde!
>
> (VII 413–16, 424 [B² 1603–6, 1614])

So much is obvious, and has been often noted. What is important to see, however, is what happens to language when people try to pass off this kind of order as moral. Puns become perverse, or threatening, rather than clues to the secret harmony of the universe. "Cosynage" equates the bond of family, in which one should be able to feel most secure, with precisely that kind of fraud by trickery which especially depends upon and exploits the feeling of being secure. If sex is merely "taillynge," then the woman who suggests the arrangement has reduced herself to mere flesh, or she has dignified bookkeeping by calling it orgasmic—and, indeed, her husband does seem to be better in bed when he has just been triumphant in the market. When the moral order is nothing but the flesh, and arrangements for it comfort, then words lose all power to save. When facts try to get along without the truth, they find that language will not only permit them to do so but will even encourage them, and will by the tricks that only language can play—puns and metaphors—make the situation worse. A part of the wife's triumph is the possibility of the pun. Without it she still may have talked her husband into reasonable good cheer about her clothing bills, but her larger audience would have been less satisfied. Language gives her a connection—accidental, untrue, degrading—which she uses, and in using, accepts.

Hell, says Charles Williams, is imprecise. So is sin. And so in real life are the intricate arrangements we make to cover the tracks of our sins and our mistakes. The very fact that in fiction always, and even sometimes in life, words will go along with these intricate imprecisions through metaphors and puns, in ways which have about them a quality of wit, adds a dimension of rightness to the wrong and begins to redeem it. When, in the beginning of the story, we are told of the troubles husbands have with their wives' expenditures on clothing, we smile in recognition. When Priest John giggles at his risque language we smile again. And when the possibility of this tallying knits up the feast, and makes an end, our satisfaction is as much with the moral power of words to be neat as it is laughter at the immoral power of people to keep their original private little worlds going, more or less in order, for a while.

The moral group, then, is a group of marriages. Chaucer chose this particular human experience as the paradigm for particular morality because marriage so perfectly combines the particularity of the flesh with the narrative intentionality of the vow—that is, because it combines words with things; and because marriage, of all human institutions, best admits to allegorical or analogous or typical resonance without surrendering its existence as a daily set of facts which unify two people with past and future, constituting social history. His examples occur in descending order; we have called the series an enthymeme both because of that figure's connection with rhetoric and because of the fact that in series a detail from one story becomes the whole of the next. Throughout, there is one game being played with the presence and power of God, or his pagan substitute; another is played with what may be most generally called allegory—that is, the resonant relation, positive or ironic, between the facts of a story and the truth which the story might exemplify. Both these games are right, at this place in Chaucer's Canterbury collection, because it is private moralities which have the most ambiguous, or dubious, relation to God, and because the test which these particular assertions of order demand by wishing to be true is the test of allegory. That all of them, except the *Man of Law's Tale*, are found wanting should be no surprise; only Saturn was right, and no shrine was built to him. Lesser daemons may make their promises, but none will come true unless Saturn wills it. Men may make their marriages, playing God or playing pimp, as the case may be, but we only discover what it all means after it is all over, Constance has come home, and she finds that God has a use for the fact that Alla loves her truly still.

1. The term *frame* comes from Erving Goffman, *Frame Analysis: An Essay on the Organization of Experience* (Cambridge, Mass., 1974). In using it we do not intend to import into the analysis of Chaucer a sociological anachronism. But if we discount the phenomenological dimensions of Goffman's analysis, the notion of the framed event—the event whose shape and significance depend largely (or even partially) on the assumptions or truth systems of the actors and audience (if any)—nicely defines medieval morality. The medieval frame, of course, was ontologically grounded.

2. *The Waning of the Middle Ages,* passim.

3. Chauncey Wood, "The Man of Law as Interpreter," *Traditio* 23 (1967): 149–90.

4. Explained in helpful detail by Emerson Brown, Jr., in a series of articles: "*The Merchant's Tale:* Why Is May Called 'Mayus'?" *Chaucer Review* 2 (1967): 273–77; "*The Merchant's Tale,* Januarie's 'Unlikely Elde,'" *Neuphilologische Mitteilungen* 74 (1973): 92–106; "*The Merchant's Tale:* Why Was Januarie Born of Pavye?", *Neuphilologische Mitteilungen* 71 (1970): 654–58; "Hortus Inconclusus: The Significance of Priapus, and Pyramus and Thisbe, in the *Merchant's Tale,*" *Chaucer Review* 4 (1969): 31–40. See below, note 30.

5. If we may trust the pun established in the *Miller's Tale* and the *Wife of Bath's Tale,* then the Merchant speaks more truly than he knows, because the "queynte world" for whose good order he is concerned will to his loss come to include the world of "queynte."

6. Thus, in the *Ovide moralisé,* the romance of Mars and Venus is discussed as a conjunction of planets, which govern the "colerique" and "pasibile" temperaments (2:131 lines 1489-96). This relation between emotions and temperaments, and the stars, for the Middle Ages is explored in Curry, *Medieval Sciences.*

7. See below, in the Epilogue, for a fuller treatment of this dimension of marriage imagery and the intimate connection between Chaucer's understanding of human marriage and the power of story.

8. Of Chaucer the narrator E. Talbot Donaldson remarks, "It is almost as if the Creator were watching with loving sympathy and humorous appreciation

the solemn endeavors of His creatures to understand the situation in which He has placed them" (*Chaucer's Poetry: An Anthology for the Modern Reader* [New York, 1958], p. 944).

9. Emelye's two potential mothers-in-law, if we take the easiest implication of Chaucer's pedigree for Palamon and Arcite—"... of the blood roial / Of Thebes, and of sustren two yborn" (I [A] 1018-19)—were Antigone and Ismene. The disorder that intricately and incestuously ravaged Thebes has now been pushed back to far distant borders. Emelye is almost as passive as Constance. Theseus's project in making his ward's marriage is like the emperor's in sending Constance to the sultan, in that he has succeeded in consolidating his border states, Amazonia and Thebes, much as the emperor hoped to Christianize the pagan realms and eventually succeeds in doing so in his daughter's second marriage. Constance's adventures are alternate.

10. This lesson, that allegory cannot be identity, is of course the one that Walter, in the tale immediately following, violates—as we shall see, with interesting consequences for the enterprise of interpretation.

11. Thomas H. Bestul, "The Man of Law's Tale and the Rhetorical Foundations of Chaucerian Pathos," *Chaucer Review* 9 (1975): 216-26, makes the valuable point that the Man of Law may not be skilled in the rhetoric of display, but reveals a talent for the medieval art of evoking pathos.

12. R. K. Root calls the tale "a splendidly pictured tapestry" (quoted by Muscatine, *Chaucer and the French Tradition*, p. 176). The nonsequential character of the *Knight's Tale* is also stressed by Muscatine in his own treatment of the poem, which he finds more appropriately understood as a "poetic pageant" than as a story organized around plot and character development (p. 181).

13. Donaldson, *Chaucer's Poetry*, 2d ed., p. 1082.

14. Ibid., p. 1081.

15. The problem of the folktale origins of the tale is treated, with a helpful bibliography, by J. Burke Severs in *The Literary Relationships of Chaucer's Clerk's Tale* (New Haven, 1942), pp. 4-6. Severs discusses the various types of folktale traditions which have been offered as suggesting key elements in the tale, including the Cupid and Psyche tales and those of the Calumniated Wife and the Intended Bride. Severs concludes, along with W. A. Cate, "The Problem of the Origin of the Griselda Story," *Studies in Philology* 29 (1932): 399, that the story "is derived from a special development of Cupid and Psyche folktales." The Griselda story is not entirely faithful to the Cupid-Psyche pattern because Griselda never fails in her duty to her husband, whereas Psyche does and must win back his love. See Margaret Schlauch's discussion of the tests which Psyche traditionally must undergo before winning Cupid back, in *Chaucer's Constance and Accused Queens* (New York, 1927), p. 54. Stith Thompson classifies the Griselda story among the tales of wives tested by husbands who feign illness, and so forth, in order to prove their brides' worth; see his *Motif-Index of Folk-Literature* (Bloomington, Ind., 1955), 3:415. One crucial element of the story, that is, the presumption of Walter's efforts to play God, could be due, at least in part, to the story's folktale backgrounds, in which the actions of the superhuman character are not explained or ac-

counted for but only serve as the impetus for action. At the same time, stories of the tested wife sometimes deal explicitly with this question of why the test should be conducted at all. Don Juan Manuel, in *El Conde Lucanor,* an early fourteenth-century Spanish story collection, tells a story analogous to the *Taming of the Shrew,* but without the shrew as an excuse for the harsh treatment. The husband explains that after testing his wife in examples of arbitrary demands on her obedience, he could have confidence in her judgment at all times. From the number of folktale analogues catalogued by Cate, it seems likely that Chaucer could have known the story in other forms. At any rate, he seems aware of the dual aspect of Walter's character as both man and God.

16. "I truste in Goddes bountee, and therfore / My mariage and myn estaat and reste / I hym bitake; he may doon as hym leste" (IV [E] 159–61). The Latin of the source is less open-ended a commitment: "Illi ego et status et matrimonii mei sortes, sperans de sua solita pietate, commiserim; ipse michi inveniet quod quieti mee sit expediens ac saluti" (Bryan and Dempster, *Sources and Analogues,* p. 300).

17. This definition was documented in connection with our discussion of the *Knight's Tale.*

18. Robert Kaske, in his article "Chaucer's Marriage Group," draws a similar conclusion as an explanation for the various tensions between literal story and allegorical meaning established within the tale.

19. Walter's usurpation of the place and activity of God has been often enough noted. See especially Jordan, *Chaucer and the Shape of Creation,* p. 198, and the scholarship that Jordan cites.

20. William Peraldus, *Summa virtutum ac vitiorum* (Lyons, 1668), p. 302. "Since by the virtue of justice we give back to everyone what we owe, justice is divided according to those things which we owe, and to whom we own them. Therefore it should be understood that we owe certain things to everyone, as affection, truthfulness, and faithfulness: but certain things we do not owe to everyone and among them we owe something to someone superior, to someone below us, and something else to an equal. Next we owe something special to our relations and friends, as to our relatives and to our countrymen, which debt is paid by dutiful conduct, as Macrobius and Cicero say concerning it. Next we owe something to those who give benefits, that is, thanks, about which Cicero speaks. And something to those who try to do evil, that is, defense, about which Cicero also speaks. And something also to those who endure or suffer evil, that is, mercy."

21. Ibid., p. 305. "The third is to commit our life to God. For one who knows through faith that he has his life from God, wishes to offer it to him, and by prayer and supplications brings about that it is directed by God. Tob. 4. Bless God all the time, and desire of him to direct your ways, and that all your counsels may abide in him."

22. If reference may be made to the analogous claims made about *Gawain and the Green Knight* in *The Friar as Critic* (pp. 145–49), one might say that Walter, throughout the tale, has the status of the Green Knight when he first comes to Arthur's court. It is as if the Green Knight had come, made his

challenge, lost his head to Gawain's stroke, and had then said, putting his head back on, "All right, boys, I was only kidding, to see if you were really brave. Now where's my chair?"

23. *Ovidius moralizatus*, p. 71. "Or say that these are Echo: certain litigious and quarrelsome women, or also certain complaining servants, who always wish to have the last word, and answer back to whatever their husbands or lords say, and if they are reproved by them always grumble. Against them [see] Lev. 19: Do not be a detractor or whisperer among the people."

24. In T. H. White's *The Book of Beasts* (New York, 1954), a translation from a medieval Latin bestiary, camels are described as beasts both swift and strong, although they "cannot be given loads beyond what is fitting, nor are the latter willing to do more than the accustomed distances" (p. 80). Isidore of Seville, *Etymologiarum* 12.1, gives the standard explanation of the camel's name, based on a Greek word meaning humble, because the camel kneels to accept its burdens. See also Florence McCulloch, *Medieval Latin and French Bestiaries* (Chapel Hill, 1960), who cites a probable origin for the majority of the camel's traits in Pliny *Historia naturalis* 8. 18 (p. 102).

25. White, *Book of Beasts*, pp. 12–13: "Tigris the Tiger gets his name from his speedy pace. . . . When he perceives that the mother is close, he throws down a glass ball, and she, taken in by her own reflection, assumes that the image of herself in the glass is her little one."

26. Ghisalberti, "Arnolfo," p. 209. "Echo means a man's good reputation, which should love the proud [Narcissus] and extol him with blessing lest he prefer himself above all and have contempt for good reputation. Because she was held in contempt, she hid, saying nothing good of him."

27. Bersuire, *Ovidius moralizatus*, p. 72. Echo's wanderings through the mountains and forests and along the riverbanks are allegorized as the following of the flatterer after all classes of people in society, the prelates and religious and secular individuals. Echo is described as repeating back their words.

28. Bersuire, *Reductorium morale*, p. 643. "Thus, certainly, the truly patient ought to be agile in the quickness to obey and should sustain the burdens of penance and the attacks of the enemy with patience and steadfastness. Whence Galatians, 6, 'Each one will bear his own burden.' And so when the master of the camel, that is, the prelate or priest, or also when God names, enjoins, and sends some work of penance, work, or trouble, immediately we must bow down through humility, obedience, and submissiveness, and bend our knees, through the action of grace." The allegorization that accounts for the camel's unwillingness to bear unreasonable burdens is directed to the edification of the ruler, not to permitting the subject to answer back: "Verumtamen magister Cameli, idest praelatus non debet plus debito imponere vel iniungere, alioquin Camelus, idest subditus forsitan non impleret, immo totum reiiceret, et nihil de impositis perficeret, et sic gravius delinqueret, et peccaret" (p. 643). "Nevertheless the master of the Camel, that is, a prelate, ought not to impose or enjoin as an obligation something too difficult, lest the Camel, that is, the penitent, by chance should not do it, on the contrary reject it entirely, doing none of the things required, and thus fail and sin even more gravely."

29. Philosophically, an isolated particular must always be ironic, since it cannot be the basis of true knowledge, which is of universals, whether it insists on its particularity or not. But the irony is a redeeming one, which delivers us from the necessity of a thoroughgoing skepticism. For an opposing view, which takes Chaucer's arrays of particulars and alternatives as skeptical, see Sheila Delany, *Chaucer's House of Fame.*

30. This relation between January-May and Joseph-Mary is discussed briefly by Emerson Brown in "Biblical Women in the Merchant's Tale: Feminism, Antifeminism, and Beyond," *Viator* 5 (1974): 387–412. Brown offers a suggestion valuable for the *Merchant's Tale,* and for the other tales as well, when he remarks that, "Perhaps the time has come to move beyond arguing whether the *Merchant's Tale* is either 'dark' or 'mirthful'" (p. 411). That is, judgments based on "dramatic" questions of mood and self-revelation have tended to distract attention from the stories as stories. Brown's article should also be consulted for a summary of critical opinions on the tale. The burden of Brown's argument on the tale's meaning is that the allegorical overtones of the tale establish equations between May and Mary, and January and some diabolical or otherwise evil figure, in order to undercut the narrator's misogyny and give some overtone of Boethian hope to an otherwise pessimistic narrative by promising that alternative, and purer patterns of life, could obtain. This is certainly true, and one must always try to say something about the divine order of things in the midst of human circumstances, however sordid. At the same time, it should be possible to use the same technique of allegorical irony, plus the allegorical structuring which this book defines, to let the Merchant tell us something about marriage as well, and the intentional earthly order of which it is a part—sub specie aeternitatis, of course, but still real and necessary on its own.

31. Ibid., p. 403: "The connection between the Virgin and the woman of Genesis 3:15 is unmistakeable in the first illustration of the *Biblia Pauperum.* This commonly presents the beginning of New Testament history with a central picture of the Annunciation. To the left of this is an illustration of Genesis 3:15, often with the woman in a tree, trampling the head of the serpent coiled about the trunk." The position of the snake in the tree is further testified to by the plate on p. 10 of *Biblia Pauperum: The Esztergom Blockbook of Forty Leaves* (Corvina Press, 1967). In parallel with the central panel of Christ's temptation in the desert is the right-hand depiction of Adam and Eve eating the forbidden fruit, while Satan, coiled about the tree trunk, looks on. Cf. also p. 25 of the *Biblia Pauperum,* when Christ on the cross is linked with the episode of Exodus 7:9, the plague of serpents. In the illustration a snake is elevated on a branched rod, while on the ground below snakes devour the Egyptians. The identification of the figure in the tree as a snake, with whom the woman Eve makes her sinful agreement to the detriment of her husband, Adam, suggests obviously the parallel between Damian and the snake, a parallelism which is supported by the *Merchant's Tale* itself (Brown, p. 406). On the other hand, if the parallel is to suggest Christ, Mary, and Joseph, then the figure of the snake must, in some sense, be connected with January, and through him to Joseph. Brown, p. 406 n, suggests the possible double association of January with both Adam and the snake. The possibility that the man in the tree is God, and that the snake is either coiled at the tree's base or

standing beside it, making his arrangements with Eve, is suggested by the plate, taken from a Dresden manuscript and presented on p. ii of the *Biblia Pauperum*, in which God looks down from the tree on Eve and the snake. January's posture in the tale, "He stoupeth doun, and on his bak she stood" (IV [E] 2348), might well have been suggested by the curving figure of the snake.

32. For a discussion of this tradition, which relates the child in the tree of the fall to the Christ in the tree of the cross, and which stems ultimately from the Gospel of Nicodemus, see Esther Casier Quinn, *The Quest of Seth for the Oil of Life* (Chicago, 1962).

33. *Biblia sacra, cum glosa ordinaria et expositione lyre litterali et morali*, vol. 5 (Basel, 1498), fol. a7v-a8r. "But it might be asked here why Mary did not tell him the divine secret. It must be said that such things are not to be revealed, except as much as the divine will permits. And for that reason the holy virgin was silent, believing firmly that, just as the secret had been revealed to St. Elizabeth, as it is told in Luke 1, so it would be revealed to others at the right time from the goodness of the divine will. Similarly it might be asked why Joseph did not ask her? He would have asked in vain, because he would not have believed Mary speaking for herself. And so it was done through the divine dispensation, so that through the revelation of an angel, Joseph was assured that he would not be able to doubt concerning these things in any way."

34. Ibid., fol. a8v. "By Joseph, who was thinking of putting Mary away but accepted her as wife when the angel convinced him of the miracle, is signified a man who, doubting about faith or morals, is confirmed in the faith by a preacher or a good confessor, and submits himself to him in matters pertaining to orthodox faith."

35. This desire to place one's moral choices outside the judgment of God or man is connected with the theme of "pryvytee," man's secret knowledge or inner convictions, which we considered in the first fragment. The connection is especially clear in the story of January and his private garden, in the *Merchant's Tale*.

36. Harwood, "Language and the Real," pp. 268-79, which raises the same question of defending poetry as accurate reportage which we considered in chap. 2 with regard to the General Prologue, Miller's Prologue, and Retraction.

37. George Economou, "Chaucer's Use of the Bird in the Cage Image in the *Canterbury Tales*," *Philological Quarterly* 54 (1975): 679-84.

38. Robertson says of the Wife that she is the "literary personification of rampant 'femininity' or carnality" (*Preface to Chaucer*, p. 321).

39. The entire collection, in fact, turns on the testing of an ideal—that married people live happily ever after—against the harsh, perhaps the harshest, tests.

40. Except to effect the transformation of the crow. But Chaucer's language radically obscures the miraculous dimension of that transformation and describes the metamorphosis as if it were merely physical aggression:

And to the crowe he stirte, and that anon,
And pulled his white fetheres everychon,
And made hym blak, and refte hym al his song,
And eek his speche, and out at dore hym slong
Unto the devel.

(X [H] 303-7)

41. For instance, in "A prayer of the Five Wounds" Jesus is the lemman: "Ihesu cryst, myn leman swete." In "Christ Pleads with His Sweet Leman" the term is applied to the other member of the relationship: "Lo! lemman swete, now may þou se" (*Religious Lyrics of the XIVth Century*, ed. Carleton Brown [Oxford, 1957], nos. 52, 78).

42. George Cary, in his *Medieval Alexander*, ed. D. J. A. Ross (Cambridge, 1956), examines the medieval treatment of an episode in Alexander's career which had been for the authors of antiquity a serious mark against him, an instance of a foolish mismanagement of the emperor's high trust. Cary suggest that in Chaucer, on the contrary, as in most medieval treatments, the story reflects the emperor's courage rather than his error (p. 252).

43. Chaucer's Apollo becomes still more ironic when we note that Chaucer has neglected to mention Aesculapius, the child who resulted from this relationship. Bersuire's interpretation establishes the parallel with politics to which medieval marriage was so amenable: "Recte tales corvi sunt adulatores et verborum relatores: qui soli idest dominis suis semper nituntur referre adulteria quae committunt concubinae eius idest mala que committunt subditi eius: et hoc ut eis placeant: et gratiam ab eis obtineant. Sed quandoque fit quod tales relatores poenam portant: unde premium reportare crediderant. Nam quando homines vident propter malam relationem et informationem talium se male egisse ipsos odiunt et quandoque ipsos puniunt: et nigros id est viles et pauperes faciunt" (*Ovidius moralizatus*, pp. 54-55). "Rightly such crows are flatterers and tellers of tales: to him, that is, to their masters they always attempt to reveal the adulteries which their concubines commit, that, is the evils which their subordinates do. They do it to please their master, and obtain favor from them. But it sometimes happens that such tale-tellers carry sorrow, where they had believed to receive a reward. For when men see that on account of the bad report and information of such creatures they have done evil themselves, then men hate them and punish them, and make them black, that is, cast down and poor."

44. Albert H. Silverman, "Sex and Money in Chaucer's Shipman's Tale," *Philological Quarterly* 32 (1953): 329-36.

7

The Varieties
of Interpretation

The final group of tales we have called the interpretation group. It is the group which corresponds to the last section of the *Knight's Tale,* in which Arcite wins and dies, Palamon loses and wins, and Theseus makes the Boethian application. This group, therefore, is particularly focused upon outcomes—upon what happens in the end—and upon what one must make of them. The first tale here, as in the past two groups, is a saint's life—the story of a largely passive innocent, enduring inexplicable or unjustifiable dangers and trials which only make sense afterwards. Constance witnesses by her life; Cecilia and the clergeoun witness by their deaths; but this difference, essentially, is insignificant. What matters is that all their lives involve the enduring of worldly events in expectation of an end directly involving, and only made explicable by, the will and nature of God.[1]

The problem, of course, is that ordinary human beings do not live and think, clearly and consciously, sub specie aeternitatis. The will and nature of God are often hidden behind events and can only be seen by the eyes of informed faith, which can interpret seemingly random, meaningless, calamitous, or fortuitous events as the results of Providence. And more often than not, that informed faith offers no really developed interpretation. Job is the paradigm.

To walk by faith and not by sight is often to persist in faithful behavior even when it seems imprudent or even absurd to do so, blindly trusting that it is the right kind of behavior even when it seems most wrong. From the point of view of the visibilities of this world, Egeus is right:

"Right so ther lyvede never man," he seyde,
"In al this world, that som tyme he ne deyde.
This world nys but a thurghfare ful of wo,
And we been pilgrymes, passynge to and fro.
Deeth is an ende of every worldly soore."

(I [A] 2845–49)

And Theseus, though he professes to believe in the order that the First Mover arranges in his "faire cheyne of love" (I [A] 2991), must in the end make "vertu of necessittee" (I [A] 3042).

For both Theseus and Boethius, belief in order is something philosophically achieved and affirmed, as it were, in the teeth of the facts. The *Consolation of Philosophy* uses particular facts of experience—of suns and stars, of clouds and storms and unstable ocean—as epistemological metaphors, but the perfect good is beyond facts. For the medieval Christian all this is true too, yet the Incarnation forces a certain adjustment, and nominalism imposes at least a slightly different style. The relation between facts and truth, between any given event and its full meaning, is always slippery, even when the Incarnation guarantees that the truth has a use for the flesh, and the doctrine of personal salvation guarantees that particulars have an absolute right to existence. The precedent of the *Knight's Tale* and the *Prioress's Tale,* taken together as a definition, would seem to tell us that as long as we remain puzzled by events, the Boethian posture, which simply affirms the orderly good, is the right one; and that when we find an event intelligible, it will be an event in the life of a saint. Either one sees the crown of roses and lilies on Cecilia's head or one does not. There would seem to be no middle ground.

But of course there is. One finds the middle ground, in the context of the unintelligibilities of life, by telling stories about them.[2] The means by which we understand what the stories mean and how to use them is the subject of the whole of this book, and we shall not, at this point, explain that. Rather, we believe that in the interpretation group Chaucer presents an array of tales suggesting an array of interpretative postures, all but one more or less wrong, and all related by the usual Chaucerian irony to the answer. The saint's life, first of all, recommends an attitude toward life which cannot be, in the Christian present of Chaucer's culture within which the tales exist, deliberately adopted. Sainthood is something given, not aspired to; in fact, the vanity of aspiring to it is the very pride which guarantees that it will not be achieved. Sainthood, in the Christian society, is the interpretation which overtakes life while it is busy doing something else.[3] The little clergeoun, in his innocent and heedless devotion to the Virgin, exercised without thought of danger from the Jews,[4] becomes an existence out of harmony with his compromised and fallible world and is, from the point of view of that world, destroyed. But the truth is larger than that world knew—though it should have known—and the miraculous fate of the little clergeoun reminds them. The finest and best interpretation is the one provided by God, which intrudes into the world the divine order which the human order all too often misinterprets as miracle. The human order is, for the nonce, set right, and understanding is cultivated thereafter by telling the story of the saint.[5] Telling the story does not necessarily make it easier to understand any other given vicissitude of life, but at least it encourages us to think that understanding will be given, perhaps even miraculously, in the final outcome.

It is when we decide that this meaning is not enough that we get into trouble. Both the consolation of philosophy and the consolation of sainthood are extreme cases, and though we may and must in ordinary times appreciate them for their high purity and remember them for the glory they shed around the ordinary events between birth and death, we are tempted to ask for meanings more locally applicable. And so we tell other stories and seek for other, less demanding paradigms.

In the *Thopas,* the *Melibeus,* the Monk's tragedies, the *Nun's Priest's Tale,* and the Parson's sermon, we have Chaucer's analysis of what happens to us when we do tell stories. The *Thopas* is a parody of popular romance; the *Melibeus* is a collection of proverbs, loosely hung on an allegory; the Monk's tragedies are exempla *de casibus;* the *Nun's Priest's Tale* is both a beast fable and (rhetorically) an epic. All of them, as well as the Parson's sermon, are popular genres—one might even say that here we have all but one of the genres which in fact were most prized by medieval people below the aristocracy, without a reputation for cultivation to keep up.[6] All of them except the *Thopas* (and that for good reason, as we shall see) were genres explicitly associated with moralizing interpretation. And all of them are, in their various ways, excellently done.[7]

In the saint's life, as we have said, the act of interpretation is easy, direct, and obvious, but the lesson one learns is so general as to function more as comfort or inspiration than as moral guidance. The following tales attempt this moral guidance more directly but fail. Their failures, however, are themselves instructive because they release the usual Chaucerian irony, and in recommending various reductionist or pseudoabsolute interpretations, they warn us that the right way to be instructed is through acceptance of stories. The *Thopas* and the *Melibeus*, which must be taken as a matched pair, attempt to isolate sentence from solace, and present each separately. The Monk, the only pilgrim to imitate Chaucer by telling a set of stories, fails because his array is not normative but merely miscellaneous. The *Nun's Priest's Tale*, the subtlest and best of the lot, invites a bad, reductionist allegory. The *Parson's Tale*, worst of all, breaks the frame, rejects story, and tries to address itself directly to the pilgrims (and to us) in penitential generalizations which reject the flesh, reject embodiedness, reject, ultimately, the structures of society in whose patterns we accept definition.[8]

The *Thopas* is a metrical romance, or, rather, a parody of one. As a genre medieval romance was the particular vehicle of two values—the value of idealism and the value of adventure. The world of romance was one whose business was love and battle, carried on by good knights whose purpose was to become better knights—if possible ideal ones. In addition, the action of romance tended to be adventure in the radical sense—arising out of situations that just happened to happen. Arthur's delaying the feast until the adventure appeared is a ritualization of this quality; a knight's riding miscellaneously over terrain differentiated only by the fountains, bridges, trees, and castles where adventures happen is its typical form. In these two ways—that it is the vehicle for the celebration of ideals and that its action is given, rather than caused or arranged—the romance is a secular equivalent of the saint's life and is therefore generically appropriate as Chaucer's second tale of interpretation.

In the sentence-solace doublet, the *Thopas* is solace. It is for this reason, we think, that Chaucer chose for this position not just romance but parody of romance. Properly, sentence arises out of solace; the two are inseparable, different effects of the same form of words. Solace, which includes a range of human experiences from entertainment to the feeling of being comforted or consoled, is in essence the state of mind or personality which arises from the recognition of something in the universe that is in some way right. Recognition, of course, includes glad assent—to experience "solaas" is to be glad that one has done or heard or read (and solace usually comes to an audience of some sort) something transfigured by the quality of its truth.[9] Medieval stories tend so often to be moralized, or to end with a blessing, or to include much discursively sententious material, or to digress into parallel exempla, because the decorum of medieval words emphasizes so much this component of truth. The chief pleasure of an analogizing mind is that analogies can be made, can be seen; the chief pleasure of a civilization that believed in providential justice was being permitted to see, in either story or in life, that a given turn of events did in fact harmonize with the definitions by which ideal justice is known. Thus medieval stories please by neatness, as modern ones often please by evocative open-endedness.

Solace, then, consists in the recognition that the story to which one is attending has a sentence—exists in parallel to the truth. But the *Thopas* is pure solace. And therefore it must be a parody, because parody generates the experience of pure parallel, emptied of direct sententious reference. For the experience to work, of course, one must know the genre, and preferably the text, being parodied, because the delight of the thing arises out of one's constant awarenss of allusions that at once fit and distort. Given this knowledge, parody has a double effect; seeing the original genre (in this case, romance) in the ridiculous guise of parody, one can detect in it elements of real weakness which serious presentation would have obscured, without necessarily being given the normative sentence justifying the judgment. At the same time, the internal consistency and verbal exuberance of the parody itself generates an experience of decorum, of verbal intention, which is normative in form, even though without content. A Flemish wrestler knight is a contradiction in terms, three ways; furious pricking leads merely to a nap; a ride into faerie leads to postponed adventure because Thopas has neglected to bring his armor—these and other parodic elements are obvious, and obviously wrong. We know they are wrong because we have attended to other romances. At the same time, these comic assertions have the manner of serious romances and demand, poetically, to be taken as seriously as all other things of the same manner. The result is laughter—the laughter shared by a poet and an audience who have in common the perception that everything has gone wrong, and that they know it. To have this knowledge—to be in on the secret, to be thus right when everything has gone wrong—is as pure as solace can be.

The *Melibeus* is the other half of the equation. In the context of the other *Canterbury Tales*, it is hardly a tale at all. Rather, as befits something sententious, it is a vast collection of sapiential lore attached to a rudimentary narrative outline. Of all the tales, it is the one least adapted by Chaucer;[10] aside from a sentence or two, and the crucial assignment of the name Sophie to the wounded daughter of Melibeus, Chaucer's most significant contribution to the tale is the context in which he put it and, by so putting it, asserted that it belonged. Its significance as a thing by itself is neither simple nor obvious, though once pointed out it is convincing enough, as Strohm and Owen have shown.[11] Our concern here, however, is with that meaning only as it illuminates the tale as one of a series, placed not in association with the Man of Law[12] but as a doublet with the *Thopas*, "diminished [in] its impact as overt morality."[13]

So placed, what the Melibeus does is define, in a remarkably subtle way, the value and clarity of sapiential lore as a practical interpretation of, and guide to, ordinary human actions. Chaucer's interest in this material is only natural. In the later Middle Ages, sapiential material received increasing attention, as Beryl Smalley has shown.[14] After the twelfth century popes tended to be canon lawyers. Books on the virtues and vices proliferated. Dante's great *Commedia* is only the noblest evidence of a general interest in precise moral values and detailed moral guidance. All these tendencies added up to an increased interest in this life and an increased use for materials in the area of what can reasonably be called worldly wisdom. Such popularity must from time to time have been thought overdone—for one medieval reader there were "so manye bokes & tretees of vyces and vertues and of dyuerse doctrynes, þat þis schort lyfe schalle raþere haue anende of anye manne þanne he maye owþere studye hem or rede hem."[15] Chaucer's subtle and often ironic treatment of other medieval conventions requires us to expect, or at least suspect, subtlety here—and that a subtlety at the expense of conventional wisdom.

The plot of the Melibeus is simplicity itself: the household of Melibeus is attacked by enemies and his daughter is wounded. His wife then talks him out of revenge and helps him achieve a reconciliation with his enemies. In the course of the tale, we are given an explicit allegorization: Melibeus, the drinker of honey, that is, the enjoyer of temporal pleasures, has sinned, and the three enemies of mankind, the world, the flesh, and the devil, have attacked him through the windows of his body, that is, through his senses. Thus, it would seem, the end of the literal tale must allegorically recommend that one reconcile himself, at the spiritual level, to the world, the flesh, and the devil—a manifest absurdity. Chaucer gives some comfort to this absurdity in naming Melibeus's daughter Sophie, or wisdom. Clearly, Melibeus's enemies do not attack his household because Sophie is already wounded, but rather in order (among other things) to wound his wisdom.[16] If he is to reconcile himself to the enemies who wounded his wisdom, then the rules of one-to-one personification allegory would require that this reconciliation signify an accommodation with the forces of evil.

Strohm opposes this absurdity by arguing that the reconciliation which Prudence advises properly signifies that Christian resignation which refuses vengeance and leaves it to the grace of God to cope with one's spiritual enemies. Owen, developing this interpretation, shows that the *Melibeus* is not conventional personification allegory but something rather more figural. In these terms, the story of Melibeus has its own integrity, and Prudence's vastly proverbial peacemaking may be perfectly appropriate. That these events correspond, up to a point, to an allegorical description of Melibeus's spiritual condition need not require a one-to-one equivalent ending. One must always oppose the world, the flesh, and the devil, whether by spiritual combat or by the resignation that trusts God's grace; one must also love one's enemies. Success in the first fosters success in the second; the two are parallel, but not necessary congruent. What Chaucer seems to be telling us is that sententious wisdom can counsel right action and right attitude, but not when understood in an overliteral way. If the allegory is simple, direct, and one-to-one, it creaks, and leads to bad advice; if the figures give good advice, it is only on the basis of resignation, trust in grace, and a very subtle and insightful interpretation.

What one wants out of proverbs, of course, is both—something simple, direct, easily understood, and also profitable. This desire the tale of Melibeus pretends to satisfy—and misleads, at least, the Host. But it is ultimately a desire which neither language nor reality can satisfy. The connection between universals and particulars—in this case, between proverbs and their application—is at once necessary and impossible, at once obvious and incredibly complex. There is no rule but charity which particulars can perfectly trust, and that trust is possible only because it is, in medieval terms, dogmatically guaranteed. Such a rule, like the pardon which Piers Plowman tore, is difficult to apply. On the other hand, any particular proverb which seems to talk generally about particulars must always admit of exceptions. The truth, like the law, proceeds case by case, and when sentence is imposed, there is almost always, even in the best of worlds, a bit of imposition involved. What one can trust is the combination of sentence and "solaas"—a particular, or better, an array of particulars, that is, stories which please by being right, from which one can analogize to one's own story without having to go too trustingly through generalization. By separating sentence and "solaas," and by letting both his Host and his persona misjudge what he has done,

Chaucer emphasizes the impossibility of the separation; and at the same time, by putting these examples so close to his paradigmatic saint's life, he has shown how high and plausible is the temptation to try to make it.[17]

The Monk gets right at least that the truth is in story. But the array of tragedies which he tells is not normative; it is not even, as he admits, properly ordered.[18] The arrangement of the Monk's collection has already been sufficiently analyzed,[19] and there is no need here to repeat that analysis. The Knight's judgment is much to the point:

> "I seye for me, it is a greet disese,
> Whereas men han been in greet welthe and ese,
> To heeren of hire sodeyn fal, allas!
> And the contrarie is joye and greet solas,
> As whan a man hath been in povre estaat,
> And clymbeth up and wexeth fortunat,
> And there abideth in prosperitee.
> Swich thyng is gladsom, as it thynketh me,
> And of swich thyng were goodly for to telle."
>
> (VII 2771–79 [B² 3961–69])

And the Host's judgment underlines the game plan of the whole: "Swich talkyng is nat worth a boterflye, / For therinne is ther no desport ne game" (VII 2790–91 [B² 3980–81]).[20]

It is true that collections *de casibus* were popular in the Middle Ages and are a valid, though negative and backwards, way of talking about the ultimate importance of heaven and the life to come. It is also true that one possible way to deal with the eternal potential of man's life is to meditate *de contemptu mundi*. But neither way is Chaucer's. He knows that this life is provisional, certainly—he could have learned as much from the death of his friends at the hands of the Merciless Parliament, if not from less firsthand history. At the same time this life is something for whose good order one can and should be properly concerned, and the Incarnation, if not the doctrine of creation, assures that if properly ordered it is true. Even failed orders have an ironic power to be true. The interpretation which the Monk invites is that life does not make sense. It is an interpretation to which many medieval readers would have assented. In Chaucer's series of interpretations, it is lower than the *Melibeus*, because it offers no guidance at all for this life; it is still lower than the *Thopas*, because it offers no "solaas"; it is still more below the tale of the little clergeoun, whose real life was interpreted as good and true by an intrusive miracle of the Virgin.

The Monk himself exists as a contradiction of his tale, exactly appropriate to it. In both the general prologue and the prologue of the tale, the Monk is presented as an excellently appropriate human stud. If he would engender children, our heirs would not be "so sklendre / And feble that they may nat wel engendre" (VII 1957-58 [B² 3147-48]). This antinomy between the unfortunate death which overtakes all and the devout engendering which conquers death and keeps the human race alive is the one which in Chaucer's tradition is more blatantly defined by the *Romance of the Rose*. It is a false antinomy, but it is one made necessary if either of its sides is affirmed. A purely sexual set of values leads to meaningless death, and meaningless death encourages merely sexual vitality. One partial view deserves the other, and neither permits a correct interpretation and acceptance of this life. To put both, as Chaucer does, in the fragment that extends from the *Prioress's Tale* through the *Nun's Priest's Tale* tells us what those partial views are worth, as soon as we see that the tales, in series, are for each other a set of interlocked glosses.

The *Nun's Priest's Tale* is one of the most complex in the whole of Chaucer's collection. In part this complexity derives from the fact that the tale is so well written—the sheer verbal and parodic virtuosity of Chaucer's art, his easy ability to do everything at the same time, and everything right, is perennially fascinating. Even more, however, the tale is complex because there has been so much doubt as to how to take it—that is, as to what its proper interpretation should be.

This controversy over interpretation was at its height not many years ago but seems now somewhat abated, we think because the enterprise of interpretation itself was shown to be one of the objects of Chaucer's irony.[21] Some points made then need to be repeated here. First of all, it is obvious that Chaucer invites interpretation: "Taketh the fruyt, and lat the chaf be stille" (VII 3443 [B² 4633]). As his language and his allusion to the Bible make clear, Chaucer instructs his readers to allegorize according to the modes defined by the fruit and chaff, husk and kernel, *integumentum* and *sententia* method as defined in the great tradition from Augustine's *De Doctrina Christiana* through Hugh's *Didascalicon* and as later recommended by Robertson. Chaucer permits—even encourages—a certain confusion between the literal allegory of the poets and the spiritual allegory of the theologians, which itself leads to the contradictory willingness to want a Christian allegorical meaning (which must be based on the exegetical procedure which prizes the letter) and the willingness to treat the letter as discardable chaff (which is based on the reductionist hermeneutic of the allegory of the poets).[22] What he recommends has led to the indulgence of much modern learning in showing that Chauntecleer is an allegory—usually of Christ or of the Christian preacher. But the clues that permit one to interpret Chauntecleer as Christ or as the preacher, though they are in the text, are also under-cut by other details, so that every attempt to allegorize is explicitly made unprofitable or meaningless by a contradictory part of the lit-eral story. Thus Chauntecleer both must and cannot be allegorical.

What Chaucer is telling us here, negatively, about interpretation is that reductionist interpretation is perverse. He denies that one must see the world only in order to see through it, discard it, leave it behind. By giving us an incredibly attractive beast fable—a genre conventionally moralized—and by giving us an explicit invitation to reductionist moralization which, when tried, does not work, Chaucer leaves us with the attractive beast fable and implicitly tells us that that is what should be able to satisfy us. The fruit, as Talbot Donaldson so wisely observed, "is its chaff."[23] Therefore the world, and the stories we tell about the world, must be taken as valuable, not discardable, as something acceptable and in some manner good and true, not as mere means to truth. In this series of stories of interpretation, the next to last and next to most perverse form of interpretation is the allegorical reductionism which tells a story only in order to reject it. The only thing which can be worse, as we shall see, is to reject story without telling one, as the Parson does.

If we do not reject or reduce the *Nun's Priest's Tale*, but accept its chaff as its fruit and its folly as our truth, what we get is a beast fable that is also a mock epic. Here, properly more than anywhere else in Chaucer's work, the full dimensions of his art come into focus, and we learn fully and clearly, even if with some dependence on irony, what it means to be in story. We are all Chauntecleers, in our various ways, and the power of story to make this equation between chickens and people not only true and instructive but also enjoyable, also a cause of "solaas," is, we think, Chaucer's point. Two disparities are here bridged, even while they are accepted and displayed—the disparity between chickens and men, and the disparity between chickens (and implicitly men as well) and the words of epic atmosphere and high style, appropriate to noble deeds. These disparities are at least analo-gous to, and probably even examples of, the fundamental disparity of Chaucer's time—that persistent yet redeemable disparity between particulars and the nominalist words which gave to particulars their meaning, definition, and truth. Therefore, to display before us a chicken, in whose case and in whose story these disparities are accepted at maximum strength, even made the occasion of exuberant verbal revel, and to use irony and the true allegory of structure to overcome these disparities, is to give hope also to men, who in their own stories confront the same disparities and seek the same victory.

In confronting the problem of the relation between words and things, we transcend the medieval context. This is a universal problem, which every age solves, or fails to solve, or refuses to face, in its own way. The late medieval attempt at solution is, we think, more nearly successful than most, and Chaucer's Canterbury collection of tales, more profoundly than any other long poem except perhaps the *Commedia*, is the celebration and the embodiment of that attempt. But since the problem is universal, and since the *Nun's Priest's Tale* is Chaucer's extreme or test case, it is necessary here to pursue some larger-than-usual comparisons, in order to make the distinctive medieval character of Chaucer's project and his achievement completely clear.

Chaucer's mock epic chickens are instructively framed by two other great poems, also mock epics, from two other ages very different from the medieval and very different from each other—the classical *Metamorphoses* of Ovid and the neoclassical *Rape of the Lock* of Pope. In the *Metamorphoses* of Ovid, when Apollo chases frantically after Daphne, or when Juno dispels the suspicious clouds to find an embarrassed Jupiter with an inexplicable cow, the result, according to Brooks Otis, is mock epic. "The epic style of life simply cannot maintain itself under erotic stress. . . . Love is not 'funny' *per se*, but divine majesty is not set up to include love."[24] He comments later, "Ovid knew well enough that though one may archaize the modern, . . . one cannot modernize the archaic without making it ridiculous."[25]

Geoffrey Tillotson, in his introduction to the *Rape of the Lock*, would probably call this technique burlesque—it is Dido speaking "like a fishwife." His definition of mock epic is rather the reverse of Otis's—it is a "trivial subject comically exalted by the epic manner, or, conversely, an exalted manner comically degraded by a trivial subject."[26] Either way, the essential disparity is between manner and matter, and the effect depends upon one's seeing the disparity as absolute, as impossible of reconciliation. But both modes, subject exalted and manner degraded, would seem to fit Otis's category of archaizing the modern, which he apparently thought could be seriously done.

Tillotson goes on to beg a central question—the question of the relation between words and things—in order to define the ironies of mock epic as both unredeeming and irredeemable. "The triumph of the mock-heroic," he says, "is not its mockery of a literary form. The mock heroic poets laugh at the epic form but also at men. . . . Poets mock at the literary form for carrying the contemporary 'low' human material, but they mock more severely at the material for being so unworthy of the form."[27] He thus solves the problem of whose ox is gored by concluding both, but one far worse than the other. It is a conclusion which Pope's mode of art and the literary and philosophical assumptions of his age make seem wholly natural. But it is not the proper medieval conclusion.

On the face of it, it seems obvious enough that epic conventions, when used to describe a high society haircut, will make that haircut look silly. But there is no a priori reason for presuming that this disparity, or any other, will necessarily be left absolute and reproving. If low behavior, as in the *Metamorphoses*, mocks an epic character, then the disparity is contained within the action; if epic manner in word and metaphor mocks the low actions of the people it describes, then the disparity is between form and content, or words and things. In neither case is the mockery inevitable, however. Washing feet is a low action, but there is no mockery when Christ does it;[28] the baseness of Milton's Satan and the childishness of the Earl of Bridgewater's vacationing children are concealed, not mocked, by Milton's exalted language—and whatever ironies affect Satan or whatever sincere praises affect the children are generated not by the disparity itself but by realities beyond it. How then can we be sure we are supposed to laugh at Belinda, or at Chauntecleer, or at Apollo? High language might as well redeem its subject as mock it. And once we know we are to laugh, how can we be sure which end of the combination is normative and which is mocked?

The initial disparities in the *Metamorphoses* are disparities between a character (specifically, a god) and his behavior—proper gods do not fall in love like men and chase girls. The disparities of the *Rape of the Lock*, on the other hand, tend to be metaphoric: when "awful Beauty puts on all its arms,"[29] what is actually being put on is perfume and jewelry and all the other things which make real women fully decorous triumphs of art as well as of nature. The epic level thus exists as metaphoric vehicle; the subject matter is the perfectly consistent (if slightly immoral) behavior of the coquette—it functions as tenor. The point of the combination is that it does not work—the too obvious reality of the coquette intrudes upon what is demanded of it as tenor, and the result is mockery.

Such metaphors, however, do not always mock. When the same combination of consistent action and high metaphoric manner is made in the *Metamorphoses*, the result is often high seriousness. Even the miraculous metamorphoses which come to many of Ovid's characters are extensions of metaphor. Niobe, in the midst of her slaughtered family, rigid with grief, bloodless, pale of face, with her tongue in the stillness past lamenting, is imperceptibly real stone.[30] The headlong flight of Procne and Philomena is suddenly and without transition a real one with real wings. Io, once more a woman and afraid to speak for fear of mooing,[31] recalls a predicament funny only because we see it in the context of the ridiculous antics of the gods. When Actaeon is torn by his own hounds, his real condition is an overwhelming reminder that metaphors implying the frailty of man have some basis in reality more profound than the disparity between man and the form of a deer.[32] In these metamorphoses the "barrier between species"[33] is indecorously leaped, but the result is not necessarily mockery. It is rather often apotheosis like the hack epic epithet "wingage of oars," suddenly real in the flight of Dante's angel ship, coming from Tiber beach to Purgatory; metaphor is the deep truth rather than the mocking ornamental container.

Belinda is mocked by her metaphors; Chauntecleer, and through him mankind, is somehow redeemed by his. The predicament of the eighteenth century was that literary oxen will usually gore real ones; the glory of the Middle Ages and, in a different way, of classical times is that both will join together under the yoke of reality. Perhaps better than any other late medieval poem, the *Nun's Priest's Tale* makes clear the reason why. Fortunately, the *Nun's Priest's Tale* exists in a neoclassical version. Dryden translated it into his own couplets, expanding slightly and adding a new moral; in the process he totally changed the character of the poem. In Chaucer's version the chickens are chickens, in spite of all the rhetoric, learning, and high atmosphere. Dryden, on the other hand, does all he can to reduce the chicken level to mere metaphor, and gives us real people described as if they were chickens. This is a distinction difficult to make theoretically, but absolutely crucial to the argument. In a sense, both Chaucer's and Dryden's Chauntecleers are metaphors. But in Chaucer's case the whole story, which is consistently about chickens, can be taken as analogous to some whole story about a man—there are, implicitly and (in the structural sense) allegorically, two stories, independent of each other and both real, one of which is evoked by the other. In Dryden's case there is just one story, a story about foolish people who are made even more foolish by the persistent and arbitrary trick of calling them chickens. Writing thus is to deny the ontological validity of the comparison even as it is made.

The point should be clearer in examples. Dryden's Chauntecleer, for instance,

> ... had a high Opinion of himself:
> Though sickly, slender, and not large of Limb,
> Concluding all the World was made for him.[34]

To be thus bird-legged loses all its point on a real bird and must therefore apply to a man. Again, Chauntecleer's father, according to Dryden's fox, was

> A Peer deserving such a Son, as you:
> He, with your Lady-Mother (whom Heaven rest)
> Has often grac'd my House, and been my Guest.[35]

Chaucer's point, that the father and mother "han in myn hous ybeen to my greet ese" (VII 3297 [B² 4487]), correctly implies that real chickens visit foxes only once. Again, Chauncer's Chauntecleer simply had "sevene heenes for to doon al his pleasaunce, / Whiche were his sustres and his paramours" (VII 2866–67 [B² 4056–57]). Dryden digresses to justify this behavior by the example of Ptolomeys and other royal lines, and expands mention of Chauntecleer's sexual prowess with the entirely human explanation that Pertelote

> Resolved the passive doctrine to fulfil
> Tho' loath: And let him work his wicked will.
> At Board and Bed was affable and kind,
> According as their Marriage Vow did bind,
> And as the Churches Precept had enjoined.[36]

Again, when Chaucer says, "For thilke tyme, as I have understonde, / Beestes and briddes koude speke and synge" (VII 2880–81 [B² 4070–71]), we have the impression of a time ancient in myth and magic. When Dryden, on the other hand, says, "For in Days of Yore, the Birds of Parts were bred to Speak, and Sing, and learn the libral Arts," we think no further back than the education of the Renaissance man.

The result of these differences is a difference of moral. Dryden's is clear, direct, and predictable—the epic atmosphere condemns its content and teaches us to beware of the examples it contains. Dryden has fallen into Chaucer's trap; he wishes to take the morality, take "the fruyt, and lat the chaff be stille." Given his version of the poem, he is right, because he has transformed Chaucer's subtlety into something admittedly witty and delightful, but much simpler. Chaucer's moral, on the other hand, finds value in the folly itself. As ironies accumulate rhetoric is mocked, learning is mocked, even the procedures of biblical allegory are mocked. But chickens are not mocked, and all the mockery adds up to no real condemnation. Rather, it is a part—necessary, but only as a part—of the definition of the world.

Essentially, the *Nun's Priest's Tale* is a beast fable. Far more profoundly than Dryden, whose bird metaphors are merely local and verbal, Chaucer's tale asserts that beast fables are both possible and true—that is, there is a real connection between chickens and foxes, on the one hand, and people, on the other, which makes it morally valuable for the one to attend to the adventures of the other. Sub specie aeternitatis, merely human heroism is a folly, but a good folly, because it may lead to story in this world and wisdom in the next, and both are very important. From the point of view of man, chicken-heroism is a folly, but a good folly, because it generates both story and insight. Man can only see himself whole by looking through analogy down the great chain of being. The *Nun's Priest's Tale*, then, contains man, distanced, visible, whole, under the species of a chicken. In writing it, and in putting it in this fragment so preoccupied with stories of interpretation, Chaucer reminds us once again of the true subject of his Canterbury collection—man, not God; human order in this life, not that heretical preoccupation with salvation before which this life is a distraction rather than an instrument.

The *Nun's Priest's Tale*, therefore, teaches us in a way how to interpret all the stories. Like the tale of Chauntecleer, they all demand to be accepted, not reduced, heard as stories, not as the husk of allegories or the too easy platforms of oversimplifying generalizations. As stories they contain behavior capable of existing in parallel—like the beast fable, they exist to be analogous—to each other, and to all stories, most importantly including our own stories, which are their nonreductive tropology, as they are ours. This mortal life of ours is surrounded, as was Chaucer's, with both the security of words and the threat of Fortune's wheel. Rhetoric, learning, allegory, and high sentence are the words with which we buttress our lives; what eventually actually happens is the result over which those words have no final power. That Chauntecleer and Pertelote are learned and heroic is at once their glory and their foolishness, and both must be accepted.

Analogously, the game we call life, which death and salvation will use as an instrument of preparation even though they make it appear to be a folly, is both glorious and foolish, and must always be played as both. This is the highest and best point of Chaucer's habitual ironic pose—that it is a commitment to life which is at once real and not absolute, and which can see good and truth in what he already knows is (for its actors) provisional, because of those actors and their acts he can make, or analogize, a story.

There is no need to pause long over the *Parson's Tale*. Once one grants what it is, one can see many virtues in it. That use of life which one might call Augustinian, which survives in Catholic Jansenism and in various rigorous and self-denying fundamentalisms of protestantism, finds in the *Parson's Tale* what one can without irony call happy expression. Connoisseurship of sermons still survives in some Western cultures, even into this last third of the twentieth century, and public fascination with confessions of political sins during the Nixon presidency, almost as if the television were the confessional and the public were a vast collective priest, proves that even twentieth-century people can be fascinated with the process by which one finds out precisely how much his deeds are worth. The eloquent analysis and denunciation of sin, though now more frequently heard from political than religious pulpits, makes delightful hearing both for the Pharisees whose superiority seems confirmed as others are blackened and for the sinner whose repentance demonstrates that he is important enough for the direct attention of God himself. The penitential exhibitions of modern Spain, in particular, obviously give the participants a good deal of temporal as well as spiritual satisfaction. All these survivals, in this secular age, of the peculiar attitudes which would have made the *Parson's Tale* admired should convince us that there is no reason to resort to the "boring tales for boring people" argument as a justification for the presence of this treatise in Chaucer's Canterbury collection. As a treatise on penance and the seven sins, it is effective, well organized, competently and occasionally eloquently expressed, and doctrinally reasonable.[37] People did, and do, believe, and believe they should believe, these things.

Chaucer is another matter. England has been described as a naturally Pelagian country. The Bradwardine to whom Chaucer ironically refers in the *Nun's Priest's Tale* devoted very considerable theological energies to denouncing as Pelagians many of the important theologians of his day—the generation just before Chaucer.[38] No label will perfectly fit Chaucer, but the label of Pelagian is certainly helpful here because it helps one to see how the *Parson's Tale* might have been included, not as the absolute truth with which to end the pilgrimage, but as a party document, excellent of its kind, but partisan, to be received ironically rather than straightforwardly.

As a tale of interpretation the *Parson's Tale* is certainly last, lowest, and least. It denounces tale-telling without telling one. It attempts to break the frame of tellers and tale by imposing teller values on, or in, the tale. Worse than the quiters, who tell good tales and then misappropriate them to ulterior and limited uses, the *Parson's Tale* exists as an actual surrender to that misappropriation. It is an attempt to apply generalizations directly to particulars, rather than indirectly through the principle of analogy and normative array, which the tales up to this point have established. So, of all the interpretations, it is the worst.

Fortunately, for so radical a point there is external as well as internal evidence.[39] Chaucer's largest single contribution to the borrowings which make up the *Parson's Tale* is the text with which it begins: "State super vias, et videte, et interrogate de viis antiquis que sit vita bona, et ambulate in ea; et invenietis refrigerium animabus vestris, etc." (Jeremiah 6:16; "Stand on the ways, and see, and ask for the old ways which is the good way, and walk in it, and you will find rest for your souls"). But the Parson's application of this text to penance occurs in only one traceable context of medieval exegesis, and there with radically different spirit. And the Bible commentary which might well be described for Chaucer's day as the latest and best variorum, the compilation supervised by Hugh of St. Cher between 1230 and 1235, explicitly denies the Parson's application.[40] Explaining the "old paths," *viis antiquis*, Hugh says: "Antiquis/quia ut dicitur vulgariter: Antiqua via melior est, et securior. Contra illa, qui semper adinventiones vanas in poenitentia, vel in religione adinvenerunt, et fabricant novas Religiones."[41] He goes on to explain himself, possibly with some topical sensitivity to the new orders of friars, by distinguishing between a real innovation and an innovation such as holy poverty which simply restores an ancient custom of the saints. But there is nothing in this explanation which would qualify or mitigate his disapproval of "adinventiones vanas in poenitentia."

The way which leads to *refrigerium* for Hugh is not penance; one goes rather "per rectam viam, scilicet, per viam fidei, et charitatis" ("by the right way, that is, by the way of faith and charity"). This is a cliché, of course, and yet the tone is different. Here is no *contemptus mundi*. In fact, "cum viam invenit, consolationem recepit propter spem veniendi cito ad finem, quasi, bene erit vobis, et veniet vobis prosperitas, et temporalis, et spiritualis."[42] Temporal and spiritual prosperity indeed. The tone is positive, not negative. The earthly pilgrimage, if it be one on which good stories are both told and acted, and acted in order to be told, is continuous with the heavenly, and not its rival. It is all one way, this way of faith and charity, which has a proper use for heaven, of course, but also, and most importantly, a proper use of earth.

In Hugh's reproof we have Chaucer's subject: "Bene erit vobis, et veniet vobis prosperitas, et temporalis, et spiritualis." ("It will be well with you, and there shall come to you prosperity, both temporal and spiritual.") Chaucer's subject is the prosperity of the world, as it is capable of being the ground and exemplum of the true. He is therefore constantly exhibiting to us the particulars of this world's prosperity, or lack of it, with a gently ironic affection which accords to each its worth, and only its worth, knowing that a sufficient and a sufficiently well chosen array will indeed be normative and will permit us to find light as well as empathy in the ironies Chaucer shares with us. Of this light the only fit interpreter is God, as and if he intrudes into someone's story with the news that it is the story of a saint. Beyond this, all interpretations are at once provisional and necessary. We must seek to understand, as well as do, and at the same time we must accept the fact that the decorum of our doings is more likely to be good for the truth than the decorum of our interpretations, if only because of the greater commitment necessarily involved. We may, however, seek refuge in mere amusement, hoping that lack of action may permit lack of outcome and therefore lack of calamity. But the Host will disapprove of our vulgarity. We may take refuge in the conventional wisdom of conservative sententiousness. We may decide that death means that the world makes no sense at all. We may feel so guilty about our follies that we allegorize them away, and so lose all profit from them. Or we may reject the whole show, with the Parson. And we will be wrong. But had we been so wrong in medieval England, we would at least have had the hope that Master Geoffrey would have heard of our wrong, and would have told its story and made it right, and worthy to "drawen to memorie."

1. On the portrayal of the ideal of Christian passivity through the figure of a woman, see Sheila Delany, "Womanliness in the Man of Law's Tale," *Chaucer Review* 9 (1974): 63–72.

2. The imagery of sight, linked to the theme of justice, predominated in the first two groups of tales, particularly in the tales of magic. Here, in the final group of tales, we will be concerned primarily with the imagery of the tongue, linked to the human act of interpretation. Thus, the collection begins with the tale of the clergeoun; it includes several heated conversations about the proper use of words, particularly in the tales of Chaucer the pilgrim; and we have the tricks of Chauntecleer, whose glib speech saves him from the mouth of the fox.

3. This is patently true of the clergeoun, but also of Cecilia and Constance, who are pursuing their private lives, not seeking the cross of martyrdom.

4. Critics who are distracted into discussions of medieval anti-Semitism have missed the point. Chaucer knows what he is doing. The Jewish ghetto is a thing "Sustened by a lord of that contree/For foul usure and lucre of vileynye,/Hateful to Crist and to his compaignye" (VII 490–92 [B² 1680–82]). Its modern moral equivalent is not the Jewish (or black) section of town, where live the helpless victims of majority prejudice, but rather the red-light district, run by the Mafia or its equivalent and winked at by the city fathers because its existence is good for the convention trade. Ethnically, the population did happen to be Jewish, against whom prejudice is in absolute terms a sin, but ethically they were the people to whom society turned to provide needed services (as it happens, banking) which respectable people wished to have done but were too ethically pharisaical to do for themselves.

5. Chaucer's art in this tale has been the subject of praise; Donald W. Fritz, "The Prioress' Avowal of Ineptitude," *Chaucer Review* 9 (1974): 166–81.

6. That the tales of this group represent a catalogue of medieval genres has been noted by Baum, *Chaucer,* pp. 74ff; and Gaylord, "*Sentence* and *Solaas* in Fragment VII of the *Canterbury Tales,*" pp. 226–35.

7. To defend their quality is to admit that it needs defending, perhaps. But one should not make modern tastes absolute either, since they might be, in the whole economy of art, the ones least absolute. Sententious literature—proverbs, fables, and sermons—are at present seriously out of favor, but there was far more art in them than in our analogous wearing of slogans on shirts and car bumpers. And no age which spends good money on Andy Warhol should look down on the *Thopas.* For the fairest possible estimate of Chaucer's achievement in these tales, one should come to them from extensive reading in such books as the *Summa Praedicantium,* the *Gesta Romanorum,* Robert Holkot's *Moralitates,* or anything from Lydgate.

8. Repeatedly, in this study, we have suggested that the quiter's error is to misappropriate stories for the sake of merely local attack. The Parson is the worst quiter of them all, because he attacks the company as storytellers with a treatise which is no story at all.

9. Aristotelian catharsis would be solace, if experienced in the cognitive way defined by O. B. Hardison in his commentary *Aristotle's Poetics: A Translation and Commentary,* with Leon Golden (Englewood Hills, N.J., 1968). Non-cognitive or purely emotional catharsis, in the way understood by romantic and postromantic critics, would violate the medieval habit of finding emotional and rational harmoniousness inseparable. Such a cognitive catharsis is a

component of medieval experience; it is defined, however, primarily within the tradition of medicine. For a discussion, see Patrick Gallacher, "Food, Laxatives, and Catharsis in Chaucer's Nun's Priest's Tale," *Speculum* 51 (1976): 49–68.

10. Cf. Dolores Palomo, "What Chaucer Really Did to *Le Livre de Melibee*," *Philological Quarterly* 53 (1974): 304–20.

11. Paul Strohm, "The Allegory of the *Tale of Melibee*," *Chaucer Review* 2 (Summer 1967): 32–42; Charles A. Owen, Jr., "The *Tale of Melibee*," *Chaucer Review* 7 (Spring 1973): 267–80.

12. Charles A. Owen, Jr., "The Earliest Plan of the Canterbury Tales," *Mediaeval Studies* 21 (1959): 202–10.

13. Owen, "The *Tale of Melibee*," p. 271.

14. Beryl Smalley, "Some Thirteenth-Century Commentaries on the Sapiential Books," *Dominican Studies* 2 (1949): 318–55; 3 (1950): 41–77, 236–74, and "Some Commentaries on the Sapiential Books of the Late Twelfth and Early Fourteenth Centuries," *Archives d'histoire doctrinale et littéraire du Moyen Age* 18 (1950): 103–28.

15. K. Horstmann, "*Orologium Sapientiae, or the Seven Poyntes of Trewe Wisdom* aus MS. Douce 114," *Anglia* 10 (1887): 328.

16. A possible source for Chaucer's identification of Melibeus's daughter with wisdom, by name, is Hugh of St. Victor's *Soliloquium super arrham animae*, PL 176, col. 961, in which the picture of death and sin invading the soul through the senses is also evoked. The *Soliloquium* was one of Hugh's most popular spiritual treatises. Cf. Kevin Herbert, *Soliloquy on the Earnest Money of the Soul* (Milwaukee, 1956), p. 11.

17. Surrender to which temptation is, we think, the cornerstone of the reductionist allegorizing of critics deriving from the theories of D. W. Robertson.

18. "Though I by ordre telle nat thise thynges" (VII 1985 [B² 3175]).

19. William C. Strange, "The Monk's Tale: A Generous View," *Chaucer Review* 1 (1967): 167–80.

20. Cf. the discussion of "ernest" and "game" in chap. 2 above.

21. Allen, "The Ironic Fruyt."

22. In the interests of brevity, there is here an inevitable oversimplification. For a full analysis, see Allen, *The Friar as Critic*, pp. 3–28.

23. E. Talbot Donaldson, "Patristic Exegesis: The Opposition," in *Critical Approaches to Medieval Literature*, ed. Dorothy Bethurum (New York, 1960), p. 20.

24. Otis, *Ovid as an Epic Poet*, p. 104.

25. Ibid., p. 351.

26. Alexander Pope, *The Rape of the Lock and Other Poems* (London, 1954), p. 117.

27. Ibid., p. 118.

28. Cf. the helpful discussion of the "sermo humilis" as rhetorical model in Erich Auerbach's *Literary Language and Its Audience in Late Antiquity and the Early Middle Ages* (New York, 1965), pp. 150–65.

29. *The Rape of the Lock,* line 139.

30. *Metamorphoses* 6. 303–12.

31. Ibid. 1. 745.

32. Ibid. 3. 198–252.

33. Otis, *Ovid as an Epic Poet,* p. 364.

34. "The Cock and the Fox, or the Tale of the Nun's Priest," lines 656–58, *Poetical Works of John Dryden* (London, 1893), pp. 335–46.

35. Ibid., lines 608–10.

36. Ibid., lines 73–77.

37. Siegfried Wenzel, "Chaucer and the Language of Contemporary Preaching," *Studies in Philology* 73 (1976): 138–61; Susan Gallick, "A Look at Chaucer and His Preachers," *Speculum* 50 (1975): 456–76.

38. Gordon Leff, *Bradwardine and the Pelagians* (Cambridge, 1957). One of Bradwardine's more important opponents was Robert Holkot, a skeptic and storyteller whose genial literary tastes are much like Chaucer's. Leff discusses Holkot, pp. 216–27.

39. This evidence is fully presented in Allen, "The Old Way and the Parson's Way," pp. 255–71.

40. The influence we are claiming here for Hugh is not a matter of general meaning but of precisely verbal influence. The same sort of influence can be presumed in the case of the *Nun's Priest's Tale* as well. Statistically, it takes very few independent cases of this kind of correspondence to make direct influence quite certain.

41. *Opera omnia,* vol. 4, fol. 194r: "because, as it is proverbially said, the old way is the safest and best. Against those who find vain inventions in penance or religion, and make up new religions."

42. Ibid., fol. 194v: "when he finds the way, the hope of coming quickly to the end is consolation, as if [to say]: it will be well with you, and there shall come to you prosperity, both temporal and spiritual."

Epilogue

A search for the unity of the *Canterbury Tales* is by no means an unfamiliar occurrence in twentieth century Chaucer studies. The stature of the poem has seemed to many readers, as well as ourselves, to justify the hope that in addition to all its other excellences of wit and characterization the *Canterbury Tales,* albeit unfinished, is outstanding in organization and thematic coherence as well. But whereas other researchers have concentrated on the pilgrims and their journey, we have preferred to search among the tales themselves for the unifying qualities that relate the stories one to another in ways that harmonize the entire collection. An examination of medieval literary criticism, particularly the commentary tradition of Ovid's *Metamorphoses,* and of medieval love allegory, especially Dante's *Commedia,* has provided evidence that techniques of order and arrangement based on analogical associations between story elements were available to Chaucer. Our examination of the *Canterbury Tales* in the light of this medieval literary precedent reveals this type of association within the work. The arrangement of tales used in our reading, while not demonstrably Chaucer's own, does throw into sharp relief the patterns of connection present in the tales. These patterns are the mortar, as it were, to bind the blocks of story Chaucer was assembling for his grand design.

Although our reading has focused on a general theme of the collection, that is, the formation of a good human community, primarily we have concentrated on a principle of structural rather than thematic unity. The patterns of relationship uniting the tales not only produce a well-ordered collection, however, but yield a coherent, ethical statement as well. The variety of the poem is not miscellaneous but harmonious. Chaucer adduces so many contradictory human testimonies about life, especially conflicting evaluations of love in the family, in the confidence that a broad and purposeful sampling of human experience will yield insights, reducing confusion to order and understanding. In these final pages, a few of the thematic elements of the poem illuminated by our method of structural interpretation will be discussed. The ideas about poetry and marriage, as subjects of the *Canterbury Tales,* which are presented here, are the direct and necessary outcome of our approach to the work as an ordered collection of exemplary stories.

It may seem a bit dangerous to suggest that Chaucer, valued today as the supreme ironist and tolerant humorist, is supplying an ethical judgment on his fellow men. In addition, our structural argument which supports this conclusion is liable to arouse opposition because it appears to limit Chaucer's innovation by arguing that his poetry is, in some ways, dependent on cultural tradition. A balance must be struck between our recognition of Chaucer's creative genius and his vital role, one he eagerly sought, as a transmitter of Western culture. The wealth and variety of the tradition available to Chaucer, and his own powerful reworking of it, forbid any reduction of his ethical poetry to axiomatic moralizing and guarantee an originality in itself much greater than the inventiveness often praised in his work as its highest merit.

To say that the *Canterbury Tales* is ethical and exemplary is not to suggest that Chaucer is repeating or embroidering formulas of right and wrong. He chose to speak ethically in stories, and he warns his readers repeatedly of the dangers involved in leaping too lightly from exemplum to moral. Chaucer makes story's interaction with life one of his subjects, especially in the prologues; he counsels great care in relating story to life, not because he supposes that the stories are an evil influence but rather because their precious import can so easily be lost in the transfer from fictional exemplum to man's particular experience. The poem is ethical because it supposes that a proper openness to the text awakens the reader to his responsibility to act ethically, to relate the poem creatively to his own life as a source of ethical insights. The *Canterbury Tales* illuminates and orders life; that is its ethical character.

The question of Chaucer's indebtedness to tradition is slightly more complex. First, Chaucer's development of the story collection, in its selection and manipulation of exemplary narrative units, is as extraordinary in his age as critics have long recognized his technique with the frame to be. Our emphasis on medieval parallels to various elements of Chaucer's technique was not intended to detract from this originality; rather, it seemed necessary to examine the backgrounds of poetry employing exemplary narrative units in order to justify a reconsideration of the story collection, a genre whose qualities had been firmly codified in other terms within Chaucer scholarship. While recognizing the work's originality, it is essential as well to appreciate Chaucer's evident pride in the time's traditions of expressive language and his desire to preserve and advance, rather than contradict and remove, the techniques and ideas available to him from his culture. The optimistic vision Chaucer presents of the blending of word and deed, of vow and fulfillment, of good action and its exemplary preservation in memory, springs from a culture which was rich in voices proclaiming the sacramental power of the word. The *Canterbury Tales* is rooted in an atmosphere of confidence in a harmonious creation and, in fact, affirms that this harmony is accessible to man through a proof of Chaucer's own making.

The starting point for this harmony is love in marriage. Chaucer is not alone among the great medieval love poets in broadening his studies of love to a consideration of the place that loving couples occupy within the larger frameworks of society and creation. Like Dante and Jean de Meun, Chaucer does not abandon love as a focal point when he expands his gaze to encompass all of human society, but rather seeks to reconcile the qualities of private love with the love which, according to philosophers and theologians, harmonized the universe and regulated the affairs of God and man. The *Canterbury Tales* stands out among the poet's works as an attempt to draw together all of life into a harmony based on love. The work is notable among late medieval allegories, also, in that Chaucer chooses to speak specifically about love in marriage; although by no means the only medieval love poet to speak of married love, Chaucer is the only one of the three poets we have been discussing together throughout this study—that is, Chaucer himself, Dante, and Jean de Meun—to make the love he uses as a principle of universal harmonies the love to be found in the marriage relationship.

The *Canterbury Tales* has been identified as marriage poetry in various ways. On the one hand, there are allegorical interpretations which neglect Chaucer's realistic observation and appreciation of the concrete diversity of human relationships. On the other hand, emphasis on the personalities and quarrels of the pilgrims has reduced Chaucer's metaphorical expansions on the idea of marriage to a one-dimensional argument about the marriage debt. The married couple is the focal point of Chaucer's investigation, around which both allegorical analogies and the practical realities of everyday experience are arranged. In all this patterning, Chaucer never loses sight of real marriage; it is central because he perceives it to be both literally the building block of the human community he would set in order and metaphorically the widest reaching and most richly developed symbol he could employ to name all that human relationships involve. The allegory of marriage presented in the *Canterbury Tales* develops its image of the married state within these defining limits to ensure that neither the commonsense understanding of the union nor the deeper, spiritual harmonies it represents is absent from the final synthesis.

Chaucer defines love anew within the context of marriage. The questions of social responsibility and moral accountability which marriage raises frequently are presented by medieval love poets as threats to true love. Chaucer, far from placing love at war with these considerations, insists that love can and must permeate all aspects of the marriage relationship. The love which may sustain a couple in all of life's tasks and against blows of chance differs from the love of courtship, precisely because both partners have moved from the state of desiring an unpossessed and unknown experience of union to the reality of partnership.

The defining instances of human relationship which Chaucer collects in the *Canterbury Tales* all reflect on marriage, precisely because of the nature of marriage as a permanent, abiding unit with an essential function in larger orders of social and cosmic harmony. Around the married couple Chaucer arranges other relevant examples of union—the marriage of Christ and the soul, of a priest and his congregation, of a lord and his country—along with several concrete instances of loving and unloving arrangements contracted within and outside of marriage. The difficulties man and woman encounter in establishing and then maintaining their relationships involve clashes between promises and temptations, between illusions and experience, between ideals and practice; these conflicts are played out within individual tales and also serve as the connecting points between various tales, as they present diverging testimony about married life and its trials. From even the most satisfactory of resolutions Chaucer counsels at most a cautious selectivity in accepting any one element of the marriage as paramount; from the least satisfactory he draws the truth that all elements of the relationship may be used for ill but each remains essential to the whole.

With marriage rather than love only as his subject, Chaucer treats the figures of man and woman precisely as they function within such an abiding, socially integrated relationship. What this means for woman has been discussed a good deal, because Chaucer has been so highly regarded for the female characters in the *Canterbury Tales;* what is often absent from this praise, however, is an appreciation of all the aspects of the wife which Chaucer enumerates. Essentially, the married woman commands the respect and admiration, the reverence and worship, which were her due in the poetry of the love of courtship. Arveragus and Dorigen propose to continue loving one another in the same fashion they had known before marriage. Within marriage, Valerian follows the path from human love to divine through the guidance of woman that was set forth in much poetry of the love quest. In addition to these testimonies to a continuity of emotional and spiritual attachment between courtship and marriage, Chaucer presents woman as lover in her own right and, especially, as an eager participant in the mutual pleasures of sexual love; the many roving wives encountered in the collection represent the reality of woman's role, as not only the object of desire but also an independent self with needs and desires to be realized. Chaucer's passive heroines, like Constance and Griselda, and the martyred children, like Virginia and the litel clergeon, prompt the reflection that what a wife may contribute as inspiration and as active partner in marriage requires a husband lover whose partnership frees a woman to love fully and to be fruitful both in children and in good works.

Perhaps more significant than Chaucer's profound sensitivity to woman's role in marriage is the balancing insight he brings to the role of the husband. The poem has received much less attention on this subject, and yet it is more in his assertion of the dignity of man's love in marriage than in his view of woman that Chaucer stands out among medieval poets. The poetry of his age had canonized the aspirations of man in courtship; it had gone on to couple with this a deepening appreciation of the spiritual fruits of this purifying aspiration. What is rare before Chaucer, although by no means absent altogether, is the praise of the husband, too, as true lover. In this Chaucer forshadows the Renaissance, with its schema of intimately related natural, human, and divine planes within which man's God-ordained task is to perfect himself in his humanness and to minister as governor to God's creation. In some tales the husband seems in large measure a prolongation of the knightly wooer or the idealizing dreamer in service to his lady. Even in these stories, however, marriage brings with it the transformation from the task of seeking love to the work of preserving it. In the fabliaux primarily, in the figure of the failed husband, Chaucer ironically evokes the promise of the true male role in marriage. He draws together the metaphor of Christ's union with his church and the outrageous errors of lecherous old men and their amorous, unfaithful wives, because he would blame the men not for sexual desire, precisely, but rather for the selfishness and unloving greed which lie behind their pursuit of a wife. Behind January, for example, a failed Adam and a failed Christ, hovers the model of a true husband, a paterfamilias and husbander of the family garden whose direction is taken from love, presented in the metaphor of the nurturing, supporting love of Christ for his church. The figure of the husband does not reflect primarily the lessons of the church's teaching on male superiority or authority in the partnership, or the mutual exchanges of the marriage debt—these aspects of marriage wisdom are present in the collection, usually with a rather doubtful eye to their efficiency or correctness—but rather is modeled on the figure of Christ as husband and lover which emerges from medieval spirituality. This application of the spiritual marriage to human marriage, although justified in some measure by the commentary tradition of the Song of Songs imagery which Chaucer introduces in the fabliaux, yet is primarily Chaucer's own in its effort to discover the spiritual dignity of the love known in marriage. Thus, in the role of the husband, Chaucer draws both on the lessons of secular poetry's aggrandizement of the male desire for love and on the spiritual tradition which suggests the possibility of channeling this desire into the new role of a husband now called on to preserve and maintain love in marriage.

Chaucer presents marriage as both the living heart and the fullest image of the good human community. He promises that within it man encounters the most profound range of meanings to be discovered in existence, meanings which not only enrich his private experience but also serve as a guide to his appropriate actions as member of society. When marriage is less than it might be, Chaucer points primarily to the failure of the partners to contract a true marriage or their inability to remain faithful to their promises. For Chaucer the vow is a prediction that reveals to man in advance the nature of the relationship he is entering; the promise is, moreover, the best protection the relationship has against collapse. The tie between the vow and married life is not a simple identity. As Chaucer shows repeatedly, even the most zealously loving couples find themselves precipitated against the black rocks. The word of the promise, like the word of a story, exists as a metaphor for life and must be creatively applied as life unfolds.

The allegorical tie between promise and deed, present in so many of the tales of faltering marriages, is in small an image of the relationship between language and life on all levels and especially between Chaucer's own writing and its audience. Real associations between elements of creation make verbal analogies not only possible but deeply revelatory. At the same time, allegorical statement is perceived always as a complex parallelism which can elucidate but not reduce life. Within individual tales particular marriages are surrounded by allegorical parallels underscoring the general significance of the struggles the particular couple endures. Between tales the same sort of reverberation is established. And on the final and deepest level, Chaucer looks to his readers to bring the experience of the poem and their own lives into meaningful parallel.

In some respects Chaucer's use of allegory resembles the poetic strategies to be found in other late medieval love poetry; a consideration of some similarities between the *Canterbury Tales* and the love allegories of Dante and Jean de Meun will be helpful in measuring the originality of the method in Chaucer's work. All three writers display a reverence for expressive language and a confidence in their ability to communicate effectively, through language, important insights on the human condition. All are innovative practitioners of the new vernacular literature and eager defenders of its dignity; interestingly, though, an essential part of their innovation as vernacular poets is the determination to transfer the Latin cultural heritage into a new language, for a new readership. At the same time that they advance the cause of the vernacular against the Latin tradition, they are also concerned to defend the integrity of the poetry of this tradition against the encroachments of dialectic. They affirm that a specifically analogical process of understanding, coupled with an eloquent appeal to man's conviction, remains a powerful and efficacious method of expression and communication. They practice their art under the guidance of a tradition of rhetorical literature founded in the classical poets but enriched as well by philosophers and moralists within the Christian tradition.

Three markedly different works emerge from this common background, and they testify strongly to the need in modern research to replace the long-standing assumption of a unitary medieval literary theory and to open research into the evolution of the many currents of rhetorical expression present during the period, especially in the years 1150–1400. The three poets being examined here exemplify very well the range of possibilities for allegorical poetry during the Middle Ages. In the *Romance of the Rose,* a vernacular dream vision is continued under the rubric of philosophical poetry presenting quests after knowledge, especially the knowledge of the harmony of creation. Jean de Meun, writing during the thirteenth century, deliberately returns to models of rhetorical poetry especially identified with the School of Chartres; in adapting Latin culture to the vernacular, he challenges his time's prevailing interest in dialectic as the most effective linguistic tool of expression, and proposes as an alternative the rhetorical method of learning from previous literary works and adapting their insights and techniques to new human problems. Jean illuminates the essential nature of love by contrasting its meaning within the secular tradition of love poetry with the natural and cosmic significance it held in the works of Boethius and Alan of Lille. In the *Commedia* poetry again is made new under the inspiration of ancient and medieval examples, and its subject is the interrelationship of personal love and cosmic love. Here, however, the source of expression and the lessons of love's deeper significance come from specifically Christian, biblical, and theological sources rather than from philosophy. In Chaucer a great change occurs, in that his focus moves from the love quest, which provides narrative continuity in both the *Romance* and the *Commedia,* to a panorama of life. Whereas both Jean and Dante link the lover's quest to poetic forms in which a hero receives instructions and performs a series of tasks, Chaucer chooses as his model an epic of many stories, many heroes: the *Metamorphoses.* Chaucer links this model to a contemporary literary phenomenon, the multiplicity of stories he finds in all genres and types of writing which take as their primary focus the relationship of man and wife. Tapping the philosophical and Christian sources of wisdom his predecessors had consulted, he reached farther than they in attempting his own harmony of this wisdom with love, both idealized and in its full, concrete, various reality.

The task of making insight fresh and relevant goes hand in hand with the task of reworking the traditions of expressive language in order to embody these insights effectively. Chaucer extends his command of language not only into the provinces of God's own words in the Bible but also to the most humble human utterances, in order to find just the right way to reach the truth of life and then reveal it to mankind. Unless the truth speaks, it cannot shape the lives of his listeners, and those lives are his most significant goal, for in them, in the private dramas of a thousand households, Chaucer discovers the true substance of human society.

For Chaucer the fundamental human entity is a married couple whose vows have conquered the tragic human condition of isolation, both physical and spiritual, and have given man and woman a territory in which to work and to dream. Chaucer does not suggest that life's difficulties are ended with a promise of marriage; rather, he perceives that man, by nature, is incomplete, and that a commitment to marriage begins a life of commitment to completion, through communicating and sharing with all of creation and ultimately with the Creator. Chaucer discovered in the human institution of marriage a paradigm of life which would enable man to touch both heaven and earth in his every conscious choice and willed action. The otherness of things lies within man's understanding and reach when that otherness is acknowledged as the necessary complement to human nature's inadequacies. Any society or community is plagued by the very differences among its members, which make their cooperation and union such a desirable goal. Man, for whom it is not good to be alone, has the power in his life-giving words to make lasting contact with things outside himself, with people and with ideas. Chaucer offers the description of such a way of life in the *Canterbury Tales*. It is a world rich in permutations on the essential human fact of making contact. There are false starts and poor finishes, there are grandiose schemes which collapse and modest suggestions which gain unexpected success. There is even the Knight, who in his life and tale is that rare object, a good man. In its pleasing wholeness, which defies the mundane fact of Chaucer's death, the *Canterbury Tales* holds the whole of the human condition, which may be failed by some of its participants, but which in itself offers hope for every man.

Bibliography

Manuscripts

Assisi. Biblioteca communale. MS 302. Commentary on the *Thebaid* of Statius.
———. MS 309. Commentary on the *Poetria nova* of Geoffrey of Vinsauf.
Florence. Biblioteca Laurenziana. MS Plut. 36.3. Commentary on the *Metamorphoses* of Ovid.
Leiden. University Library. MS BPL 95. Commentary on the *Metamorphoses* of Ovid.
Oxford. Magdalen College Library. MS lat. 18. Commentary on the *Thebaid* of Statius.
Paris. Bibliothèque nationale. MS lat. 8010. Commentary of William of Theigiis on the *Metamorphoses* of Ovid.
———. MS lat. 8300. Commentary of Robert of Sorbona on the *Anti-claudianus* of Alanus de Insulis.
———. MS lat. 15136. Commentary on the *Metamorphoses* of Ovid.
———. MS lat. 16089. Commentary of Bartholomew of Bruges on the *Poetics* of Averroes.
Vatican City. Biblioteca Apostolica Vaticana. MS Vat. lat. 1479. Commentary on the *Metamorphoses* of Ovid.
———. MS Vat. lat. 1598. Commentary on the *Metamorphoses* of Ovid.
———. MS Vat. lat. 2781. Commentary on the *Metamorphoses* of Ovid.
Venice. Biblioteca Marciana. MS lat. XII. 61 (4097). Commentary on the *Thebaid* of Statius.

Printed Works

Adams, J. F. "Structures of Irony in the Summoner's Tale." *Essays in Criticism* 12 (1962): 126–32.
Abelard, Pierre, and Heloise. "The Personal Letters between Abelard and Heloise." *Medieval Studies* 15 (1953): 47–94.

Aegidius Romanus. *De regimine principum.* Rome, 1607. Reprint. Aalen, 1967.

———. *In epistolam B. Pauli Apostoli ad Romanos commentarii.* Rome, 1555. Reprint. Frankfurt, 1968.

Allen, Judson B. "Commentary as Criticism: Formal Cause, Discursive Form, and the Late Medieval Accessus." In *Acta Conventus Neo-Latini Lovaniensis,* edited by Ijsewijn Kessler and E. Kessler, pp. 33–39. Munich, 1973.

———. *The Ethical Poetic of the Later Middle Ages.* Forthcoming.

———. *The Friar as Critic.* Nashville, 1971.

———. "The *Grand Chant Courtois* and the Wholeness of the Poem: The Medieval *Assimilatio* of Text, Audience, and Commentary." *L'Esprit Créateur* 18 (1978): 5–17.

———. "Hermann the German's Averroistic Aristotle and Medieval Poetic Theory." *Mosaic* 9 (1976): 67–81.

———. "The Ironic Fruyt: Chauntecleer as Figura." *Studies in Philology* 66 (1969): 25–35.

———. "The Old Way and the Parson's Way: An Ironic Reading of the Parson's Tale." *Journal of Medieval and Renaissance Studies* 3 (1973): 255–71.

———. Review of *Chaucerian Fiction,* by Robert Burlin. *Speculum* 54 (January 1979): 116–18.

———. Review of *Rhetoric in the Middle Ages,* by J. J. Murphy. *Speculum* 52 (April 1977): 411–14.

Allen, Judson B., and Gallacher, Patrick. "Alisoun through the Looking Glass; or, Every Man His Own Midas." *Chaucer Review* 4 (1970): 99–105.

Amoils, E. R. "Fruitfulness and Sterility in the Physician's and Pardoner's Tales." *English Studies in Africa* 17 (1974): 17–37.

Aquinas, Thomas. *In 4 de Sententiarum. Opera Omni,* vol. 10. London, 1873.

Auerbach, Erich. *Literary Language and Its Public in Late Latin Antiquity and in the Middle Ages.* New York, 1965.

Augustine. *De Civitate Dei Libri. Corpus Christianorum Series Latina,* vol. 14.

Baldwin, Ralph. *The Unity of the Canterbury Tales.* Copenhagen, 1955.

Baugh, A. C. *Chaucer's Major Poetry.* Englewood Cliffs, N.J., 1963.

Baum, Paul F. *Chaucer: A Critical Appreciation.* Durham, N.C., 1958.

Beidler, Peter G. "The Pairing of the Franklin's Tale and the Physician's Tale." *Chaucer Review* 3 (1969): 275–79.

Benson, Larry D. *Art and Tradition in Sir Gawain and the Green Knight.* New Brunswick, N.J., 1965.

Benton, John F. "Clio and Venus: An Historical View of Medieval Love." In *The Meaning of Courtly Love,* edited by F. X. Newman, pp. 19–42. Albany, 1968.

Bersuire, Pierre. *Dictionarium seu reportorium morale.* 3 vols. Venice, 1589.

———. *Metamorphosis Ovidiana moraliter.* Paris, 1509.

———. *Ovidium moralizatus: Reductorium morale.* Book 15, cap. ii–xv, Werkmateriaal (2). Utrecht, 1962.

———. *Reductorium moral super totam Bibliam. Opera Omnia Totam sacrae scripturae, morum, naturae historiam complectentia.* Cologne, 1631.

Bestul, Thomas H. "The Man of Law's Tale and the Rhetorical Foundations of Chaucerian Pathos." *Chaucer Review* 9 (1975): 216–26.

Biblia sacra, cum glosa ordinaria et expositione lyre litterali et morali. Vol. 5. Basel, 1498.

Biblia sacra, cum glosa ordinaria . . . et postilla Nicolai Lyrani. Vol. 3. Lyons, 1520.

Blodgett, E. D. "Chaucerian *Pryvetee* and the Opposition to Time." *Speculum* 51 (1976): 477–93.

Bloomfield, Morton W. "The Miller's Tale—An UnBoethian Interpretation." In *Medieval Literature and Folklore Studies: Essays in Honor of Francis Lee Utley,* pp. 205–11.

Boer, C. de. *"Ovide Moralisé": Poème du commencement du quatorzième siècle.* 5 vols. Amsterdam, 1915–38.

Boetius de consolatione . . . novissime cum Sancti Thomae philosophi profundissimi commentariis. Venice, 1524.

Boggess, William F. "Aristotle's Poetics in the Fourteenth Century." *Studies in Philology* 67 (1970): 278–94.

———. "Averrois Cordubensis Commentarium Medium in Aristotelis Poetriam." Ph.D. dissertation, University of North Carolina at Chapel Hill, 1965.

Booth, Wayne C. *The Rhetoric of Irony.* Chicago, 1974.

Bowden, Muriel. *A Commentary on the General Prologue of the Canterbury Tales.* New York, 1948.

Brandt, William J. *The Shape of Medieval History: Studies in Modes of Perception.* New Haven, 1966.

Bronson, Bertrand H. *In Search of Chaucer.* Toronto, 1960.

Brooke, Christopher. *The Twelfth Century Renaissance.* London, 1970.

Brown, Carleton, ed. *Religious Lyrics of the Fourteenth Century.* Oxford, 1957.

Brown, Emerson, Jr. "Biblical Women in the Merchant's Tale: Feminism, Antifeminism, and Beyond." *Viator* 5 (1974): 387–412.

———. "Hortus Inconclusus: The Significance of Priapus, and Pyramus and Thisbe in the Merchant's Tale." *Chaucer Review* 4 (1969): 31–40.

———. *"The Merchant's Tale:* Januarie's 'Unlikely Elde.'" *Neuphilologische Mitteilungen* 74 (1973): 92–106.

———. "The *Merchant's Tale:* Why Is May Called 'Mayus'?" *Chaucer Review* 2 (1967): 273–77.

———. "The Merchant's Tale: Why Was Januarie Born 'Of Pavye'?" *Neuphilologische Mitteilungen* 71 (1970): 654–58.

Brown, William, Jr. "Chaucer's Double Apology for the *Miller's Tale.*" *University of Colorado Studies: Series in Language and Literature* 10 (1966): 15–22.

Bryan, W. F., and Dempster, Germaine, eds. *Sources and Analogues of Chaucer's Canterbury Tales.* London, 1941. Reprint. 1958.

Burrow, J. A. *A Reading of Sir Gawain and the Green Knight.* New York, 1966.

Carruthers, Mary. "Letter and Gloss in the Friar's and Summoner's Tales." *Journal of Narrative Technique* 2 (1972): 208–14.

Cary, George. *Medieval Alexander.* Edited by D. J. A. Ross. Cambridge, 1956.

Cate, W. A. "The Problem of the Origin of the Griselda Story." *Studies in Philology* 29 (1932): 389–405.

Clawson, W. H. "The Framework of the Canterbury Tales." In *Chaucer: Modern Essays in Criticism,* edited by Edward Wagenknecht, pp. 3–22. Oxford, 1959.

Clogan, Paul. "The Figural Style and Meaning of *The Second Nun's Prologue and Tale.*" *Medievalia and Humanistica* 3 (1972): 213–40.

Cox, Lee Sheridan. "A Question of Order in the Canterbury Tales." *Chaucer Review* 1 (1966–67): 228–52.

Cummings, Hubertis M. *The Indebtedness of Chaucer's Works to the Italian Works of Boccaccio.* New York, 1965.

Curry, Walter Clyde. *Chaucer and the Medieval Sciences.* Rev. ed. New York, 1960.

Dahlberg, Charles. *Romance of the Rose.* Princeton, 1971.

Dante Alighieri. *Opere.* Edited by E. Moore and Paget Toynbee. Oxford, 1953.

Dantis Alagherii Epistolae. 2d ed. Edited by Paget Toynbee with C. G. Hardie. Oxford, 1966.

David, Alfred. *The Strumpet Muse: Arts and Morals in Chaucer's Poetry.* Bloomington, Ind., 1976.

Delany, Sheila. *Chaucer's House of Fame: The Poetics of Skeptical Fideism.* Chicago, 1922.

———. "Undoing Substantial Connection: The Late Medieval Attack on Analogical Thought." *Mosaic* 5 (1972): 31–52.

———. "Womanliness in the *Man of Law's Tale.*" *Chaucer Review* 9 (1975): 63–72.

Delasanta, Rodney. "Sacrament and Sacrifice·in the *Pardoner's Tale.*" *Annuale Medievale* 14 (1973): 43–52.

Dempster, Germaine. "A Chapter in the Manuscript History of the *Canterbury Tales.*" *PMLA* 78 (1963): 456–84.

———. "Manly's Conception of the *Canterbury Tales.*" *Modern Language Notes* 61 (1946): 379–415.

———. "On the Significance of Hengwrt's Change of Ink in the *Merchant's Tale.*" *Modern Language Notes* 63 (1948): 325–30.

———. "A Period in the Development of the *Canterbury Tales* Marriage Group of Blocks B² and C." *PMLA* 68 (1953): 1142–59.

———. "The Problem of Tale Order in the *Canterbury Tales.*" *PMLA* 64 (1949): 1123–42.

Dionysius the Carthusian. *In omnes beati Pauli Epistolas Commentaria.* Paris, 1540.

Dobson, R. B., ed. *The Peasants' Revolt of 1381.* London, 1970.

Donaldson, E. Talbot. *Chaucer's Poetry: An Anthology for the Modern Reader.* New York, 1958.

———. *Chaucer's Poetry: An Anthology for the Modern Reader,* 2d ed. New York, 1975.

————. "Chaucer the Pilgrim." *PMLA* 69 (1954): 928–36.

————. "The Ordering of the *Canterbury Tales*." In *Medieval Literature and Folklore Studies in Honor of Francis Lee Utley*, edited by Jerome Mandel and Bruce A. Rosenberg, pp. 193–204. New Brunswick, 1970.

————. "Patristic Exegesis: The Opposition." In *Critical Approaches to Medieval Literature*, edited by Dorothy Bethurum. New York, 1960.

Dragonetti, Roger. *Aux frontières du langage poétique*. Romanica Gandensia 9. Ghent, 1961.

Dronke, Peter. *Medieval Latin and the Rise of European Love Lyric*. 2 vols. Oxford, 1965.

Dryden, John. *Poetical Works*. London, 1893.

Duncan, Charles F. "'A Straw for your Gentillesse': The Gentle Franklin's Interruption of the Squire." *Chaucer Review* 5 (1970): 161–64.

Economou, George. "Chaucer's Use of the Bird in the Cage Image in the *Canterbury Tales*." *Philological Quarterly* 54 (1975): 679–84.

Fisher, John H., ed. *The Complete Poetry and Prose of Geoffrey Chaucer*. New York, 1977.

Fleming, John V. *The "Roman de la Rose": A Study in Allegory and Iconography*. Princeton, 1969.

————. "The Summoner's Prologue: An Iconographic Readjustment." *Chaucer Review* 2 (1967): 95–107.

Foucault, Michel. *The Order of Things*. New York, 1973.

Fowler, Alastair. *Spenser and the Numbers of Time*. London, 1964.

Fritz, Donald W. "The Prioress' Avowal of Ineptitude." *Chaucer Review* 9 (1974): 166–81.

Frost, William. "An Interpretation of Chaucer's *Knight's Tale*." In *Chaucer Criticism*, vol. 1 edited by R. J. Schoeck and J. Taylor, pp. 112–15. Notre Dame, 1960.

Fyler, John M. *Chaucer and Ovid*. New Haven, 1979.

Gallacher, Patrick. "Food, Laxatives, and Catharsis in Chaucer's Nun's Priest's Tale." *Speculum* 51 (1976): 49–68.

Gallick, Susan. "A Look at Chaucer and His Preachers." *Speculum* 50 (1975): 456–76.

Gardiner, F. C. *The Pilgrimage of Desire: A Study of Theme and Genre in Medieval Literature*. Leiden, 1971.

Gardner, John. "The Case against the Bradshaw Shift; or, The Mystery of the Manuscript in the Trunk." *Papers in Language and Literature* 3 (Supplement, 1967): 80–106.

Gaylord, Alan T. "The Role of Saturn in the Knight's Tale." *Chaucer Review* 8 (1973): 171–90.

————. "*Sentence* and *Solaas* in Fragment VII of the Canterbury Tales: Harry Bailly as Horseback Editor." *PMLA* 82 (1967): 226–35.

Geoffrey of Vinsauf. *Poetria Nova*. In *Les Arts poétiques du XIIe et du XIIIe siècle*, edited by Edmund Faral. Paris, 1923.

Ghisalberti, Fausto. "Arnolfo d'Orleans, un cultore di Ovidio nel secolo XII." In *Memorie del Reale Istituto Lombardo di Scienxe e Lettere, Classe di Lettere, science morali et storiche*, vol. 24, 15 of series 3, fasc. 4. Milan, 1932.

————. "Giovanni del Virgilio espositore delle 'Metamorfosi.'" *Il Giornale Dantesco* 34 (1933): 3–110.

————. "Medieval Biographies of Ovid." *Journal of the Warburg and Courtould Institutes* 9 (1946): 10–59.

Gilson, Etienne. *History of Christian Philosophy in the Middle Ages*. New York, 1955.

Goffman, Erving. *Frame Analysis: An Essay on the Organization of Experience*. Cambridge, Mass., 1974.

Graef, Hilda. *Mary: A History of Doctrine and Devotion*. Vol. 1. New York, 1963.

Green, R. H. "Classical Fable and English Poetry in the Fourteenth Century." In *Critical Approaches to Medieval Literature*, edited by Dorothy Bethurum. New York, 1960.

Haller, Robert S. "The *Knight's Tale* and the Epic Tradition." *Chaucer Review* 1 (1966): 80–81.

Halverson, John. "Aspects of Order in the *Knight's Tale*." *Studies in Philology* 57 (1960): 606–21.

————. "Chaucer's Pardoner and the Progress of Criticism." *Chaucer Review* 4 (1970): 184–202.

Hardison, O. B. *Aristotle's Poetics: A Translation and Commentary*, with Leon Golden. Englewood Cliffs, N.J., 1968.

————. "The Place of Averroes' Commentary on the *Poetics* in the History of Medieval Criticism." In *Medieval and Renaissance Studies: Proceedings of the Southeastern Institute of Medieval and Renaissance Studies* (Summer 1968), edited by John L. Lievsay. Durham, N.C., 1970.

Harwood, Britton J. "Language and the Real: Chaucer's Manciple." *Chaucer Review* 6 (1972): 268–79.

Herbert, Kevin. *Soliloquy on the Earnest Money of the Soul*. Milwaukee, 1956.

Hill, Thomas D. "La Vieille's Digression on Free Love: A Note on the Rhetorical Structure in the *Romance of the Rose*." *Romance Notes* 8 (1966): 112–15.

Hipolito, T. A. "Chaucer and the School of Chartres." Ph.D. dissertation, University of California, 1971.

Hoffman, Richard. "Jephthah's Daughter and Chaucer's Virginia." *Chaucer Review* 2 (1967–68): 20–31.

————. *Ovid and the Canterbury Tales*. Philadelphia, 1966.

Hoffmann, Arthur W. "Chaucer's Prologue to Pilgrimage: The Two Voices." *ELH* 21 (1954): 1–16.

Holkot, Robert. *In librum Sapientiae*. Basel, 1586.

Hollander, Robert. *Allegory in Dante's Commedia*. Princeton, 1966.

Horstmann, K. "*Orologium Sapientiae, or the Seven Poyntes of Trewe Wisdom* aus MS. Douce 114." *Anglia* 10 (1887): 323–89.

Howard, Donald R. "The Canterbury Tales: Memory and Form." *ELH* 38 (1971): 319–28.

————. "The Conclusion of the Marriage Group: Chaucer and the Human Condition." *Modern Philology* 57 (1960): 223–32.

————. *The Idea of the Canterbury Tales.* Berkeley and Los Angeles, 1976.

Hugh of St. Cher. *Opera Omnia,* 8 vols. Venice, 1732.

Huizinga, John. *The Waning of the Middle Ages.* London, 1924.

Huygens, R. B. C., ed. *Accessus ad auctores, Bernard d'Utrecht, Conrad d'Hirsau, Dialogus super autores.* Leiden, 1970.

Isidore of Seville. *Etymologiarum sive originum.* Book 20. Edited by W. M. Lindsay. 2 vols. Oxford, 1957.

Jauss, Hans-Robert. "The Alterity and Modernity of Medieval Literature." *New Literary History* 10 (1979): 181–229.

Jordan, Robert. *Chaucer and the Shape of Creation.* Cambridge: 1966.

————. "The Question of Genre: Five Chaucerian Romances." In *Chaucer at Albany,* edited by R. H. Robbins. Albany, 1975.

Joseph, Gerard. "Chaucerian 'Game'—'Earnest' and the 'Argument of Herbergage' in the *Canterbury Tales.*" *Chaucer Review* 5 (1970): 83–96.

Josipovici, Gabriel. *The World and the Book: A Study of Modern Fiction.* Stanford, 1971.

Kane, George, and Donaldson, E. T., eds. *Piers Plowman: The B Version.* London, 1975.

Kase, C. Robert. "Observations of the Shifting Position of Groups G and DE in the Manuscripts of the *Canterbury Tales.*" In *Three Chaucer Studies,* edited by Carleton Brown. New York, 1932.

Kaske, R. E. "The Canticum Canticorum in the *Miller's Tale.*" *Studies in Philology* 59 (1962): 480–85, 479–500.

————. "Chaucer's Marriage Group." In *Chaucer the Love Poet,* edited by Jerome Mitchell and William Provost, pp. 45–65. Athens, Ga., 1973.

————. "The Knight's Interruption of the *Monk's Tale.*" *ELH* 24 (1957): 249–68.

Kean, Patricia M. *Chaucer and the Making of English Poetry.* London and Boston, 1972.

Kee, Kenneth. "Illusion and Reality in Chaucer's *Franklin's Tale.*" *English Studies in Canada* 1 (1975): 1–12.

Kelly, Henry Ansgar. *Love and Marriage in the Age of Chaucer.* Ithaca, 1975.

Kittredge, G. L. "Chaucer's Discussion of Marriage." In *Chaucer: Modern Essays in Criticism,* edited by Edward Wagenknecht, pp. 188–215. New York, 1959.

Klibansky, Raymond; Panofsky, Erwin; and Saxl, Fritz. *Saturn and Melancholy.* London, 1964.

Laird, Edgar S. "Astrology and Irony in Chaucer's 'Complaint of Mars.'" *Chaucer Review* 6 (1972): 229–31.

Leff, Gordon. *Bradwardine and the Pelagians.* Cambridge, 1957.

Levitan, Alan. "The Parody of Pentecost in Chaucer's Summoner's Tale." *University of Toronto Quarterly* 40 (1970–71): 236–46.

Levy, Bernard. "Biblical Parody in the Summoner's Tale." *Tennessee Studies in Literature* 11 (1966): 45–60.

Leyerle, John. "The Heart and the Chain." In *The Learned and the Lewed: Studies in Chaucer and Medieval Literature,* edited by Larry D. Benson. *Harvard English Studies* 5 (1974): 113–45.

––––––. "Some 'Subtile Knyttynges' in the *Canterbury Tales.*" Paper delivered at the Chaucer session of the Medieval Academy, 11 May 1974.

Logan, F. Donald. *Excommunication in the Secular Arm in Medieval England.* Toronto, 1968.

Lumiansky, R. M. *Of Sondry Folk: The Dramatic Principle in the Canterbury Tales.* Austin, 1955.

Lydgate, John. *Siege of Thebes.* Edited by Axel Erdmann. Early English Text Society, ES 108. London, 1911.

Macaulay, G. C., ed. *The Works of John Gower.* 4 vols. Oxford, 1899–1902.

Macrobius. *Commentary on the Dream of Scipio.* Translated by William Harris Stahl. New York, 1952.

Manly, John M. *Some New Light on Chaucer.* New York, 1926.

Manly, John M, and Rickert, Edith. *The Text of the Canterbury Tales.* Vol. 2. Chicago, 1949.

Mann, Jill. *Chaucer and Medieval Estates Satire.* Cambridge, 1973.

Mannucci, Vincentio, ed. *Petri Alleghierii super Dantis ipsius genitoris comoediam commentarium.* Florence, 1845.

Marot, Clement. *Le Roman de la Rose.* Vol. 1. Milan, 1957.

Marshall, Linda. *The Garments of Philosophy: A Study of Philosophical Myth in the Twelfth Century.* Ph.D. dissertation, University of Toronto, 1974.

Mathew, Gervase. "Marriage and *Amour Courtois* in Late Fourteenth-Century England." In *Essays Presented to Charles Williams,* pp. 128–35. Oxford, 1947.

Matthews, William. "The Wife of Bath and All Her Sect." *Viator* 5 (1974): 413–44.

McCormick, Sir William, and Heseltine, Janet E. *The Manuscripts of Chaucer's Canterbury Tales: A Critical Description of Their Contents.* Oxford, 1933.

McCulloch, Florence. *Medieval Latin and French Bestiaries.* Chapel Hill, 1960.

McGinn, Bernard. *The Golden Chain: A Study in the Theological Anthropology of Isaac of Stella.* Washington, D.C., 1972.

Migne, J. P. *Patrilogiae Cursus Completus, Series Latina.* Paris, 1878–90. 222 vols.

Miller, Robert P. "Chaucer's Pardoner, the Spiritual Eunuch, and the Pardoner's Tale." *Speculum* 30 (1955): 180–99.

Mitchell, Jerome, and Provost, William, eds. *Chaucer the Love Poet.* Athens, Ga., 1973.

Moritz, Theresa. "The Metaphor of Marriage in the Spiritual Writings of Willia of St. Thierry." *Cistercian Studies* 4 (1976): 290–308.

––––––. " 'Nothing Comes from Nothing': The Structure of Jean de Meun's *Roman de la Rose.*" Paper delivered at the Medieval French section of the Medieval Institute, May 1973, Kalamazoo, Mich.

Murphy, J. J. *Rhetoric in the Middle Ages.* Berkeley, 1974.

Muscatine, Charles. *Chaucer and the French Tradition.* Berkeley and Los Angeles, 1966.

Nardi, Bruno. "Osservazioni sul medievale 'Accessus ad Auctores' in rapporto all' Epistola a Cangrande." In *Saggi e Note di Critica Dantesca.* Milan, 1966.

Nichols, Robert E., Jr. "The Pardoner's Ale and Cake." *PMLA* 82 (1967): 498–504.

Nims, Margaret F., trans. *Poetria Nova of Geoffrey of Vinsauf.* Toronto, 1967.

Nogara, B. "Di alcune vite e commenti medioevali di Ovidio." In *Miscellanea Ceriani.* Milan, 1910.

Olson, Glending. "The *Reeve's Tale* as a Fabliau." *Modern Language Notes* 35 (1974): 219–30.

Otis, Brooks. *Ovid as an Epic Poet.* Cambridge, 1970.

Owen, Charles A., Jr. "The Design of the *Canterbury Tales.*" In *Companion to Chaucer Studies,* edited by Beryl Rowland, pp. 192–207. Oxford, 1968.

———. "The Earliest Plan of the Canterbury Tales." *Mediaeval Studies* 21 (1959): 202–10.

———. *Pilgrimage and Storytelling in the Canterbury Tales: The Dialectic of "Earnest" and "Game."* Norman, Okla., 1977.

———. "The *Tale of Melibee.*" *Chaucer Review* 7 (Spring 1973): 267–80.

Palomo, Delores. "What Chaucer Really Did to *Le Livre de Melibee.*" *Philological Quarterly* 53 (1974): 304–20.

Pearsall, D. A. "The Squire as Story-teller." *University of Toronto Quarterly* 34 (1964): 82–92.

Peraldus, William. *Summa virtutum ac vitiorum.* Lyons, 1668.

Perella, Nicholas J. *The Kiss Sacred and Profane.* Berkeley and Los Angeles, 1969.

Peterson, Joyce E. "The Finished Fragment: A Reassessment of the Squire's Tale." *Chaucer Review* 5 (1970): 62–74.

Pochoda, Elizabeth T. *Arthurian Propaganda: Le Mort Darthur as an Historical Ideal of Life.* Chapel Hill, 1971.

Pope, Alexander. *The Rape of the Lock and Other Poems.* London, 1954.

Pratt, Robert. "The Order of the Canterbury Tales." *PMLA* 66 (1951): 1141–67.

Pratt, Robert A., and Young, Karl. "The Literary Framework of the Canterbury Tales." In *Sources and Analogues of Chaucer's Canterbury Tales,* edited by W. F. Bryan and Germaine Dempster, pp. 1–81. London, 1941. Reissued 1958.

Preston, Raymond. *Chaucer.* London and New York, 1952.

Quain, E. A. "The Medieval Accessus ad Auctores." *Traditio* 3 (1945): 215–64.

Quinn, Esther Casier *The Quest of Seth for the Oil of Life.* Chicago, 1962.

Reiss, Edmund. "Chaucer's *fyn lovynge* and the Late Medieval Sense of fin amor." In *Medieval Studies in Honor of Lillian Herlands Hornstein,* pp. 181–92. New York, 1976.

Riedel, William, ed. *Commentum Bernardi Silvestris Super Sex libros Eneidos Virgilii*. Gryphiswald, 1824.

Robbins, R. H. *Historical Poems of the Fourteenth and Fifteenth Centuries*. New York, 1959.

Robertson, D. W., Jr. *A Preface to Chaucer*. Princeton, 1962.

———. "Why the Devil Wears Green." *Modern Language Notes* 69 (1954): 470–72.

Robinson, F. N., ed. *The Works of Geoffrey Chaucer*. 2d ed. Boston, 1957.

Root, R. K. "Chaucer and the Decameron." *English Studies* 44 (1912): 1–7.

Rosenberg, Bruce. "The Contrary Tales of the Second Nun and the Canon's Yeoman." *Chaucer Review* 2 (1967): 278–91.

Rougemont, Denis de. *Love in the Western World*. Rev. ed. New York, 1940.

Ruggiers, Paul. *The Art of the Canterbury Tales*. Madison, 1965.

———. "Some Theoretical Considerations of Comedy in the Middle Ages." In *Versions of Medieval Comedy*. Norman, Okla., 1977.

Sandkühler, Bruno. *Die frühen Dantekommentäre und ihr Verhältnis zur mittelalterlichen Kommentartradition*. Munich, 1967.

Sayce, Olive. "Chaucer's 'Retractions': The Conclusion of the *Canterbury Tales* and Its Place in Literary Tradition." *Medium Aevum* 40 (1971): 230–48.

Schlauch, Margaret. *Chaucer's Constance and Accused Queens*. New York, 1927.

———. "The Marital Dilemma in the Wife of Bath's Tale." *PMLA* 61 (1946): 416–30.

Severs, J. Burke. *The Literary Relationships of Chaucer's Clerkes Tale*. New Haven, 1942.

Shoaf, Richard Allen. "*Mutatio Amoris:* Revision and Penitence in Chaucer's *The Book of the Duchess*." Ph.D. dissertation, Cornell University, 1977.

Silverman, Albert H. "Sex and Money in Chaucer's Shipman's Tale." *Philological Quarterly* 32 (1953): 329–36.

Singleton, Charles. *Dante Studies I, Commedia: Elements of Structure*. Cambridge, Mass., 1965.

———. "The Irreducible Dove." *Comparative Literature* 9 (1957): 129–35.

Sledd, James. "The *Clerk's Tale:* The Monsters and the Critics." In *Chaucer Criticism*, vol. 1, edited by R. J. Schoeck and J. Taylor, pp. 160–74. Notre Dame, 1960.

Smalley, Beryl. *English Friars and Antiquity in the Early Fourteenth Century*. Oxford, 1960.

———. "Some Commentaries on the Sapiential Books of the Late Twelfth and Early Fourteenth Centuries." *Archives d'histoire doctrinale et littéraire du moyen âge* 18 (1950): 103–28.

———. "Some Thirteenth-Century Commentaries on the Sapiential Books." *Dominican Studies* 2 (1949): 318–55.

———. "Some Thirteenth-Century Commentaries on the Sapiential Books." *Dominican Studies* 3 (1950): 41–77, 236–74.

———. *The Study of the Bible in the Middle Ages*. 2d ed. Notre Dame, 1964.

Stevens, Martin. "Chaucer and Modernism: An Essay in Criticism." In *Chaucer at Albany*, edited by Rossell Hope Robbins. Albany, 1975.

Stokoe, William C., Jr. "Structure and Intention in the First Fragment of the Canterbury Tales." *University of Toronto Quarterly* 21 (1952): 120-27.

Strange, William C. "The Monk's Tale: A Generous View." *Chaucer Review* 1 (1966): 167-80.

Strohm, Paul. "The Allegory of the *Tale of Melibee.* " *Chaucer Review* 2 (Summer 1967): 32-42.

Szittya, Penn R. "The Friar as False Apostle: Anti-Fraternal Exegesis and the Summoner's Tale." *Studies in Philology* 71 (1974): 19-46.

―――. "The Green Yeoman as Loathly Lady: The Friar's Parody of the Wife of Bath's Tale." *PMLA* 90 (1975): 386-94.

Tatlock, J. S. P. "The *Canterbury Tales* in 1400." *PMLA* 50 (1935): 100-39.

Thilo, G., and Hagen, H., eds. *Servii Grammatic; qui feruntur in Vergilii Carmina Commentaril.* Vol. 1. Leipzig, 1881.

Thompson, Stith. "The Miller's Tale." In *Sources and Analogues*, edited by W. F. Bryan and Germaine Dempster, pp. 106-23. London, 1941. Reprint, 1958.

―――. *Motif-Index of Folk Literature.* Vol. 3. Bloomington, Ind., 1955.

Thorndike, Lynn. "Unde Versus." *Traditio* 11 (1955): 163-92.

Traugott, Lawler, trans. *The Parisiana Poetria of John Garland.* New Haven, 1974.

Trimpi, Wesley. "The Ancient Hypothesis of Fiction: An Essay on the Origins of Literary Theory." *Traditio* 27 (1971): 1-78.

―――. "The Quality of Fiction: The Rhetorical Transmission of Literary Theory." *Traditio* 30 (1974): 1-118.

Tupper, Frederick. "Chaucer and the Seven Deadly Sins." *PMLA* 29 (1914): 93-128.

Turner, Frederick. "A Structural Analysis of the *Knight's Tale.*" *Chaucer Review* 8 (1973): 279-96.

Tuve, Rosemund. *Allegorical Imagery.* Princeton, 1966.

―――. "Spring in Chaucer and Before Him." *Modern Language Notes* 52 (1937): 9-16.

Ullman, B. L., ed. *Colucii Salutati de laboribus Herculis.* Zurich, n.d.

Vance, Eugene. "Mervelous Signals: Poetics, Sign Theory, and Politics in Chaucer's Troilus." *New Literary History.* 10 (Winter 1979): 293-337.

Vinaver, Eugene, ed. *The Works of Thomas Malory.* London, New York, Toronto, 1954.

Vogt, G. M. "Gleanings for the History of a Sentiment: Generositas Virtus, non Sanguis." *Journal of English and Germanic Philology* 24 (1925): 102-23.

Wenzel, Sigfried. "Chaucer and the Language of Contemporary Preaching." *Studies in Philology* 73 (1976): 138-61.

Westlund, Joseph. "The *Knight's Tale* as an Impetus for Pilgrimage." *Philological Quarterly* 43 (1964): 526-37.

Wetherbee, Winthrop. *Platonism and Poetry in the Twelfth Century: The Literary Influence of the School of Chartres.* Princeton, 1972.

White, Gertrude M. "The *Franklin's Tale:* Chaucer and the Critics." *PMLA* 89 (1974): 454–62.

White, T. H. *The Book of Beasts.* New York, 1954.

Whiting, B. J., ed. *Proverbs, Sentences, and Proverbial Phrases.* Cambridge, 1968.

William of St. Thierry. *The Golden Epistle: A Letter to the Brethren at Mont Dieu.* Translated by Theodore Berkley. Cambridge, 1971.

————. *Un Traité de la vie solitaire: Epistola ad Fratres de Monte-Dei.* Edited by M. M. Davy. Paris, 1940.

Wimsatt, James. "Chaucer and the Canticle of Canticles." In *Chaucer the Love Poet,* edited by Jerome Mitchell and William Provost, pp. 69–90. Athens, Ga., 1973.

Wood, Chauncey. "The Man of Law as Interpreter." *Traditio* 23 (1967): 149–90.

Woods, Marjorie Curry. "The *In Principio Huius Libri* Type A Commentary on Geoffrey of Vinsauf's *Poetria Nova:* Text and Analysis." Ph.D. dissertation, University of Toronto, 1977.

Yates, Frances. *The Art of Memory.* Harmondsworth, Eng., 1966.

Index

This compelling reading of the *Canterbury Tales* is new in three important respects: It goes beyond the critical truism that Chaucer was fond of Ovid to discover, in medieval analyses of the form of the *Metamorphoses* as a collection, basic guidance for understanding the form of Chaucer's own aggregation of tales. It proposes, in light of this evidence, a new order or sequence for the tales that is based neither on the mute witness of some single "good" manuscript or group of manuscripts, nor on the geography between London and Canterbury. And, instructed by the inconclusive results of merely internal evidence, it establishes an ordering grounded primarily in external evidence — in medieval literary commentaries and manuals and in the *Metamorphoses* itself, which defined medieval principles of literary organization.

By reading the *Canterbury Tales* as a normative array of exempla in four groups, which exploit the literal and analogical significance of the structure of marriage in order to arrive at a definition of social order, Allen and Moritz are able to posit a medieval unity for Chaucer's fair chain of narratives. The first of the four exhibits a clearly logical coherence that is Chaucer's own creation and an obvious adumbration of his intention for the whole. The succeeding three are the heuristic constructs of Allen and Moritz, who, while respecting the integrity of each of Chaucer's fragments, reorder them according to the example provided by his own medieval editors. The classification of Chaucer's tales into the four Ovidian categories — natural, magical, moral, and spiritual — obeys both the method and the specific content of medieval literary criticism.